MW01115035

Angels ON HIGH

Walt Deecki Sr.

ISBN 978-1-64140-300-9 (Paperback)
ISBN 978-1-64140-301-6 (Digital)

Copyright © 2017 by Walt Deecki Sr.
All rights reserved. No part of this publication may be reproduced, distributed, or transmitted in any form or by any means, including photocopying, recording, or other electronic or mechanical methods without the prior written permission of the publisher. For permission requests, solicit the publisher via the address below.

Christian Faith Publishing, Inc.
296 Chestnut Street
Meadville, PA 16335
www.christianfaithpublishing.com

Printed in the United States of America

DEDICATION

This book is dedicated to my father.

Thanks, Dad, for the stories you shared with me as I was growing up. Your wisdom, strength, and faith were the inspiration for the characters' warmth and compassion that are shared throughout this story.

CONTENTS

ACKNOWLEDGMENTS

God has blessed me with a very special friend and companion, my wife Debbie, who has encouraged me every step of the way in the development of this book. She has supported me by reading my unreadable handwriting, doing late-night proofreading, and, most of all, assisting with many computer malfunctions.

Thanks to my daughter, Dawn, and granddaughters—Chelsae, Brooklyn, and Cheyenne—for their smiles and the excitement that I see in their faces and their beautiful eyes that are evident in the female characters in this story.

Thanks to my sons—Walter Jr., John, and Jason—and my grandson, Walter III, for they are all, in some way, responsible for the personalities of the young male characters.

To all of you who read this book, may God's grace shine upon you and your loved ones.

PART 1

LAUGHTER, TRAGEDY, TEARS, DREAMS, AND HOPE

INTRODUCTION
TO PART 1

This story is about a very special friendship between a thirteen-year-old boy named Jimmie and an elderly man named Samuel Pulaski. Samuel shares stories about his life with all who are willing to listen but mostly with his young friend Jimmie in exchange for the young boy's companionship. He shares his trials and tribulations and the effects they have had on his beliefs, faith, and trust in the Lord. However, Samuel is unaware of the impact he has had on Jimmie's life as he grew up. This would be recorded by Jimmie many years later.

Perhaps you have reached a point in your life when you weren't sure of your faith because of some incident that occurred. Did a tragedy occur where you just couldn't understand how it happened to you? Perhaps someone you loved died, became seriously ill, or was injured. And you found yourself asking the question, "Why me, Lord?" You may have been so angry and hurt that you felt God owed you an explanation. Did you demand an explanation, and if it didn't come, did you give up praying or trusting in God? Did you give God the silent treatment?

I can tell you from experience that God is patient. The fact is, however, he has a tendency to give you a little nudge through some small miracle that encourages your return. He may even have sent an angel to help you with whatever conflict you were going through to help point you in the right direction. Sometimes that return may take a few days, weeks, or even years; but time is irrelevant when it comes to God's love. When you experience a terrible situation, no matter how difficult it may be to accept, God wants you to put your trust in him. He wants you to trust him by your own free will. The following example is only one possible scenario. Think about the last time you watched a movie, and the guy looked at the girl during a life-threatening situation, and he said to her, "Do you trust me?" She said, "What?" Maybe it was too noisy or perhaps she was hard of hearing; however, most likely, it was in the script, and he had to repeat himself, "Do you trust me?" She would ask, "Why?" (Stick with me on this one; I'm almost finished.) He'd respond, "Don't say anything. I'm asking you to trust me no matter what happens. Now do you trust me?" She looks into his eyes and says, "Yes!" Then he yells, "Okay then. Hold on and don't let go!"

We know what's going to happen, even if we hadn't read the script or seen the movie before. They survive their situation because of some spectacular rescue by the hero or heroine. What about God? We don't know what's going to happen, but he's asking us to trust him, to believe in him no matter what happens, and to not let go. But unfortunately, sometimes we do let go because we want answers. And when we don't get them, we do it alone.

Why? Because we don't understand how he could let bad things happen to us. But if we hang on, at some point in this life or the next, we will find out why. It's not a movie but real life. And real life does not give us a pass on not experiencing anything bad. But God grants his love for us, forgives us, and promises us a life in his glorious presence if we accept him. However, if we do it alone, our situation will worsen. Trust God and believe in his Holy Son, Jesus Christ, and you will have eternal life. That—is—his—promise.

With this in mind, here's my second question. Have you ever wished you could go back in time to a special moment or time in your past when you were so happy that you wished the time would never end? It may have been during the birth of a child, your wedding day, or maybe it was as far back as when you were a young child growing up. There were several times I wanted desperately to return to more pleasant times, but we can't. Time travel isn't possible, except in our dreams. Our lives are full of hopes, dreams, and prayers. As time passes us by, we experience special moments, moments that bring joy and happiness. Other times are sad, and we grow older, finding ourselves reliving all the moments of our lives.

The times of great pleasure, as well as the times of sorrow, flood the memory banks of our minds. They remain with us in every path we walk through in life. Sometimes we are able to pinpoint the exact times those memories occurred and remember exactly how the event transpired. Perhaps you never really got to say a final good-bye or have the opportunity to say you loved him or her one last time.

When my mother passed away from cancer, I talked to her on the phone the night before her surgery. I told her everything would be all right. I didn't take all our children with us the day of her surgery because I decided they could see her on the weekend. And I didn't want them to miss school, but that day never came; she passed away during the night. I received the phone call from my brother early that morning; I couldn't believe it. I didn't want to believe it.

After the funeral, we returned home. For weeks, sleep was too difficult as I wrestled with making the wrong decision. I prayed every night for God to help me. I spent twenty years in the military, which allowed my family and me to only visit once a year. After my retirement, the opportunity came for us to transfer closer to family with my new job. We were only three hours away from my immediate family. But the new job required many hours, and time just continued slipping by with few visits throughout the year. I never expected my mother to leave us so soon. Until the night that she left us to be with our Father in heaven, I thought that we had plenty of time.

One night unexpectedly, God granted me a prayer. I fell asleep after my usual prayer, and I dreamt that my mother and I were walking together in a park as we talked. I told her how sorry I was that we didn't get to spend more time together, especially with her grandchildren. I also told her that I was so very sorry that I wasn't able to visit her and Father more often and how sorry I was that my children didn't have the opportunity to grow up with their grandparents, except for our occasional visits. But most of all, I told her how much I missed her. And in my dream, she smiled at me and assured me that everything was going to be all right. She told me how much she loved me. When I woke up the next morning, I felt like a giant weight had been lifted from my shoulders. I had been given the opportunity to say good-bye.

Although some of you may believe that what I experienced was only a dream, I know that God had given me the time I needed with my mother. I really believe that God gave my mother and me the chance to walk together one last time. I believe that I experienced a wonderful miracle that night. It wasn't the first miracle I experienced in my life, but it was the most significant.

This is just one of the reasons I know that angels are with us all the time. And I know these following things to be true: Jesus is with us when we call on him from our hearts; God our Father is loving and caring; you only have to believe and trust in him, who made the heavens and the earth; and anything is possible through the grace of God.

With all this in mind, there is just one last point I'd like to make before getting into the story. While I was working for a nonprofit organization, I worked with many different types of people and families. I was blessed to be a counselor for an eight-year-old boy who lived with foster parents. He was the happiest child I ever worked with. You would have never guessed he was a foster child who moved from home to home. The family he was living with at the time provided a home for him that was very loving and caring. If he didn't tell you he was a foster child, you would never have known.

One night while we were at a party where the children were required to make a cake with minimal help from their parents, this little boy came up to me with the biggest eyes and a smile as big as the Grand Canyon. "Mr. Walt, I'm going to be adopted!" The foster parents had already adopted five other children over the years and were going to make this wonderful child a permanent part of their family too.

Isn't that wonderful? And to know that our Father in heaven wants us to be a permanent part of his family is the greatest feeling in the world. I know he must get very excited when people pray and ask him to come into their hearts, to forgive them, and to hold them in his hands. To know that each one of us is a part of his wonderful family forever is awesome, isn't it?

If you're reading this book because you're looking for answers, I pray that you find them. But most of all, I pray that you find comfort in the fact that you're not alone. God is always with you. He carries you through the troubled times when you're tired. Please hang on to your faith in the Father and his Son.

Through this faith in the Father and his Son, just like Samuel, the elderly man in this book, you can overcome any tragedy that you face. But you have to be willing to tell God about it and give it to him. Thus, even though the elderly gentleman in this book is a kind man, he is not without tragedy. Neither was Job or Moses. Are you upset with God and giving him the silent treatment? Break that silence and talk to him. Tell him how you really feel. "Lord, I'm angry with you right now. Lord, I'm scared. God, I don't understand why this has happened!" He loves you, and he is by your side now and forever, always, forever and ever. He told us he was.

Now with these few thoughts in mind, let's get started on our journey through life with these two special friends. I pray that you find a common bond with them as you read. We'll talk again before part 2.

CHAPTER 1

Fishing with Mr. Pulaski

*When it was full, the fishermen pulled it up on the
shore. Then they sat down and collected the food fish
in baskets, but threw the bad away.*
—Matthew 13:48, New International Version

It was early morning, and the sun was beginning to caress the horizon. The last few stars disappeared one by one. The first bird lifted his head with the anticipation of the rising sun and began his morning song. The other birds joined in. I arose from my bed, dressed, and was downstairs before Dad was even up. I even had Dad's coffee brewing when I heard the creak of the first step as he descended the stairs. It was only a few months since school began, but our little town was already feeling the chill usually reserved for late fall. The warm weather slipped by so quickly that I didn't realize it was gone until I heard everyone in town talking about the holidays and getting ready for Thanksgiving.

This past summer was the best one I'd ever had. For the first time in years, Dad and I were able to go fishing every other weekend, and this was to be our last father-and-son fishing trip for the season. We were both almost out the door too when the phone rang. It was Dad's work. I could tell because they were the only ones that ever called that early in the morning, except when Aunt Lilly thought someone was trying to break into her house, and it would only turn out to be her cat that she had accidentally locked in the basement.

"Good morning, Mike!"

The only Mike I knew was the one that worked for Dad.

As I waited for Dad to get off the phone, I sat down at the kitchen table. I laid my tackle box in front of me, leaning the fishing pole against my leg. Somehow, I knew what was about to happen— our last dad-and-son fishing trip had to be postponed. I made sure I sat facing him in the hope that he would see the disappointment on my face as he talked. It seemed that some of the trucks wouldn't start, and they couldn't figure out why. Dad hung up the phone as he turned and glanced at me. He didn't look very happy, and neither did I.

"I'm sorry, Jimmie. I guess you know what that phone call was about."

I just hung my head and nodded.

"Our first snowfall could only be a week or two away," he continued. "I'm a little surprised we haven't had it yet, but we have to have the trucks ready to go at any time!"

"I know, Dad." I smiled for his benefit, not mine. "We sure had a great summer, didn't we?" I tried not to sound too disappointed.

"We sure did! Caught some big ones too, huh?" replied Dad.

"You mean I caught some big ones!" I said pointedly.

He laughed and agreed, "Yeah, you caught some big ones."

"So can I still go fishing?" I asked, knowing that it wouldn't be the same without Dad. But I was thinking about the big catfish that I'd seen the last time we went. It must have weighed at least forty pounds. Maybe fifteen, but it was really big and nearly snapped my pole in half before it got away.

Dad put his hand on the back of my head and rubbed my hair. "Sure, Jimmie, just be careful."

I didn't like it much when he did that. His hands were rough from working on the trucks all the time. I can't ever remember seeing his hands really clean, except when we went to church on Sundays. And that was only because Mom made him scrub his hands, sometimes three or four times, and then made him use a brush to get the grease out from under his nails. I always thought it was funny when she'd make him show her his hands, and if she wasn't satisfied, she'd scrub them for him. He never argued with her either. He said it would waste too much energy, and he wouldn't win anyway because it was useless to argue with someone as good-looking as Mom.

Not wanting to waste time on all the mushy stuff, I just rolled my eyes and grabbed my fishing pole and tackle box as I walked out. As I walked by the kitchen table, I grabbed a banana from the fruit bowl and quietly closed the door so as not to wake up Mom. The early morning air was just cool enough to see your breath. A thick fog slowly drifted all around me as the cool fall air slightly pushed it across the ground.

The best place to fish was a quarter of a mile below the falls where the river bent around a small island. The river had cut a shallow ravine in the riverbank, and the water swirled as if it was trapped. That was where the big fish liked to stay.

As I passed Mr. Pulaski's house, I decided to take a chance and see if he might be awake. I knew he got up early sometimes to sit on the front porch. He was an early riser because he always said, "If you don't get up early, you miss the best part of the day."

Although I visited him often, we hadn't fished together since late spring. So I tiptoed up the front steps and tapped lightly on the door. I figured if he was awake, he'd hear me, and if he was sleeping, then I wouldn't disturb him. I waited for a minute or two, and then as I turned and started down the steps, the porch light came on, almost blinding me. As I put my hand over my eyes, I dropped my tackle box, and my hooks and lures flew everywhere. The door opened, and Mr. Pulaski stood leaning against the open door.

"Jimmie! What are you doing up so early?"

I fumbled to pick up my tackle box and quickly threw everything back in it. "I didn't mean to wake you, Mr. P, if you were still sleeping! Dad was going to go with me, but he was called into work. He said I could go by myself, but as I was passing your house, I thought maybe you'd like to go!"

Mr. Pulaski smiled, rubbed his chin with his fingers, and said, "You know, Jimmie, I couldn't sleep, so I was sitting in the living room looking out the window, thinking to myself how nice it would be to go fishing this morning!"

"Really?" I replied.

"You bet," Mr. Pulaski answered. "It will only take me a minute or two to get my fishing pole and tackle box."

He was right; he was only gone a few seconds. I think he kept his fishing gear in the closet by the front door.

"I'm ready!" he said, and the two of us started on our way.

We'd made this trip so many times during the past few years that it didn't matter that the mist was so thick you couldn't see your hand two feet in front of you. We could probably find our way blindfolded.

As we left the main road, we could barely make out the outline of a few deer grazing in the small field just ahead. We always tried to see how close we could get to the deer before they got spooked and ran. Because of the fog, we were able to get a lot closer than usual. But they finally sensed our presence, and with one graceful leap, they disappeared into the fog-hidden trees.

Leaving the deer behind, Mr. Pulaski and I continued on our way to our fishing destination at the river. It was a good thing we wore boots because the grass was at least eight inches high and very wet. Once we entered the edge of the woods, it was necessary to go down a short embankment, cross a small stream, and scramble about ten steps up the other side. I didn't want Mr. Pulaski to fall, so I found a sharp rock and dug foot holes for him to use as steps. I knew that if he fell and hurt himself, I'd never be able to carry him out by myself.

It wasn't that he was overweight or anything; it's just that I barely came up to his waist. As a matter of fact, Mr. Pulaski must have been at least six feet tall. He was not quite a slender man, and his upper body leaned slightly forward because of his arthritis. He had pure white hair, and if his beard was longer, I imagine he'd look sort of like Moses. I'm not sure if Moses had blue eyes or not, but Mr. Pulaski's blue eyes sure did match his kind and gentle personality. I'm almost sure that he must have been at least sixty years old, but I never asked him because Mom always told me it wasn't polite to ask older people their age. And if there was anyone in the world I respected as much as my mom and Dad, it was Mr. Pulaski. I guess you could say he was my best friend.

After we crossed the stream and made it to the top of the hill, it was only a few yards to the edge of the river. Mr. Pulaski laid his tackle box down in his favorite spot and sat on a rock that he said was made just for him. He claimed it was in the perfect spot because it was exactly where the biggest fish were. I smiled and climbed out on a massive fallen tree trunk.

I always told Mr. Pulaski that it must be as old as him. He always laughed at me too.

I made the first cast, and Mr. Pulaski made his cast. He pushed a stick shaped like a slingshot into the ground and then leaned his pole against it.

As we both sat quietly, the mist hid our lines so that we couldn't see them. Within an hour, the sun's rays pushed their way through the mist and brought the daylight. As the dawn broke through the early morning darkness, the birds began to let the world know that it was time to start the day. While they sang, we could hear the soft trickle of the crystal-clear river as it flowed over the rocks. Then the fish began jumping. A big one jumped right below me and startled me so much that I almost fell out of the tree into the river. I tried not to make it obvious to Mr. Pulaski that I was anxious to catch the first one, but it was hard. He always bragged about being a pro at fishing, and if I watched him closely enough, I could be one too.

"That's what my dad always said," I told him.

After about a half hour, I looked over at Mr. Pulaski. It was still a little hazy, but it looked like he was sleeping. I quietly made my way back to the edge of the river, picked up a rock, climbed back out on the tree, and then dropped it in the river as close to him as I could reach. He jumped up, grabbed his pole, and yelled, "What was that?"

"It was the biggest fish I ever saw, Mr. P, and it was right by your line! You should have seen it. You would have too if your eyes were open!" I couldn't keep from laughing because of the look on his face.

Mr. Pulaski smiled and said gruffly, "You threw a rock in, didn't you, you little varmint?"

All of a sudden, my pole jerked.

"I got a bite!" I yelled, and then I jerked back on the pole.

"Keep it tight, Jimmie. Don't let it get away!" Mr. Pulaski yelled. "Hang on tight. Reel it in, reel it in!"

I thought how difficult it was to concentrate when a pro is yelling instructions at you. You'd think I never fished before. I have to admit I didn't think I'd ever get that one in, but after a great fight, I managed to bring it in close enough to pick it up with my net.

"Holy cow, look at that trout, Mr. P!"

"I think it's the biggest one I've ever seen, Jimmie, except for the one Antonio caught when he was thirteen." Mr. Pulaski helped me put it on the stringer.

I rebaited my hook, and said, "Now it's your turn, Mr. P!"

"I'll see what I can do," he said.

Just then, a man passed by on his way downstream. "The fishin' any good?" he asked.

Mr. Pulaski looked at him and shook his head. "Not for me, but my friend Jimmie here just caught a big trout. It's there on the stringer on the edge of the bank."

The man looked over, let out a low whistle, and moved a little farther downstream.

Right after he left, Mr. Pulaski smiled. "I remember when I used to take the boys from the youth center fishing. That was a long time ago, but I can remember it like it was yesterday. Once in a while, my wife Maria went with us most of the time. She'd bring her favorite book, a chair, and a picnic basket with more food to eat than you ever saw. She'd just sit patiently with intentions of reading. But I seem to remember we, I meant her, talked most of the time. And if I managed to catch a fish, even if it was big enough to keep, she'd usually talk me into letting it go. Occasionally, I talked Maria into fishing with me, but it just wasn't her sport."

He paused and then continued, "She really wasn't much for baiting the hook. She tried casting a few times, but she never could get it any farther than six feet from the river bank. Then if she did catch one, I'd help her reel it in and take it off the hook."

I laughed at Mr. Pulaski's expressions as he was talking.

"Sounds like you did the fishing," I said. "All she did was holding the pole!"

"Yes, Jimmie, I suppose it does, but I loved every minute I spent with her. It didn't matter if I caught anything or not because we were together. Lord knows I'd give anything to relive those days."

It was getting toward midmorning, and I began to feel the hunger pains. I only had the banana that I had grabbed on my way out the door. Mr. Pulaski had a thermos of coffee and some cookies. After I polished off the banana, I ate most of the cookies too. I only did it because Mr. Pulaski said he wasn't very hungry. He said he could only eat one or two, and he didn't want to carry them back home, so he gave them to me. Finishing up our snack, we noticed that the day was starting to warm up just a little, and the fish had stopped biting, so we figured we'd call it a day. We had fun that morning; I only wished I didn't have to go back to school on Monday.

On our way home, Mr. Pulaski seemed to be quieter than usual.

"Are you okay, Mr. P?" I asked. "Are you tired? Do you need to rest?"

"No, Jimmie, I'm fine. I was just thinking about those picnic baskets Maria used to pack."

As we reached the steps leading up to his front porch, I said, "Thanks for standing in for my dad. I had a great time, Mr. P!"

"I had a great time too, Jimmie, and you're welcome any time."

Mom said she was going to take me to get more clothes and supplies for school, so I couldn't stay at Mr. Pulaski's house like I usually did. Mom never thought I had enough school supplies, so usually by the third week of school, I had enough paper and pens to supply the whole town.

I was still concerned about Mr. Pulaski, so I waited for him to go up the steps and into his house before leaving. I loved that old man. He was like a grandfather to me, and I could talk about anything with him, and he always listened. He never laughed at anything I told him unless he thought it was funny, and he never really told me what to do unless he thought it was in my best interest. He just seemed to have a way of letting me figure out the answer to my own questions. Most of the time, he just asked, "So what are you going to do?" Even if I said I didn't know, Mr. Pulaski would say, "You must have some idea," and by the time our conversation was finished, I had the answer. It may not have been the answer I was looking for, but it was the answer. I liked it most of all when Mr. Pulaski told me a story to make his point. The answer was always there somewhere within the moral of the story. Mr. Pulaski's ability to sense when something was wrong amazed me. And he was always ready with a smile and some wise words. It was truly unbelievable.

> *"Come, follow me," Jesus said, "and I will make you fishers of men."*
> —Mark 1:17, New International Version

CHAPTER 2

Thanksgiving Day

He brought me to the banqueting house, and his banner over me was love.

—Song of Songs 2:4

Mr. Pulaski woke early. Most mornings, he fixed himself a light breakfast and coffee first thing, but that morning, there wasn't any time to waste. He was in a hurry; he needed to get to the church quickly. Every Thanksgiving, Christmas, and New Year's, it was a tradition for him to cook and serve the holiday meals for the elderly who were either unable to afford to buy their own food or families that didn't want to spend the day cooking at home. But most of the families attended for the fellowship and a reason not to have to clean up after a big meal. Since Mr. Pulaski's son and daughter lived far away, he enjoyed doing this for others; besides, it made the day go faster, and he felt useful.

As Mr. Pulaski hurried out of his house that morning, he grabbed his coat, scarf, and hat. And as he was putting his hat on with one hand, he was slipping his arm in one sleeve of his coat while throwing his scarf around his neck. He picked up his cane as he was putting his other arm in its sleeve, and by the time he was out the front door and down the steps, he had it buttoned up. As he hurried down the street as fast as his old legs would go, he hadn't noticed the wintry air until his breathing increased. He wondered why it hadn't snowed yet. Since the town was so far in the mountains, sometimes it snowed as early as Halloween. I remember a few times we had snow flurries in September. As you can imagine, autumns in this town seemed to be very short.

Finally, Mr. Pulaski arrived at the church. Just before Mr. Pulaski opened the door leading into the kitchen located in the basement of the church, he glanced over his shoulder at the sunrise.

"It's a beautiful morning, Lord. I approve." He chuckled as he closed the door behind him and hung up his coat. He turned and rubbed his hands together as he held them to his face and blew into them. They were a little cold, and he was attempting to warm them up. Still rubbing them together, he grabbed an apron from the pantry and tied it around his waist. After getting his apron on, Mr. Pulaski prepared to start the meal by gathering up all the pans and other utensils that he knew he needed. Now after pulling just about every shape and size of pan down off the rack hanging over the island in front of the sink, he washed his hands, then held them up above his head, took a deep breath, and said out loud, "What should I do first? The turkeys!" he exclaimed. "It's Thanksgiving, and the turkeys will take the longest to cook!" Then he opened the door to the big refrigerator and moved the three twenty-two-pound turkeys to the counter on the side of the sink.

"It's a good thing they're not all one big turkey!" he said, leaning against the sink.

After he caught his breath, he quickly washed all three; then he put them in their pans and made the stuffing. And just as he was starting to scoop the stuffing from the pan to fill the turkeys, he was startled by a voice.

"Good morning, Samuel. Have you seen the sunrise this morning?"

Samuel jumped. "Are you trying to make me have heart failure, Reverend?"

"No way!" Pastor Foreland replied. "No one else is willing to cook three turkeys and a full-course Thanksgiving dinner for over a hundred people!"

"Well," Samuel started, "since you put it that way and you're standing here in my way, start peeling some potatoes!"

Pastor Foreland laughed. "Okay, Samuel. How many do you want?"

"Just start peeling and don't stop until I tell ya to!"

Pastor Foreland grabbed an apron, washed his hands, and followed Samuel's instructions.

Just as Mr. Pulaski finished stuffing the turkeys and putting them in the oven, Mrs. Foreland walked in, carrying two pies in her hands.

"Good morning, Samuel," she said as she set the pies down on the counter and walked over to Pastor Foreland. As he was sitting on a stool, peeling a potato, she leaned over and kissed him on the forehead. "How are you doing this morning, dear?"

"Don't stand there too long. Samuel will give you something to do," he said to her jokingly.

"That's what I'm here for," she said. "Is it okay, Samuel, if Pastor Foreland takes a break from KP and help me to bring in some more things from the car? He left in such a hurry this morning I had to load the car myself."

"It sounds to me like he was trying to get out of work. Sure, Mrs. Foreland, that's okay," Samuel replied.

By the time everything was brought in, the counter was covered with every dessert you could think of. There were apple, cherry, and pumpkin pies, banana pudding, and a very large basket of fruit. Also, there was a large bowl of gelatin with fruit in it and all kinds of cookies, candies, nuts, and a whole lot of other things. Including some things that looked like someone might have been trying some new experiments.

Not allowing Pastor Foreland to get out of helping to prepare the meal even after he sat the last armful down, Mr. Pulaski didn't let up for a second when he said, "Okay, Pastor. Back to the potatoes. There isn't much time left!"

Mr. Pulaski had the cranberries and carrots left to cook and his special favorite dish that Maria had taught him to make, a broccoli and cauliflower cheese dish. Everything was made from scratch. Maria never used canned or packaged foods, and Mr. Pulaski wasn't going to either. As he continued cooking, he couldn't help but remember Maria spending the whole day before Thanksgiving, making sure everything was just right. If she had to go to a hundred stores, she made sure everything was fresh, and no one could fool her. She knew her produce.

Thinking of his late wife Maria, Mr. Pulaski sat down on a stool next to the counter, and as he drank a glass of water, he glanced out the window. There were three more cars pulling in the parking lot at the same time.

"We have more help. Looks like Mrs. Smith, Mrs. Lynstrom, and Mr. Sikes."

Just as he called out the last name, the door opened, and Katy walked in. Katy was Mrs. Smith's twelve-year-old daughter. She reminded Mr. Pulaski of Angela, his adopted daughter, the first time he met her.

"Hi, Mr. Pulaski!" she said.

He already had his arms stretched out. She turned around from closing the door, and without hesitation, she ran over to him and hugged him.

"How is Princess Katy this morning?"

Katy took a step back, curtsied, and said, "Princess Katy is wonderful," and then the two of them laughed.

"May I set up the tables and the plates and everything."

"Sure," Mr. Pulaski said. "You know where everything is?"

"Yes, I do," she replied as she ran out of the kitchen and into the dining hall.

Mrs. Smith chuckled. "I wish she was that excited when I ask her to set the table at home."

Meanwhile, everyone continued to prepare for the Thanksgiving feast. Mr. Pulaski looked up at the clock located over the stove. He announced that there were only two and a half hours left until their guests would begin to arrive, and there was still much to do. Then Mr. Pulaski basted the turkeys once more. As he closed the oven, he announced that the turkeys were going to be done on time. Mrs. Smith had already taken over the preparation of the cranberry sauce that Mr. Pulaski had started simmering on the stove. The smell of fresh cranberries cooking, the turkey, and the bread rolls that Mr. Sikes was taking care of filled the room. Since he owned the only bakery in town, he always took charge of the rolls.

Everyone was counting the minutes until it was time to eat. Mrs. Lynstrom was taking care of heating up the broccoli and cauliflower cheese sauce and the lemon carrots. Pastor Foreland finally finished peeling and cutting up the potatoes. After he put them in the very large pot, he took a deep breath and stretched his back by leaning backward and placing his hands behind him for support. "Samuel," he said, "next year, could we use instant potatoes?"

"Absolutely not!" Samuel's eyebrows almost reached the top of his forehead.

"Don't get excited, Samuel. I just thought I'd ask."

Everyone looked at Samuel with grins. Samuel just shook his head.

"Bring the pot over here to the sink. I have to rinse the potatoes. Nobody is going to get sick from my food!" Samuel said as he wiped his hands with his apron.

Pastor Foreland struggled, but he managed to get the pot to the sink. It wasn't long before the potatoes were boiling.

Meanwhile, just as the potatoes had started to boil, Mrs. Foreland had finally finished cutting up the carrots for the salad and wiped her hands off. "Is the punch ready?" she asked.

"It sure is. It's already on the serving table!" Mr. Sikes answered. "Samuel, everything is cooking just fine. Why don't you sit down for a while?"

"Can't," Mr. Pulaski replied. "I have coffee and juice to get ready."

"I got the juice ready too, Samuel!" Mr. Sikes said as if he was proud of himself.

"I'll make the coffee," Pastor Foreland said.

"I've tasted your coffee, Reverend, and I believe there's a law against toxic waste!"

Pastor Foreland frowned with surprise. Mrs. Foreland put her hand over her mouth to hide her uncontrollable laughter.

"I'll make it, Samuel," Mrs. Foreland said in the midst of laughing.

"Okay, Mrs. Foreland. Just promise me you won't let your husband near it!" Samuel remarked.

"Okay, Samuel, I promise," she said, trying to control herself.

After this conversation, Mr. Pulaski sat down with a cup of punch. Katy was putting a centerpiece on the last table. She looked over the room just to make sure she hadn't missed anything.

"How does that look, Mr. Pulaski?" she asked.

"Looks wonderful, Katy!"

She smiled at Mr. Pulaski's approval. It was time to start setting the food out on the serving table.

"May I help serve," Katy asked.

"I don't see why not!" Mr. Pulaski answered as they went into the kitchen together.

Everyone hurried to get the food ready, and they all took their places ready to go. Mr. Pulaski brought in the stool for Katy to stand on so she could reach the counter.

Just then taking a deep breath, Mr. Pulaski stepped back, looked at the food, and the dining room, and then he smiled, saying, "Thanks, everyone, and I wish you to have a happy Thanksgiving!"

They all smiled and, at the same time, answered, "And we wish you a happy Thanksgiving too, Samuel!"

"Well, it is showtime!" he yelled as he threw up his hands.

People started streaming into the church hall from all directions and began picking out their seats at the tables; it wasn't long before the dining hall was filled to capacity. Pastor and Mrs. Foreland pulled off their aprons and hurried to welcome everyone. It was only a matter of minutes before everyone was seated at the tables with their families and friends. Pastor Foreland made his way to the front of the room. He raised his hands, and everyone quieted down.

Pastor Foreland put his arm around Mrs. Foreland and smiled. Pastor Foreland then proceeded to say, "It is a joy to see so many people come together just as the multitudes assembled to hear Jesus as he spoke to them on the hillside. Thanksgiving is a special time, a time for all of us to reflect on the past year of our lives and to give thanks for the joys we've shared with others and to give thanks for the not-so-good times as well and what we've learned from our experiences. Some of us have experienced a loss of loved ones, but we must give thanks that the Lord has held them in his arms and welcomed them into his home!" As Pastor Foreland raised his arms once again, he said, "Please join me in the prayer of Thanksgiving!

"Father, we come before you on this special day to give thanks for the pilgrims, who so long ago took a chance and left their homes to build new homes and to start new lives in a new land. Father, we give thanks today for this food that you have set before us, and we give thanks, Lord, for the many friends and families who have come together to share this day. I ask this in the name of your Holy Son, Jesus Christ, amen.

"Now I invite all of you to go to the back, and the kitchen staff that has so graciously put this together is ready to serve you! Please eat until it's all gone. There is no reason for anyone to leave hungry." Pastor Foreland escorted Mrs. Foreland to take their places on the serving line.

It was a wonderful afternoon. Everyone ate until they couldn't take another bite. Mr. Pulaski smiled from the time the doors opened until the last person left—an elderly man with hair as white as Mr. Pulaski's and a big smile. He turned as he was leaving, paused for a minute, and looked at Mr. Pulaski.

"It was a wonderful meal, Samuel, and I enjoyed every bite. Maria is very proud of you," he said.

Mr. Pulaski was stunned as the man left. Surprised and confused, he accidentally knocked a pan off the kitchen counter and almost tripped trying to get to the door, but the gentleman was gone by the time Mr. Pulaski opened the door to the parking lot to look for him. Mr. Pulaski turned around with a surprised look on his face, closed the door, and returned to the kitchen.

"Samuel, is everything all right?" Pastor Foreland asked.

"Yes, oh yes, everything is just fine!" Then he walked back into the kitchen to continue cleaning.

Cleaning didn't take long with everyone working as hard to put everything away as they had putting it together. The tough task of washing the pots and pans, wiping down the countertops and stove, and mopping the floor only took half the time as it did to prepare everything.

After everything was back in place, Mr. Pulaski tiredly climbed the stairs to the sanctuary and sat down in the front row. He sat staring at the big stained-glass cross behind the pulpit where Pastor Foreland stood when he preached. It was dark except for the dim late afternoon sunlight that slightly peeked through the single stained-glass window that gave a bright glow to the cross.

As Mr. Pulaski sat with his hands folded, tears rolled down his face. A quiet voice spoke to Samuel from behind as it did before.

"Are you really all right, Samuel?"

Samuel recognized that it was Pastor Foreland that spoke. He wished it was God, but Pastor Foreland would do for now.

"I'm fine, Reverend." He paused for a minute and then continued, "I thought you and Mrs. Foreland left."

"We started to, but Mrs. Foreland had a feeling that I should make sure you were okay. She's really good at sensing when something doesn't feel right."

Pastor Foreland sat next to Samuel. "It was a great afternoon, Samuel. Everything was wonderful. Did you see Mr. Sikes? He's a wonderful man, great voice in the choir, but I laughed when he went up for the fifth time."

"He didn't take any less than the first time either," Samuel added as he laughed. "Mrs. Sikes did a pretty good job keeping up with him too."

"Samuel, you know everyone has a time when they need to talk to someone, and I may not have all the answers people are looking for. But I'm a pretty good listener, at least I think I am," Pastor Foreland said, trying to provide comfort to Samuel.

Samuel smiled. "Every time a holiday comes around, I can't help but think of Maria and how much she means to me. I mean, she's always on my mind, but I seem to miss her so much more during the holidays!"

Pastor Foreland was quiet for a minute, and then he said, "I can't imagine what it's like to lose someone that close to you. I can only think how I would feel if I lost Mrs. Foreland, but I am always ready to listen."

Pastor Foreland paused once more; then he continued, "Samuel, I would very much like to hear how she died. If you don't mind telling me, I'd really like to know!"

Samuel smiled and began his story, a story that had been locked up inside of him for many, many years.

CHAPTER 3

Maria's Passing

In my Father's house are many rooms; if it were not so, I would have told you. I am going there to prepare a place for you.
—John 14:2, New International Version

"It was evening, just after six, and I returned home from work. It was a Friday, and I was ready to start the weekend. The week hadn't gone very well, and it was about to get worse. I walked in the door as usual and yelled to Maria, 'I'm home!'

"I could barely hear Maria tell me that she was in the den. I hung up my coat on the rack in the hallway. I was a little puzzled because Maria always greeted me at the door when I returned home. I made my way into the den, and as I walked in, I smiled, trying to hide my concern by saying, 'I'm really tired this evening. Today was a really long day.'

"Then I sat down next to her. I took her hand and asked her how her day was.

"'The doctor called this afternoon, Samuel, and he wants me to come in as soon as possible. As a matter of fact, he canceled his afternoon appointments on Monday.'

"'Did he say why?' I asked. I really didn't know what else to say. I was frightened, but I didn't want Maria to know."

As Samuel began to tell the story about his wife's passing to Pastor Foreland, he began to relive it as if it were just a short time ago. Then Samuel's voice became softer.

"Take your time, Samuel," Pastor Foreland said.

Samuel took a deep breath and continued, "Maria told me, 'He's concerned about my test results, and he said we need to talk!'

"I held her hand tightly and whispered as I wiped a tear from her eye. I said, 'There's nothing to worry about, Maria. Doctors just don't like to give information over the phone. Everything will be all right, I promise!'

"Pastor Foreland, I promised! But I couldn't keep it. I just couldn't protect her!" Samuel paused as he looked down at his folded hands trembling.

"That Monday, I stayed home from work. I didn't want to leave Maria by herself, and we weren't ready to say anything to Antonio or Angela until we talked to the doctor. I never felt so helpless in my life! As I was driving to the doctor's office, I looked over at Maria. Her eyes were closed, and she was praying."

Samuel smiled. "My Maria had more faith in God than anyone I ever knew. I asked her if she wanted me to pray with her, but she said that she wasn't praying for herself. 'I am praying for you and Antonio and Angela!' she said. Again, I told her that everything was going to be all right!

"After we arrived at the doctor's office, we signed in and sat down in the waiting room. It was just a short time and the nurse came out and told us that the doctor was waiting for us. 'I'm to bring you right in,' she said.

"Maria and I looked at each other. She smiled at me as she took my hand, and then we followed the nurse down the long hall to the doctor's office.

"It was very quiet, except for the ticking of the clock on the wall. Neither one of us could think of anything to say. After a few minutes, there was a knock on the door, and it slowly opened. The doctor entered, and we looked up at him as he walked over to his chair, pulled it up close to us, and said, 'Maria's tests came back, and after I looked at them, I called the specialist . . .'

"'What specialist?' I asked.

"But the doctor stood up and walked over to the window. As he stared out, he put his hand up to his mouth and said, 'This isn't easy for me to say, but . . . um . . . she . . . um . . . Maria, you have cancer!'

"And then he turned around and looked at us. 'It has spread too far for us to stop it,' he said.

"Pastor Foreland, I jumped right out of my seat! 'There must be a mistake!' I said. 'She can't . . . Do the test again!'

"But he just looked at us for a minute, put his hands in his pockets, and shook his head. 'Samuel, I already had the tests run twice just to be sure. I wanted them to be wrong. I really did.'

"My legs became weak, and I fell back in my chair. Maria looked at the doctor and quietly asked him, 'How long do I have?'

"But before the doctor could answer her, I held my fists tight." Samuel demonstrated to Pastor Foreland as he became angry.

"'When do we start her treatment? When do you do the surgery? How soon do we start?'

"Maria looked at the doctor, and in a calm voice, she whispered my name, 'Samuel.' She took my hands and held them close to her heart. 'There isn't going to be any surgery or chemo. You must listen to the doctor.'

"I closed my eyes. 'No, Maria.'

"But she put her finger to my mouth and then said, 'Hush, my love.'

"'No, Maria,' I said. 'No, not my Maria. Please, Doctor, not my Maria!' She turned and looked at the doctor.

"He nodded as he started to leave the room. 'Take all the time you want. Let me know if there's anything you need, and we'll talk again when you're ready, but I suggest you go home for the night and try to rest.'

"The doctor left the room and closed the door. Maria and I talked for a while, but no matter how hard I tried, I just couldn't believe that Maria was not going to be with me much longer. How was I going to tell Antonio and Angela? This was the second time they were going to lose their mother.

"As Maria knelt on the floor in front of me, she held my hands in hers, looked into my eyes, and said, 'I am going to see our Father in heaven. I want you to be happy for me.'

"But all I could think to say was 'How can he let this happen to us, to you?'

"Then she said, 'Don't be angry with God. He created a beautiful world, one without sickness, worry, or hate or even pain. Evil entered God's perfect world and created all sorrow and sickness. God gave us the ability to make choices, and when bad things happen, God comforts us. He saves us. So please, Samuel, do not be sad. Let your heart be filled with love for me and for God because we both love you!'"

By the time Samuel reached this point in his story, Pastor Foreland was wiping his tears with a tissue.

Samuel continued, "'Maria,' I said, 'I can't go on without you. I don't want to be alone, and I need you in my life.'

"I was convinced that God wanted us to be together; that's why he brought us together in the first place! But she said to me, 'Yes, Samuel, there was something missing in our lives, and God wanted us to find it together, and we did! Samuel, you're not alone. God is always with you, and I will always be in your heart. Now please, Samuel, let's cherish the time we have left. Tomorrow I will call Angela and Antonio and ask them to come home for the weekend from college, just so I can see them. I don't want them to know. Promise me you won't tell them until I'm ready, and then we will tell them together.'

"What could I say? I looked into Maria's eyes and agreed. 'Okay, Maria. I don't know how I'm going to hide this, but if that's what you want . . .'

"'It is, Samuel. Thank you. Now let's ask the doctor to come back in. I have some questions that I need to ask him before we go home.'

"The doctor came back in, and Maria asked many questions. I was unable to speak. I just sat in my chair and listened. It was too difficult to concentrate as they talked. All I could remember the doctor telling us was that it had spread too far.

"We spent every minute we could together for the next eight months. Angela and Antonio took some time off, but Maria made them continue college. She wanted so much to see them graduate. She made them promise that they would do well and believe in God with all their hearts. We made many trips to the hospital. I sat for hours next to her bed reading whatever she wanted me to. We talked, laughed, and cried together. I wanted to be with her every minute I could. Even when she wanted me to go to the cafeteria, I'd refuse because every minute was so precious to me. But then she'd say, 'I need some time to speak to God alone. Now go.'

"My timing was never right though. The cafeteria was always closed, except for the coffee machine. So I'd buy a cup of coffee, sit at the table in the corner alone, and count the minutes until I could return to Maria.

"I remember sitting in the cafeteria late one night. I was sitting kind of in the dark, and the only light was coming through the door from the hallway. I was sipping my coffee, and an elderly gentleman came in. I watched as he got his coffee. Then he walked over and quietly sat at the table next to me. After a minute or two, he looked at me, and I smiled the best I could. I didn't know why he picked the table next to me. There were fifteen other tables he could have chosen. He smiled back and said, 'Looks like you and I are the only ones left in the hospital visiting.'

"'I haven't noticed,' I said.

"He asked me how I was doing. Then he laughed a little sarcastically and said, 'I'm sorry, that was a dumb question. You're in a hospital, and that usually means you're not doing very well, or you are visiting someone else who is not doing very well.'

"I could feel the tears starting to form. I couldn't speak.

"'Is there something I can do to help?' he asked.

"I told him, 'No, not even God is going to help this time.'

"He looked down at his coffee and whispered, 'Do you really believe that?'

"'I don't know what to believe anymore!' I said. 'My wife, Maria, she believes, always has, and always will. She said I should be happy for her because she is going to be with the Father in heaven.'

"'You don't agree?' he asked.

"I started to get angry again. 'All I know right now, this minute, is that I am going to lose someone who is very special to me, someone who I thought was going to be with me for the rest of my life! I promised Maria that I would always believe in our Father in heaven, for myself and for her, but I am so angry and hurt. What am I going to do without her?'

"I tried to hold back the tears but couldn't.

"'What about you being with her for the rest of her life?' he asked.

"I wasn't sure what he meant at the time. Then he said to me, 'I think God brought the two of you together because he knew this was going to happen. He wanted to give her and you the opportunity to share your happiness with each other, and I can only guess that you and Maria were able to bring happiness to others as well.'

"I shook my head back and forth with my eyes closed and tilted down. 'All I can think about is that someone very special to me is in pain, and I can't do anything about it. I want so desperately to take her pain away. I asked God to let me trade places with her, and I want to do it right now!'

"'Well, first of all, you're right,' he said, 'you can't do anything about it, and you know as well as Maria does that God doesn't work like that. There are no trades. You asked God to relieve her pain, and he does, maybe not in the way you want him to, but he is answering your prayer. By taking her home, he is taking care of her! It's not going to make any sense to you right now, but someday it will. Someday, God will make it very clear to all of us. Someday, we will understand everything, but until then, we must trust in him no matter how much it hurts or how much we disagree with him!'

"Then he told me to talk to God. He told me to tell him how angry I was. He said to tell him exactly how I felt because God was waiting to listen. He stood up, put his hand on my shoulder, and smiled. Then just before he left, he said that I must never lose faith, and one day, I'd see her again.

"Maria and I spent every minute we had left together. Antonio and Angela took a semester off from college and stayed home with

Maria and me until she passed away. They went back to college, and I stayed in our house as long as I could. But after a few years, I just couldn't live there without Maria anymore. So I sold the house, put some money in a trust fund at the church we attended to take care of Maria's grave, put some in a scholarship fund in memory of Maria for kids at the center so they would be able to go to college, and I left and came here. I used to visit Maria's grave every Friday and take her fresh flowers. I would pack a picnic basket, nothing like she used to pack, but I had dinner with her every Friday, and we'd talk. I'd talk to her about Antonio and Angela and how my week had gone. You know, Pastor Foreland, she still loved to listen to me, and I could still see her brown eyes and smile.

"Anyway, now I write to her once a week and then place the letters in a box. I keep in touch with my friends at the church, and maybe someday, I'll return. I don't know when but someday."

Pastor Foreland stood up. "Thank you for sharing your story with me, Samuel. I guess we take our families and friends for granted, and we don't realize how fragile life is. Well, I better get home before Mrs. Foreland locks me out. I might have to stay at your house." Pastor Foreland smiled. "Thank you again, Samuel. I know that must have been difficult, but I am really glad that you shared Maria with me. See you Sunday."

Samuel and Pastor Foreland walked out together.

"Can I give you a ride home?"

"No, thanks, Pastor. It's a cool night, and I think the fresh air will be good for me. It keeps me young."

"Good night then, Samuel."

And they each went their separate ways.

It didn't take long for Samuel to arrive home. Just as the sun was about to disappear, he smiled and laughed to himself. "Thank you, Lord," he whispered. "It's as beautiful as you, Maria." And he watched it as it slipped away.

Samuel opened the storm door, then the front door, and went inside. He hung his coat and hat on the coat rack that stood tucked away behind the door as it opened to the entranceway, and he slowly walked down the hall to his bedroom.

CHAPTER 4

Dreams of Maria

Jesus replied, "The people of this age marry and are given in marriage."
—Luke 20:34, New International Version

Mr. Pulaski was extremely tired at the end of that special day. After preparing for bed, he poured himself a cup of hot chocolate and sat in the living room, as was his end-of-day routine. He reached over and turned on the music that he and Maria used to listen to together every night before going to bed. He sat back, closed his eyes, and pretended Maria was next to him once again. With a smile on his lips, his thoughts turned to the time when he first saw her.

He couldn't help thinking of Maria as he drifted off into a deep sleep. His dreams seemed so real to him, so much like reliving it all over again. He was sitting on a bench along the park trail that ran between the edge of the lake and the tree line of the woods where many visitors observed nature as it came together in a subtle, quiet, picturelike setting. There was no doubt that it was one of God's displays of his beautiful creation—the tall grass that hid God's smallest creatures from harm, the flowers that gave up their sweet nectar to the small flying collectors, and the sweet smell of the blossoming trees close by.

After finishing a very exhausting day, he couldn't think of a better way to end it than with a walk through the park; the peacefulness that existed there created an atmosphere where one could relax and erase the stressful day's events from one's cluttered mind. The beautiful surroundings offered refuge not only from the stress and confusion of the workday but from the whole world. Fortunately for Samuel, it was within walking distance of work and home, so he thought of this place as his sanctuary.

He was so much at peace here he often sat on the park bench, laying his head back and listening to the sounds of nature. On occasion, he became so relaxed that he'd fall asleep. But this time, as he was leaning back, he unexpectedly and for no apparent reason glanced toward the parking lot before closing his eyes. He was immediately trapped in an unbelievable trance. Totally unable to take his eyes off the vision of beauty that stood before him, he stared at a young woman not too far off in the distance. He noticed how long and soft her hair fell upon her shoulders; her smile was like no other he had ever seen. As his heart began to beat faster and faster, he became unaware of the sights and sounds that so commonly surrounded him. He only knew how he felt at that exact moment. Then unexpectedly, she turned and looked in his direction. Catching her soft brown eyes with his, she smiled slightly, as if only to acknowledge a casual greeting. Samuel smiled back and nodded slightly but was still unable to take his eyes from her.

He thought surely she must be with someone because no one as beautiful as she could possibly be alone. She began to walk past him. Samuel waited patiently as he watched in hopes that she would be alone. He didn't mean to stare at her as long as he did, but he couldn't help himself. She wore a blue Western-style dress that enhanced her long dark hair; her soft complexion offset her brown eyes that continued to captivate his attention. He remembered feeling like a mold of Jell-O, the weakness in his legs made it nearly impossible to move.

When she turned toward his direction, the low light from the evening sun reflected in her eyes, and he couldn't help but compare it to that of sparkling diamonds. At that same instant, he stood up staring at the ground as he was concentrating on his thoughts. Then he heard a soft voice.

"Excuse me, sir, do you have the time? My watch seems to have stopped."

His heart instantly fell to his feet as he looked up. "Yes," he said as he stared.

Not receiving any further response from him, she smiled. "Well, what time is it?"

"Oh, I'm sorry, it's six thirty," he replied.

She thanked him and turned to walk away. Samuel leaned against the back of a park bench. He couldn't help but feel a little embarrassed. Thinking what an idiot he was, he hit the side of his leg with his fist several times. Unable to get her out of his mind, he unconsciously yelled out, "This is unbelievable!"

A passerby turned and looked at him as if he had escaped from a mental institution, but it didn't matter. This might be his only chance, and he couldn't let her slip away. He ran toward her, and before she was able to get into her car, he called out to her, "Excuse me!" Excuse me please!"

She turned toward him as his pace slowed down, and catching his breath, he said, "I'm Samuel."

Puzzled, she said, "I'm Maria."

He removed his hat. "Hello, Maria. I know we don't know each other, but I was wondering . . . I mean . . . I was wondering if you might be so kind as to join me for dinner tonight . . . I would very much like the opportunity to learn more about you." Samuel took a deep breath. "I know this must seem strange to you. I know it does to me, and I can assure you that I've never done anything like this before . . . but I would be honored if you would please join me for dinner . . . I'm not being to forward, am I?"

Maria laughed. "I would love to, but I have something I need to do."

Samuel interrupted, "I understand."

"I don't think you do," she said, still laughing. "I mean I have something I need to do first, and then I would be happy to meet you for dinner. But you have to tell me just where it is that I am to meet you!"

Looking at her with excitement in his eyes, Samuel smiled with excitement. "Okay, great, I'll get us a table!"

She smiled back. "Okay, but you still haven't told me where I'm to meet you!"

As Maria was getting into her car, Samuel began to walk backward away from her.

"Do you know where the Rose Bud Inn is?"

"Yes. What time?"

"Is eight o'clock okay?"

"Eight o'clock is perfect!" she said with a smile.

At that moment, Samuel tripped but quickly regained his balance before falling. Still trying to regain his composure, he straightened up and began walking as if nothing had happened. Maria covered her mouth with her hand as she laughed.

Samuel was so excited he arrived at the Rose Bud Inn a half hour early, and he did it without any further incidents that might be embarrassing to him. As he was looking around the room, the restaurant host cordially met him. "Do you need a table for one?"

"Ha, not this time," he said with a smile. "Tonight, it's a table for two. And could we have that table over there in the corner?"

"Sure, follow me!"

Not only was the table located off in a semisecluded corner of the room, but it was also close to the indoor pond that provided the sound of a babbling brook as it was surrounded with a variety of colorful plants and budding flowers. It was also within sight of the door where he eagerly awaited Maria's entrance.

Samuel looked at his watch. It was exactly eight o'clock, and there she was. She had arrived as promised. Samuel closed his eyes and whispered, "Thank you, Lord, you don't know what this means to me!" He jumped up so he would be more visible to her. He just stared at her again as she moved toward him. His legs become as weak as they did the first time he saw her. He hoped that it wasn't noticeable to anyone else, especially to Maria.

Samuel smiled, pulled her chair out for her, and then sat down across from her. He really wasn't interested in dinner. It was the only way he could think of to spend time with her, but he ordered dinner anyway. Maria ordered the French onion soup with salad. Samuel thought it would be a good idea to order the same. He thought showing her that they had a common taste in foods was a good start to what he hoped would be a relationship.

For the next three hours, Samuel and Maria talked about work, their hobbies, hopes, and dreams. It was amazing to both how much they had in common. Maria was everything Samuel hoped for. It was definitely a dream come true, he thought.

The evening went quickly. Maria looked at her watch and gasped, "I have to get up early. I'm sorry, Samuel, but I have to be going. I had a wonderful time."

Samuel helped Maria with her sweater; the evening had cooled off by the time they were ready to leave. He walked her to her car. She found her keys in her purse, and Samuel opened the door for her. As she looked up with a slight smile, she said, "I really did have a wonderful time, Samuel!"

Maria paused for a few seconds before getting into her car. "I have a confession to make, Samuel. My watch was working just fine, but I couldn't think of any other way to approach you, and I think I would have been disappointed if you didn't ask me out!"

Samuel smiled. "Well then, can I see you again? Maybe we can meet at the park?"

She sat down in her car, and with a warm smile, her eyes met his. "I would like that very much."

"Good, tomorrow evening then. Six o'clock?" Samuel asked.

"Six it is. Same park bench?"

"See you then, Maria!" He closed her car door and walked away with his heart feeling like it had never felt before.

They met in the park that following evening and every weekend for the next several weeks. The visits became more frequent. Weeks turned into months. Their affection for each other grew stronger by the day, and without any warning, they couldn't stop thinking about each other. They attended church together every Sunday and Wednesday Bible study whenever they could.

All these memories continued to run through Samuel's mind as he slept. He rolled over, took a deep breath, and began talking to

Maria as he pictured the two of them walking hand in hand along the edge of the lake. In a soft voice, he said to her, "Look how the rays of the sun dance on the water as the waves move."

The sunlight sparkled as the water rippled from the slow movement of the geese. Maria smiled as she watched how slowly the geese paddled their way across the lake from one side to the other as if they had all the time in the world. Then in an instant, the geese became startled because of the excitement of young children skipping along the path that followed the edge of the shore. The young mother followed behind, holding her youngest child in a tight loving embrace as they fed breadcrumbs to the geese and ducks, with an occasional throw of a carefully picked stone that skipped across the water.

With excitement, Samuel whispered in his sleep, "Look at the leaves on the trees, Maria. See how they shimmer in the reflection of the sunlight and how their shadows overcast the water." All the wonderful sights added to the sounds of life—the subtle sounds that echoed through the air, the rustling of the leaves, and the ducks calling to one another with warning of people invading their privacy. All of a sudden, the sounds of nearby traffic and a helicopter flying overhead broke the subtleness of the natural existence of nature. These sounds, however, had no effect on the sight and smell of the freshness that he described to Maria.

He pictured Maria tilting her head back as she closed her eyes. She whispered back to him, "I can smell the clean moist air, can't you, Samuel?" With excitement in her voice, she continued, "I'm afraid the scent of autumn's dry leaves and moist air will soon give way to the scent of winter snow. Oh, Samuel, I can already feel the absence of the colorful beauty of fall and the pureness of the white winter."

At the thought of winter, Samuel reached out in his dream to feel the coolness of her face and to remember her soft skin. The images of the fall leaves losing their grip from the branches of the trees that gave them life were gradually disappearing, as was the smell for the last time of freshly cut soft grass that lay beneath their feet. The brisk wind combined with the fragrance of cherry pipe smoke slowly rose above their heads as he held his pipe in his mouth. Not wanting to, Samuel began to regain consciousness. Maria looked into his eyes, kissed his hand, smiled at him, and whispered, "I must go now, Samuel, but remember I love you with all my heart, always!"

Samuel opened his eyes as he lay in the dark. He tried reading the time on the clock, but without his glasses, he couldn't see very well. He was too tired to reach for them, so he grabbed the blankets and pulled them up around his neck, then closed his eyes, and fell back asleep.

This time, his dream took him back to when he was a young boy. It was a special time in his life that was so very long past, a time when hours sometimes turned into days when he was free to run along the trails of the mountains that rose above the valley where his boyhood town lay.

These mountains often supplied a hideaway for many people during the late fall. The trails often brought wildlife into view for all who wished to escape from the daily routines. Although the trails made it much easier to reach the top, some chose to test their strength by climbing up the steep rock side of the cliffs. High above the town, Samuel could look down and see climbers struggling to reach the top if for no other reason than to feel as though they had conquered the impossible. Samuel was very content to continue his dreams of the past and relive all the happy moments in his life.

CHAPTER 5

Visit with Jimmie

Let us acknowledge the LORD; let us press on to acknowledge him. As surely as the sun rises, he will appear; he will come to us like the winter rains, like the spring rains that water the earth.
—Hosea 6:3, New International Version

Morning came quickly for the first time in weeks for Mr. Pulaski. As he opened his eyes, he realized he had slept a bit longer than usual. Daylight was starting to break through his bedroom window. He rubbed his eyes and stretched, and as he turned over to sit up, he noticed that the sun's rays were shining on Maria's picture that stood centered, with a single red velvet rose beside it on the dresser across the room from his bed. He slowly sat up and rubbed his eyes again. After he slid his feet into his slippers, he made his way into the bathroom. He mumbled as he brushed his teeth, "I guess talking to the pastor about Maria really did help me to feel better. I haven't slept like that in years."

After he finished showering, grooming, and complimenting his reflection in the mirror, he put his glasses on and turned to walk away. Turning and glancing back one last time at his appearance, he frowned.

"I think I look better with my glasses off. Then again, maybe I look better because I can't see myself without my glasses on."

Mr. Pulaski walked down the hallway to the kitchen. He turned the water on and filled the coffeepot. As he pushed back the curtain slightly to look outside, he noticed storm clouds off in the distance.

The sun was beginning to peek above the mountains once more, but the wind quickly moved the carpet of gray-white clouds in a westward direction, as if it was hurrying to block the light before it had a chance to disperse the darkness. Mr. Pulaski adjusted his glasses and squinted, trying to see through the tree branches as they moved from the swirling wind.

"Those clouds look like they're getting ready to snow! Oh my," he said aloud to himself. *Winter is here!* he thought.

After he started the coffee, he hurriedly wiped his hands and went to the back door; he pulled the curtain back just enough to see the thermometer hanging on the tree branch just beyond the back porch.

Yep, it's going to be a cold night all right!

It seemed the temperature had dropped to thirty degrees. He turned the radio on while he was warming up some oatmeal. It was no surprise when the weather report indicated that it was not going to get much warmer throughout the day.

Mr. Pulaski cleaned up his breakfast dishes; he poured another cup of coffee and stood looking out the window.

I guess I better bring in some firewood, he thought to himself.

Just as he turned the door handle to open the door leading to the back porch, he heard a knock at the front door. As he turned around and walked back into the living room, he could see me standing on the porch through the thin window alongside the front door. I stood with my arms filled with firewood and a brown paper bag hanging from my teeth.

Samuel opened the door. "Jimmie, what are you doing here so early?"

I just stood there, lifting my chin as if to say, "Would you take this bag?"

Mr. Pulaski chuckled. "Oh, of course!" he said as he reached up and took the bag from my teeth.

"What'd ya mean, Mr. P? It's almost nine o'clock!"

"What's in the bag?" Mr. Pulaski asked as he opened the top. "Do I smell chocolate chip cookies?"

"Yeah, Mom made them first thing this morning for Dad to take with him on the road, so I asked her if she would mind if I brought some over for you."

I didn't want to tell him that I was worried about him, so I said, "Since I didn't have anything planned for this morning, I thought if you weren't doing anything and since it's Friday, we could do something together, at least until I have to meet Sam and Billy."

Mr. Pulaski smiled and said, "Well, I was just about to start up the fireplace. So why don't you go in the kitchen and get yourself a glass of milk and pour me some tea, and we'll get started."

I smiled and followed his instructions. Mr. Pulaski only drank coffee first thing in the morning and then tea, with an occasional hot chocolate for the rest of the day. He liked to sit in the living room after breakfast with a fire; it was another part of his daily routine that he'd been following for years. But today, he was happy to have someone to share it with. As Mr. Pulaski placed the wood in the fireplace, he yelled, "How are your mother and father?"

I couldn't reply right away because I had just stuffed my mouth with a cookie that was too big, and I couldn't quite fit it all in. Then I had to concentrate on balancing the plate of cookies on top of my glass of milk in one hand and Mr. Pulaski's tea in the other.

After I returned to the living room, I carefully set the milk down then lowered the plate of cookies onto the stand. Now that my hands were free, I bit off the cookie and swallowed so I could answer him.

"They're fine," I said. "Dad didn't get home until after midnight, and Mom had to leave early this morning as soon as the cookies were done, and she has to work until noon. She told me she was going to stop and pick some things up at the store, and she's going to drop my friends and me off at the movie theater. I think she's really going Christmas shopping!"

"What makes you think so?" Mr. Pulaski asked.

"Because she always starts Christmas shopping right after Thanksgiving. It's a tradition!"

He looked up at me, still leaning over the firewood. "How can you be so sure she didn't get your present already?"

"Because," I said, "I looked everywhere she hides things. Oops! You won't tell her, will you, Mr. Pulaski?"

Mr. Pulaski laughed as he nodded his head and winked. "It will be our secret."

I smiled and sat down just as he wiped his hands off and stood up.

"Christmas is a very special time of year!" he said. "My Maria always made Christmas special. Your mother's cookies remind me of Maria's baking. I remember like it was yesterday."

He closed his eyes, then smiled as he tilted his head back, and took a deep breath through his nose. "Boy, do I miss those days! She started baking weeks ahead of time and filled the freezer. Those cookies were so good that I couldn't resist sneaking one now and then. When she couldn't see me, I'd sneak one and eat it frozen for fear she'd walk in and catch me at any minute. I kind of knew that she knew I was eating them, but she never said anything except when she opened the container. She'd look inside, make a funny face, and say, 'I thought I made a lot more than this.' I'd just smile at her, shrug my shoulders. She'd smile back and start baking again without saying another word."

Mr. Pulaski picked up a cookie and took a bite as he walked over to the window. He leaned over and peeked through the blinds. "Sure looks like snow today, Jimmie," he said. Then he asked, "What time are you meeting your friends?"

"I'm meeting them between one and one thirty."

Mr. Pulaski looked at the time on the clock above the fireplace. "Well, you'd better go. It's twelve forty-five now."

"Holy cow! This morning went really fast!" I jumped up, grabbing my coat and hat. "See ya later, Mr. Pulaski." I grabbed two more cookies, one for each pocket, as I ran out the door.

Mr. Pulaski got to the door in just enough time to stop it from slamming and looked out as I was leaving. I had reached the bottom step when I stopped and turned around. Mr. Pulaski looked puzzled.

"Thanks, Mr. P, for telling me all your stories," I said. "I think they're great, and I really like hearing them."

Mr. Pulaski smiled and noted, "Thank you. I really like telling them and thank you for listening!"

I turned and ran off toward home. Mr. Pulaski just shook his head as he thought to himself, *That boy is always running.*

He made sure the door closed all the way and returned to the living room to finish his tea.

It was nearing time for Mr. Pulaski to get ready for his daily afternoon walk through town before dark. So he put the fire out in the fireplace, checked the stove, and turned down the thermostat in the living room. Then he took the last swallow of his tea, rinsed his cup, and placed it in the sink. He kept a single coat, hat, scarf, and a pair of gloves on the coat rack. It never took more than a minute or two for him to bundle up.

As he stepped out the back door, he was met by a family of squirrels that lived in the big acorn tree just a few yards from the corner of his house. He smiled and tilted his hat with his hand as he said, "Good afternoon. It's a fine afternoon for collecting acorns, isn't it?"

Then he turned and started walking toward town. Since his house was located at the edge of town next to Mr. Barrow's horse pasture, he could never resist stopping to feed the three horses carrots on his way into town every day. As a matter of fact, you could tell the horses expected it because when they saw him coming, they broke into a gallop toward him, no matter where they were. They knew Mr. Pulaski had carrots in his pocket. Once they reached him, they would lean their heads over the fence in an attempt to be the first one to reach into his pocket. He liked teasing the horses.

"Now what do you want? I have nothing in there today. Look."

Then he pulled his pocket open. As the first horse pulled out a carrot, Mr. Pulaski gasped, then scratched his head. "Now how did they get in there?"

Then he'd pull out a whole handful and shared them with all three evenly. Not one horse got more than the other two did; Mr. Pulaski always kept count to be sure. He enjoyed his visits so much that he was often unaware of the length of his visits with the horses. Sometimes time slipped by so fast that on one occasion he stayed until after sunset and never did make it to town.

> *As long as the earth endures, seedtime and harvest, cold and heat, summer and winter, day and night will never cease.*
> —Genesis 8:22, New International Version

CHAPTER 6

At the Movies

*Dear friends, since God so loved us, we also ought to
love one another.*
—1 John 4:11, New International Version

When I arrived home, Sam Bennett and Billy Smith were already at
my house waiting for me.

"Is everyone ready to go?" Mom asked as she was coming down
the steps from getting ready.

"Yeah, now that Jimmie decided to show up," Sam said as he
made a strange face.

"Do you know which movie you want to see?" Mom asked.

I rolled my eyes back and made a face at Sam. "No, just drop
us off at the cinema, and we'll pick one since there are three different
movies showing at the same time."

"Okay then, let's go," she replied.

Sam was a little taller than me, and Billy was a little shorter.
We've been best friends since the first grade. Sam was supposed to
be in the ninth grade, but he was held back a year, which was okay
with us. Most of the town thought Sam and I were brothers because
they said we looked so much alike, although I didn't understand
how. I had red hair, brown eyes, and freckles like my father. Sam, on
the other hand, had light brown hair and brown eyes. I guess it was
because we liked to do the same thing—that is, anything that had to

do with sports—and we wore the same type of clothes. Billy though was not only a little shorter than me but let's just say he liked eating a little more, and his clothes didn't always match, but that was Billy.

It was about a half an hour drive to the city, so we arrived only fifteen minutes before the movies were about to start. It was hard to make up our minds which one to see, so we spent a little time in all three. We waited until the attendant wasn't looking, and then we changed movies, about every fifteen minutes, I think. In between changing movies, we stopped by the snack counter.

First, it was chocolate, candy bars, and licorice. Then it was pretzel sticks, popcorn—the biggest bucket they had—and soda. The third trip was bonbons and nachos with cheese. Nothing really ever went together, but it didn't matter. We could never make up our minds, and we were having fun. We weren't sure when my mom was going to get back to pick us up, so we told her that if the movie finished before she was back, we would be at the pizza shop across the street. I knew Mom pretty well, and when she was busy shopping, she never kept track of the time. So it was pretty much a guarantee that she was going to be late.

I was right, the movie ended, and Mom was nowhere in sight. So we stood on the sidewalk and waited for our chance to cross the street. Traffic was really heavy, so we waited until just the right time, and then we ran as fast as we could. I guess we should have used the crosswalk, but it was a few yards away, and the fastest way to get from point A to point B is a straight line. I learned that in school; in this case, point A was in front of the movie theater, and point B was the pizza shop across the street. So it made perfect sense to us, at the time, to run straight across the street.

We raced into the pizza shop, and the three of us dashed for the chair in the corner so we could see who was coming in. It wasn't hard to decide what kind of pizza to order because it was always the same: pepperoni, sausage, and ham. I took a sip of my soda while we waited for the pizza to arrive.

While waiting for our pizza to come, our thoughts turned to our plans for the upcoming winter.

"I can't wait until the lake freezes!" I said.

Billy smiled. "Are you going to try to play hockey again this year?" he asked, laughing.

"What are you talking about? You're the one that spent most of the time lying down on the ice!" I replied.

"That wasn't me," Billy said. "That was Sam!"

Without hesitation, Sam responded, "No, it wasn't. That was you, Billy!"

The pizza finally arrived. It was the largest pizza on the menu, but it wasn't a challenge for us to eat it all. We had to wait for it to cool down some before we could bite into it, so we finished our first drink, which didn't take long. I picked up the first piece of pizza and took a bite.

Billy paused to pick up his pizza, and before he bit into it, he asked, "Are you going to spend most of your time at Old Man Pulaski's house again this year, or are you really going to play hockey?"

I tried not to get upset. "I was at every practice and game last year!"

"Yeah, but how many times did you meet us at the lake on time for practice?"

Sam and Billy looked at me, waiting for an answer.

"Mr. Pulaski has some great stories. You should go with me some time."

"No, thanks!" Billy said. "I'm not into old people's stories."

Sam just sat there eating his pizza. He never took one side or the other. We always thought he would go to college and become a politician.

"Look, Jimmie," he said, "we're all best friends, right?"

I nodded my head yes. "At least, I thought so. Now I'm not so sure about Billy," I said.

"I'm not making fun of Mr. Pulaski, but we make plans, and you're never on time. And sometimes you forget that we made plans, and Sam is no competition when it comes to hockey. We need you on the ice!"

Sam looked at Billy with his eyes wide open. "What!" Sam said.

"I'm just kidding, Sam. Don't get excited, or you'll choke."

"Listen, guys, I promise I'll do better this year, but I like Mr. P, and I like his stories. They really are good! Besides, he knows a lot about hockey. He was a coach when he worked at a youth center. If you give him a chance, I know you'd like his stories too!"

Sam looked at Billy. "All right, Jimmie, maybe someday, we'll go with you, but I'm not making any promises. It just doesn't seem like fun."

Billy finished his pizza and put his hand over his mouth. "I guess I just don't see any fun in listening to an old guy telling stories. We had to do that in elementary school, and it wasn't fun then either."

Mom pulled up in front of the pizza shop just as I looked out the window, so we got the rest of the pizza to go, but we didn't even notice that while Billy and I were talking, Sam had eaten almost the whole thing. "What happened to it?" I said.

"You snooze, you lose!" Sam said with a smile.

We put what was left in a small box and left.

"Hi, Mom!" I said as we were getting in the car.

"Did you boys have fun?"

"We sure did!" Sam answered.

Billy interrupted, "Yeah, Sam had a great time. He ate almost the whole pizza while Jimmie and I were talking."

"Like I said, you should have been paying attention!"

Mom just laughed as she drove off.

We dropped Sam and Billy off at their houses and returned home.

"Do you need me to help bring things in from the trunk, Mom?" I asked as soon as we stopped.

"No, I only have the bag on the back seat. You can bring that one in if you like."

I picked up the bag and looked into it. But I didn't see anything that resembled a Christmas present, so I got out of the car, and we went into the house. Mom knew why I was looking in the bag, but she pretended she didn't.

"I have to start dinner. Your father will be home soon," she said.

"That sounds good to me," I answered as I went up the steps to my room. "Since I only got one slice of pizza," I whispered as I closed the door.

CHAPTER 7

Samuel Encounters Tragedy

*Worship the LORD your god, and his blessing will
be on your food and water. I will take away sickness
from among you.*
—Exodus 23:25, New International Version

As I lay on my bed, facing the ceiling, I looked through one of my
sports magazines, waiting for Mom to call me for dinner. I thought
about the fun we had had that day at the movies. As we left home,
we passed Mr. Pulaski as he was standing once again at the fence of
Mr. Hansen's farm, feeding carrots to the horses. As usual, he was
visiting them first as he did on his way to the small shops in town.
He stopped at every store, which wasn't too difficult in our town,
Green of Mountain, because it wasn't very big. As usual, Mr. P
wasn't paying too much attention to time. He said that at his age,
time just didn't matter. As a matter of fact, he never even wore a
watch, so for him that's one of the reasons that some days it just
wasn't possible to complete his routine before dark. In that case,
whichever shop he stopped at, he made sure to start there the next
day.

Today though, his first shop was Mr. Michaels's grocery store.
"Hi, Peter!" he said as he walked in.
"Good afternoon, Samuel. How are you today?" Peter replied.

"I'm doing quite well. Looks like some tree branches fell last night on your roof. It looks like they're pretty easy to get down. Would you like me to take care of them for ya?" he asked.

But he didn't really give Mr. Michaels a chance to answer. "I'll just get a ladder from the storeroom and have them down in no time!"

"Thank you, Samuel, but be careful."

Mr. Pulaski didn't hear him though; he was already headed toward the storeroom.

Mr. Pulaski was right though; it didn't take long before he was on his way next door to Mr. Hanson's hardware store.

"Hi, Frank. How are you this afternoon?" Mr. Pulaski asked as he opened the door.

Mr. Hanson had gray hair. He wasn't very tall, but he wasn't short either, and he was maybe just a little husky. He often wore an apron because sometimes he had to mix paint for someone. He was usually at the counter, so Samuel didn't notice that he was busy with a customer.

"Oh, I'm sorry. Excuse me for interrupting please."

Mr. Hanson smiled at Samuel. "Hi, Samuel. I'll be right with you."

Mr. Hanson finished with Mrs. Penny, who was interested in some new wallpaper. It seems the wallpaper she had in her family room had been there since World War II, and she decided it needed to be replaced. The only problem was that she couldn't make up her mind. As a matter of fact, this was the third time within the past week that she had come in. Mr. Hanson always said it was because she couldn't remember which one she picked the last time she was in, but Mr. Pulaski thought it was for sentimental reasons.

Anyway, Mr. Pulaski apologized and then went on. "I noticed you have a loose floorboard at the front door. Would you like me to fix it for you? You wouldn't want a customer to trip on their way in, ya know!"

Mr. Hanson replied, "Sure, Samuel, that would be wonderful! Thank you. You know where the hammers are, and I'll be right with you!"

Mr. Pulaski walked into the back storeroom and looked around, but the hammer wasn't in its place. By the time he returned to the front of the store, Mr. Hanson was helping another customer. This time, it was Mrs. Sara Night who needed some picture frames. She was so proud of her grandchildren, and she had just received their new school pictures in the mail. Samuel couldn't imagine where she was going to put them. I think she had just about every wall covered with family pictures and even some that weren't family. Some of them have been on her wall so long that she couldn't remember who some of them were.

Samuel returned to Mr. Hanson and smiled. "Hello, Mrs. Night," he said as he tipped his head. "Frank, the hammer isn't in the back."

"Then just get one of the cheap ones off the shelf," he said.

Then Mr. Hanson turned back and faced Mrs. Night again. He noticed she was looking a little puzzled at him.

"I mean one of the less expensive ones," he corrected himself as he smiled at her.

Mr. Pulaski turned as he laughed to himself. Then he walked to the shelf where the stock of hammers was kept, but before he picked one up, he couldn't resist straightening out the shelf first. If there was one thing in this world he couldn't walk away from, it was straightening up and putting things back in their place. After he fixed the board, he handed Mr. Hanson the hammer and said, smiling, "Here is your cheap hammer back, and I will see you Sunday in church. You have a wonderful afternoon, Mrs. Night!"

Then Mr. Pulaski tipped his hat, turned, and walked out the door.

The next shop was Mrs. Henry's gift shop. Mrs. Henry's father started the shop at least sixty years ago. As a little girl, Mrs. Henry used to turn on all the music boxes at the same time. She said her father got so mad at her once that he moved them all to the top shelf while she was in school, thinking she wouldn't be able to reach them. But she said she climbed all the way to the top shelf one day and fell. She spent five days in the hospital and couldn't go to school for four weeks. She said her father was so angry with himself that he bought every one of them for her himself. She still has all of them on display in the front window, but they're not for sale, only show.

As soon as Mr. Pulaski walked through the door, she greeted him with a big smile, "Hi, Samuel. Are you ready to buy your Christmas presents for your son and daughter this year? I have some good sales going on right now, and time is growing short for mailing!"

Mr. Pulaski smiled and replied, "No, but I'll look around a little bit. Maybe I'll see something I just can't resist. I'm not sure what to get them this year! By the way, I noticed a lot of dirt and leaves on your sidewalk from the wind last night. Would you like me to sweep it for you?"

"If you wouldn't mind, Samuel. Thank you. My husband was going to do it when he came back, but he must have gotten delayed. Actually, he should have been back hours ago. He left early this morning to make a delivery to Mrs. Harper. Since her husband died last year, she very seldom leaves her house."

Mr. Pulaski picked up the broom and dustpan and headed out the door. He enjoyed this job the most because it gave him a chance to say hello to everyone in town who passed by. It didn't matter if he knew them or not. He always had a cordial greeting no matter who they were. It took him longer than usual that day because someone asked him how he was doing, and I know from experience, if you asked Mr. Pulaski how he was doing, you'd better have some time on your hands because he was going to tell you. He finally finished his task and carried the broom and dustpan back into the storeroom. "I'll see you in church Sunday, Mrs. Henry!"

She was in her office finishing up some bookkeeping.

As Mr. Pulaski was leaving, he heard the phone ring. "Should I stay in case you need something?" he yelled back curiously.

But Mrs. Henry was already on the phone and didn't hear him, so he waited anyway, just to make sure everything was okay. But when she hung up the phone, she looked up at him through the office window. Mr. Pulaski knew the expression on her face, and it wasn't good. He had seen it so many times before.

He slowly walked around the corner and leaned into the office from the doorway. "Is everything all right?" he whispered.

But he knew it wasn't. Tears began to form in her eyes as she stared at him. Mr. Pulaski walked over to her. Taking his hat off and tilting his head, he looked down at her. "Mrs. Henry," he said, "is there something I can do?"

With a trembling voice, she said, "James was in an accident. His car ran off the road. A deer ran out from the woods into the road and hit the front of his car. He skidded off the road. They don't know how long he's been there. Someone saw the sun reflecting off the mirror of his car. His car is leaning up on its side, and they're trying to get to him now. A rescue team just arrived, and they're trying to get him out, but the car isn't stable enough. They have to wait until they can get some cables attached to keep it from turning over and sliding down the mountain."

Samuel could hear the worry in her voice, and then she put her head down and began crying, "Oh, Samuel! what am I going to do?"

"You close up the store, Mrs. Henry, and I'll call the police and see if they'll send someone to pick you up."

Mr. Pulaski picked up the phone and dialed the police department. Officer Staples answered the phone.

"George, this is Samuel Pulaski!"

"Hi, Samuel. What can I do for you?" he answered.

"I'm here with Mrs. Henry at her shop, and she just received word from the highway patrol about her husband."

Officer Staples was quick to answer, "Yes, as soon as I heard the report over the radio, I dispatched a car to pick her up!" Officer Staples looked at his watch. "And it should be there shortly."

"Great, thank you!" replied Mr. Pulaski.

Only a minute or two after Mr. Pulaski hung up the phone, the police car pulled up out front of the store. "Are you ready, Mrs. Henry? The car is here."

Mr. Pulaski helped her into the car, and as soon as they pulled out and sped down the road, he looked toward the sky and silently asked God to protect Mr. Henry and to keep him safe. Mr. Pulaski couldn't help feeling the sorrow that Mrs. Henry felt. He remembered very well the pain of losing someone whom he loved very much. As the car drove out of sight, he was unable to leave. He remained standing on the sidewalk; with his eyes closed, he continued to pray. After he finished, he made no attempt to visit anyone else that day. Instead, he hurried to the church. As soon as he arrived, he grabbed his cleaning materials, his bucket, dust towels, and some cleaners. And he went straight to work.

Usually, he stopped there last, when he was sure everyone was gone so he could clean for Sunday morning without any distractions. After he wiped down the seats and checked the carpet for stains from the children's daycare, he sat down in the second pew from the front. He leaned forward and rested his arms and head against the back of the pew in front of him. He wasn't ready to go home yet. He wanted very much to go to the hospital; he wanted to know how Mr. Henry was, but he was afraid of the answer that he didn't want to hear. What if Mr. Henry died? What if there was nothing that could be done for him? Mr. Pulaski just couldn't face that kind of situation again. He just couldn't.

It was only a few minutes before Pastor Foreland came in through the rear of the church; he liked to practice his Sunday sermon after everyone was gone from the church late Saturday afternoons as well. Sometimes if Mr. Pulaski was still cleaning, Pastor Foreland would take a chance and ask him to comment on his sermon. But this time, Mr. Pulaski didn't see him come in. So as Pastor Foreland walked past him to get his papers that he had left on the pulpit, he asked, "How are you, Samuel?"

Mr. Pulaski was a little startled. "You have to stop doing that, Pastor Foreland. I keep thinking it's God. If and when he does decide to talk to me, I'll think it's you, and I won't pay any attention to him!"

Pastor Foreland smiled. "I'm sorry I startled you. Are you okay? You're not having a heart attack, are you?"

"No, I was at the Henry's shop a little while ago when Mrs. Henry received the call that Mr. Henry ran off the road coming down Forrest Hill."

"Oh yes"—Pastor Foreland shook his head—"I heard just a few minutes ago. I was in my office, and my wife called to let me know that Mrs. Henry asked if I could meet her at the hospital! So I'm on my way there now. I just wanted to get my notes and put them in my office. Why don't you come with me?"

Mr. Pulaski leaned back with his head bowed and didn't answer.

"Come on, Samuel, go with me. Besides, don't you visit the children's ward on Saturdays?"

"Yes, but not this late. I really don't think I'm up to it this evening."

Pastor Foreland looked at Mr. Pulaski. "You don't want to disappoint them, do you? I know they look forward to your story time, and so do you. Come on, let's go. I'll drive!"

Mr. Pulaski stood up, and they both walked out to the car.

It was a thirty-minute ride to the hospital because of the winding road down the mountain. Samuel didn't say a word the entire time. He just sat there with his hands folded together. Pastor Foreland didn't say anything either except for a smile and a message of reassurance that we are all in God's hands, and we need to trust that he will protect us. Whatever happens, God is with us in pain and happiness. Mr. Pulaski forced a slight smile as he nodded. *I've heard that before,* he thought to himself.

As they pulled into the parking spot reserved for pastors by the emergency room, they went inside. As they entered, Mr. Pulaski stopped.

Pastor Foreland looked at him, smiled, and whispered, "God and I are both with you, Samuel." And then they both walked up to the nurses' station.

"Good afternoon, Pastor Foreland," the desk nurse said. "I'm going to guess that you're here for Mr. and Mrs. Henry!"

Pastor Foreland nodded. "Can you tell me how he is doing and where they are?"

"They're still in the emergency treatment room. When they brought him in, he had a pretty bad cut on his forehead, and he was unconscious. They're running tests now. Mrs. Henry is down the hall. You know where the waiting room is. She should be there."

"Thank you!" As Pastor Foreland turned, he gently held on to Samuel's arm, and they followed the nurse's directions.

Mr. Pulaski could feel his heart starting to beat faster and faster; his anxiety level was rising rapidly.

Pastor Foreland could sense his nervous hesitation. He paused for a minute, turned toward Mr. Pulaski, and said, "Samuel, I want you to take a deep breath and slow down your breathing. The last thing I want is for you to hyperventilate."

After a minute, Mr. Pulaski nodded that he was all right and was ready to go on.

As they turned the corner to enter the waiting room, Mrs. Henry was sitting in a chair with her head leaning against the wall; her eyes were closed as if she was resting or in prayer.

Pastor Foreland gently touched her shoulder and, in a soft voice, asked, "Mrs. Henry, are you okay?"

As she opened her eyes, a tear rolled down her face. The corners of her mouth gently moved to form a smile. "Hi, Pastor Foreland. Thank you for coming and thank you, Samuel, for your help this afternoon," she said.

"How is James? Have they said anything?" Pastor Foreland asked.

Mr. Pulaski sat down on the other side of her and gently placed his hand on hers. "Is there anything I can do? Do you need anything?" he asked.

"They told us that James hit his head pretty hard. They stopped the bleeding and bandaged his head. He has a bad concussion from hitting the side of his head on the window," she said, trembling.

As she was explaining everything to Pastor Foreland, Mr. Pulaski sat in the chair supporting his head with his hand. As he leaned on the arm of his chair, he held his hat on his lap in his other hand. As he looked around the waiting room, he noticed a young mother in the corner holding a sleeping child still in his pajamas, and she looked very tired. As he listened, he heard her telling someone sitting next to her that she had been there since the night before. Her husband had fallen off a roof and had been in a coma ever since. The doctors didn't know at this point if he was going to recover. She said that her husband was a strong man and that she was sure he was going to recover, and she wanted to be there when he did.

65

On the other side of the room was an elderly woman eating a sandwich that appeared to have been brought from home and drinking a cup of water. Her husband had had a heart attack while he was fishing with a friend just a few hours ago; he was very lucky that his friend was able to get him to the hospital as fast as he did.

The hours passed slowly as they waited for news of Mr. Henry's condition. Every time the door opened, Mrs. Henry anxiously looked up with hope in her eyes. But instead, news came for the young mother that her husband was awake, but he was unable to speak. The exhausted mother put her hand to her mouth and cried, "Thank you, God! Thank you!"

As she held her young son tightly in one arm, she hugged the doctor with the other. Tears of joy ran down her face as she was escorted to his room.

After a while longer, another report came that the elderly woman would be able to visit her husband in a few short hours. His friend's quick response got him to the hospital in time, and with rest and medication, he was expected to recover. Mr. Pulaski smiled as each one left the waiting room. Mr. Pulaski, Mrs. Henry, and Pastor Foreland were the only ones left waiting. Mr. Pulaski smiled tiredly and stood up to stretch. He closed his eyes as he raised his hands up over the back of his head and rubbed his neck. Just as he opened his eyes and sat back down, the doctor came into the waiting room.

"Mrs. Henry!"

She immediately stood up and faced the doctor without saying a word.

"James seems to be stable right now, but he's still unconscious. I'm concerned that there might be some blood clotting, and so we need to keep a close eye on him. Why don't you go home and try to get some rest!"

"No," Mrs. Henry said as she tried to keep from crying. "I haven't been away from James in fifty-three years. I'm not leaving him now!"

"All right, Mrs. Henry, please try not to get upset. I don't want to have to treat you too! I'll get someone to make arrangements for you to stay here with him, but you do need to get something to eat. It's getting late."

"I'll make sure she's taken care of, Doctor!" Pastor Foreland said as he put his arm around her.

"Samuel," Pastor Foreland noticed the worry on Mr. Pulaski's face, "everything is going to be fine. Why don't you go make your visit to the children's ward? They're probably wondering where you are. I'm going to walk with Mrs. Henry to the cafeteria so that she can eat something, so take your time and try to smile for the children."

Mr. Pulaski nodded and smiled at Mrs. Henry. "I'll pray for you and James."

"Thank you, Samuel," she replied in a soft, worried-sounding voice.

Mr. Pulaski left the waiting room praying all the way to the children's ward on the third floor.

Pastor Foreland was right. As soon as Mr. Pulaski walked in, Little Frankie smiled. "What took you so long, Mr. P? We thought you forgot about us!"

Little Bobby looked up at him. "You'd never forget about us, would you, Mr. P?"

Mr. Pulaski walked over to Bobby, smiled, and rubbed his hair. "No, Bobby, I'd never forget about you guys. Never!"

Then he began his story. "I remember a long time ago when I was just a little boy in Poland . . . In fact, I was just about your age . . ."

After about an hour, he came to the end and gave each of the children a piece of candy. "I'll see all of you next week, okay?"

Just then, Mr. Pulaski heard a faint voice from the back of the room.

"You won't see me, Mr. P!"

He looked around the room until he spotted little Johnny way in the back corner.

"Why, Johnny? Are you going home?" Mr. Pulaski asked.

"No, I'm going to New York to see a specialist! Have you ever been to New York?"

Mr. Pulaski walked over to Johnny and knelt by his bed. "Yes, Johnny, as a matter of fact, I have. It's a very big city!"

Johnny smiled. Mr. Pulaski winked at him and said, "Well then, Johnny, I will see you when you get back, okay?"

"Okay, Mr. P!"

Then he gave Johnny an extra piece of candy and a hug as he whispered, "I'll pray that you get well!" Mr. Pulaski smiled and left the ward.

He returned to the waiting room just as Pastor Foreland and Mrs. Henry were returning from the cafeteria.

"Are you ready to go, Samuel?" Pastor Foreland asked.

"I think so. Mrs. Henry, are you going to be all right here at the hospital?"

"Yes, Samuel, thank you. They made up the other bed for me. I'll be just fine. I'm with James!"

"Okay then, call us if you need anything, anything at all, no matter what time it is!"

"Thank you. You both have been very good to me. I don't know what I would have done without either of you."

"Get some rest, and I'll check on you tomorrow." Pastor Foreland smiled.

Mrs. Henry shook her head yes, and Mr. Pulaski and Pastor Foreland left.

Pastor Foreland pulled up in front of Mr. Pulaski's house.

As he got out, he thanked Pastor Foreland, "I don't think I could have gone to the hospital alone."

"See you tomorrow in church, Samuel. Good night," Pastor Foreland said.

Mr. Pulaski waved as Pastor Foreland backed out of the driveway and returned home.

As Mr. Pulaski walked up the steps to his front porch, he noticed snowflakes starting to fall against the gray sky. He pulled his collar up around his neck to protect his face against the cold air. He sat down on the glider in the corner of the porch. He watched the snowflakes fall one at a time as they began to lie on the ground. He heard the church bells ring for the last time, signifying the end of another day.

It was nine o'clock in the evening. As the last bell struck, Mr. Pulaski stood up, opened the front door, and went inside. He hung his coat up on the coat rack, placed his hat on the hook above his coat, and went to bed.

> *A man's spirit sustains him in sickness, but a crushed spirit who can bear?*
> —Proverbs 18:14, New International Version

CHAPTER 8

Friday Supper at Jimmie's

For the LORD is good and his love endures forever;
his faithfulness continues through all generations.
—Psalm 100:5, New International Version

Meanwhile, it was around the same time that Mr. Pulaski and Pastor Foreland were on their way to the hospital when Mom was turning off the oven just in time for dinner.

Dad walked into the kitchen from the garage. He walked over to Mom and unbuttoned his shirtsleeves while he waited for her to take the meat loaf out of the oven. Then he leaned over and kissed her. "Hi, dear. How was your day?" he asked.

Mom smiled. "Quite busy!" she exclaimed. "I only had to work a half day today, so I was able to get a lot done around the house."

Dad walked over to the sink to wash his hands. "Did you hear what happened to Mr. Henry today?" he asked.

Mom turned around with a concerned look on her face. "No. What happened?"

Dad washed his hands, dried them off, and helped Mom carry the food in to the table. "I received an emergency call today. A car went off the road coming down the mountain. The emergency crew needed a truck with a wench and cable strong enough to keep the car from slipping down the side of the mountain any farther than it already had. The rescue team had to actually rappel down to it.

When I got there, I found out it was Mr. Henry! It took them over an hour to get down to him and get him out of the car and back up to the ambulance."

I was just about to go downstairs because I had heard Dad pull into the driveway when I heard a loud truck outside my window. I saw a big moving van go by our house, and I watched it until it turned the corner at the end of the street. I didn't know where it was going because I couldn't see it anymore after it turned the corner. I ran out of my room and down the steps in such a hurry that I missed a few in between jumps. Just as I hit the floor at the bottom, Mom was strategically standing in front of me as she was on her way to call me for supper. I stopped abruptly, smiled, and asked, "Did you see the big truck go by, Mom?"

"No, but I heard it," she said.

We all sat down to eat. Dad held his hands out to each side and bowed his head to pray. It has always been a tradition for us to hold hands as we prayed before each meal. But as Dad was praying, I whispered my own prayer thanking God that Mom forgot to yell at me for jumping down the steps. I figured that once Dad started praying, I was home free.

"Thank you, Father, for this food, your love, kindness, and the joy of living in such a beautiful world that you created for us. Bless us Lord, and we pray that Mr. Henry recovers from his accident. In the name of Jesus Christ, your Holy Son and our Lord, we pray, amen."

I was wrong. Mom added to Dad's prayer, "And, Father, please help me to teach our son the right way to walk down steps, amen."

Dad handed his plate to Mom as she served him and then me.

"By the way," she said, "that truck was a moving van. A new family is moving into the Harrison's house. Their names are Jessie and William Litchner. They have a daughter, Rebecca, whom they call Becky."

Dad and I paused from eating and looked at Mom, wondering how she knew all this already. She looked at us as she was serving herself.

"They stopped in the diner this morning for breakfast. They were so excited about moving into their first house, and we had a very nice conversation while they were eating. I told them as much as I could about the town."

"I bet that didn't take long!" I interrupted.

Mom continued, "And they said that Mr. Litchner's job transferred them here. They were expecting their furniture to arrive today."

Mom smiled as Dad and I started eating again—that is, until she said, "Oh, one more thing, I need to tell you! Becky is your age, Jimmie, and I told them that you would be happy to escort Becky to school Monday and show her around!"

I almost choked. "You're kidding, right, Mom? You're just joking. Please say you're joking!"

Dad smiled as he straightened up in his chair. "I think that's a great idea!" And then he asked, "Is she pretty?"

"Dad," I yelled, "who cares! Mom, do I have to? You know I meet Billy and Sam every morning!"

"Yes, I am aware of that!" she said. Then she said calmly, "That's why I told her that she's very lucky to have three nice, polite boys to escort her, and I mean polite, Jimmie!"

"Dad!" I exclaimed. I was looking for some support from him, but I couldn't believe he betrayed me.

"Jimmie, I think that's a great idea. Why, if I was your age . . ."—Mom looked at him with her eyes wide open, waiting for him to finish—"I'd be honored to escort the new girl in town to school." And then he smiled.

"Then you can take my place!" I mumbled as I started playing with my fork.

Dad wiped his mouth with his napkin. "Well, at least, you have tomorrow to break the news to Billy and Sam!"

Mom smiled again. "I already did," she said.

Now I was even more surprised. "You already told them!"

"No!" she replied. "I talked to their mothers."

"Great! I just can't wait to see them."

Mom got up and started to clear the table. "Is anyone ready for dessert? Al made cherry pies last night when he was baking, and he said he made an extra one. As I was leaving the diner, he gave it to me to bring home."

Dad and I excitedly said, "Yes!" at the same time.

Mom then looked at us both with a frown on her face.

"Yes please!"

Dad rolled his eyes. I'll never forget the expression on Mom's face when he did that.

Then she stood up. "Jimmie, please help me finish clearing the table."

I should have known I was going to have to work for that pie. I picked up my plate and some other items and carried them into the kitchen. Then I took the milk and the pie from the refrigerator and carried them to the table. Mom brought in the dessert plates and forks.

As she was cutting the pie, Dad asked her if she would call the hospital to find out how Mr. Henry was after we were finished eating and before it got too late.

"Oh yes!" she answered. "Mrs. Henry must be in shock. She worries about Mr. Henry all the time."

It only took a couple of minutes, and I was finished. Mom had a very small piece, and since I ate faster than she did, we finished at the same time.

"I'd like you to help me with the dishes tonight, Jimmie. I'm tired, and I want to get them cleaned up quickly."

I wasn't happy, but I reluctantly agreed; it wasn't like I really had a choice. I mumbled to myself as I returned to the table for another load, "It's times like this when I wish I had a brother or sister!"

As I entered the kitchen, Mom was wiping off her hands. "Please finish clearing the table for me, so I can take a minute to call the hospital, and then I'll be back to help you finish."

"Okay, Mom!" I said, but I knew better.

Once she got on the phone talking, she never only took a few minutes. She went into the living room and picked up the phone and dialed the number.

Dad sat in his chair across from her and listened.

"St. Francis Memorial Hospital, how may I direct your call?" a voice asked.

"Yes, I would like to find out how Mr. Henry is. He was brought in earlier today from a car accident."

"Oh yes, just a minute please. I will ring the nurses' station."

"Thank you," Mom replied as she waited.

"Good evening. Third floor nurses' station."

"Yes, this is April Jennings. I'd like to find out how Mr. Henry is doing since he was brought in earlier today from a car accident."

"I'll ring his room. His wife is in with him. Just a minute please."

The phone only rang once before Mrs. Henry picked it up. "Hello."

"Mrs. Henry, this is April Jennings."

"Hi, April," she replied.

"Mrs. Henry, I just wanted to call and find out how Mr. Henry is and if there is anything we can do for you. Would you like us to bring you anything?"

"No, April, I'm fine. James hit his head on the car window, and he had some bleeding, but he's resting fine now. They don't know how long he will be unconscious. He hit his head pretty hard. Samuel Pulaski was at my store when it happened, and he helped me close up. He even called the sheriff's office to get me a ride to the hospital. After that, he and Pastor Foreland came to the hospital. They were a great comfort, and it was so nice to have them there with me. I value their friendship."

"Yes, Mrs. Henry, they care very much, but I don't want to keep you any longer. Please let us know if there is any change or if there is anything we can do for you, and we'll keep you both in our prayers."

Mrs. Henry said thank you and smiled as she hung up the phone.

Mom explained to Dad everything that Mrs. Henry said. She then went back into the kitchen to finish helping me up after supper, but I was already finished.

Dad read the evening paper as Mom and I were wiping down the table.

"Mom!" I said.

"Yes?"

"What do you think I should get Mr. P for Christmas this year? I can't think of anything. What am I going to do?"

Mom was always very optimistic. "I'm sure you'll think of something. I believe you had this problem last year, and it worked out."

"Can we invite him over for dinner after church this Sunday?"

"I don't see why not. I plan on making a roast for dinner, and there will be plenty. But maybe you better talk to him tomorrow since it's getting so late, just in case he already has plans."

"Okay, Mom, thanks!"

I finished cleaning up. and then I hung up my towel and went back upstairs to my room. I wanted to check my hockey skates and equipment before going to bed, just in case the lake froze enough. I wanted to be sure everything was ready. I couldn't wait for the lake to freeze. I really wanted to start practicing for the games.

> *For his merciful kindness is great toward us; and the truth of the LORD endureth forever. Praise ye the LORD.*
> —Psalm 117:2, King James Version

CHAPTER 9

Saturday

Are not all angels ministering spirits sent to serve those who will inherit salvation?
—Hebrews 1:14, New International Version

Morning greeted the beginning of the day with partially blue skies and a little sunshine. Mr. Pulaski was in the process of waking up when the phone rang. He reached over and picked up the receiver.

"Hello, Samuel!" the voice said excitedly. "James is awake! He's going to be all right! They are going to keep him a few more days just as a precaution, but he's going to be okay!"

"That's great, Mrs. Henry! I'm very happy for you. If you need anything, anything at all, please give me a call."

"I will, Samuel, and thank you for everything you've done for us. It's nice to know that we have friends we can count on. Thanks again, Samuel."

"Good-bye, Mrs. Henry," Samuel replied as he hung up.

Mr. Pulaski smiled and quickly dressed, groomed, and picked up his newspaper from the front step. *If the paperboy would only aim a little higher when he throws it, he might make it to the front door*, Mr. Pulaski thought as he closed the door.

A light snow had fallen during the night but was only enough to barely cover the grass and the sidewalk. "I guess I'll have to clear the snow from the sidewalk after I finish reading," he mumbled to himself. He sat down in the living room and turned on the radio to listen to the morning news first. By the time Mr. Pulaski read through the business section, the coffee had finished brewing, so he poured a cup and was returning to his chair when he heard a strange noise outside in front of the house. Mr. Pulaski looked through the window and shook his head.

Once again, I was a step ahead of him; I was already shoveling the sidewalk.

He opened the door and yelled, "I was going to do that just as soon as I finished my paper!"

"Now you don't have to!" I yelled back.

"Well then, when you're done, come on in!"

While I was finishing up, Mr. Pulaski went to the kitchen. He heated up some milk to make some hot chocolate and placed a handful of the chocolate chip cookies that were left over from my previous visit just a few days ago onto a plate.

The snow was so light it only took me about twenty minutes to finish. I leaned the shovel against the porch and went up the steps to the front door. As I opened it, I yelled in, "Mr. P!"

"Yes, Jimmie! I'm in the kitchen. Take your shoes off and leave them by the front door on the mat!"

When I saw the hot chocolate and cookies he had brought out for me, I couldn't contain my excitement. I love chocolate chip cookies.

"Thanks, Mr. P!" I said as I tried to stuff a whole cookie in my mouth while trying to keep my eyes from popping out of my head. As I followed him into the living room, I was having just a little difficulty swallowing.

"I can't stay long," I managed to say, but I don't know if he quite understood me since I was still trying to swallow. "Mom wants to start putting up the Christmas decorations when she gets home from work. She said she wasn't going to do it herself this year."

Mr. Pulaski smiled. "It doesn't sound like you're very excited about it! I think Christmas is the best time of the year! Jimmie, you should want to help!"

Then Mr. Pulaski continued on to make his point about Christmas. "I remember our last Christmas before Maria and I adopted Antonio and Angela. Maria and I always picked out a tree and decorated it in our sitting room. It was a tall tree, but it was just wide enough to fit in the corner without taking up very much room. I remember I was standing on a step stool placing the angel on the top of the tree. I could see the anticipation in Maria's eyes. She always said that the tree wasn't complete until the angel was on the top. As I stepped down, she asked me if I believed angels really existed. I plugged the lights in and looked at her kind of puzzled. 'I never gave it much thought. Why?' I answered. She looked at me and smiled. 'I was just wondering if you believed in angels. That's all!' She reached over and held my hand. Then she said, 'I believe every one of us has a guardian angel.' I looked at her as I was trying to get the lights to come on. She smiled at me and said that she believed that God sends an angel to watch over every one of us. 'You know,' she said, 'to help us make the right decisions and to make us feel guilty when we don't. Kind of like when you have that I'm-not-sure-it's-the-right-choice feeling inside!' I laughed and said that I had never thought of it that way before. 'Well,' she said, 'I think that's when your guardian angel is encouraging you to think twice about your decision. What you choose to do is your choice to make right or wrong, but at least, your angel wants you to be positive that you want to make the wrong choice.' I always thought it was funny how Maria could think of the strangest things to say, but after I had time to think about what she was trying to say, she always seemed to make sense in her own way. After that, I always thought of her as my guardian angel, and every day, I thanked God for sending her to me."

Mr. Pulaski stood up slowly and walked over to the fireplace. He picked up the poker to move the logs around, and then he placed it back in its holder as he continued his story. "After we finished the tree and everything else Maria wanted done, she always ended the day with a wonderful dinner. That particular night while we were eating, she asked me if I was given the opportunity to be anything I wanted to be, what I would want to be. I shrugged my shoulders and told her that I didn't know I told her that I was happy just the way I was! Maria was quiet for a minute, and then she said that she'd like to be an angel. 'Angels are messengers of God,' she said. I told her that I didn't think I had ever seen an angel, but I wasn't sure and that I didn't know what to look for other than wings and a pure white robe with a bright circle of light just above their head. I don't think she heard me though since she was concentrating so hard on her thoughts of being an angel.

"She was so excited about Christmas that I was almost finished with my dinner before she took her second bite. She just kept talking about being an angel. 'Just think!' she said. 'Imagine having the ultimate responsibility of watching over all God's creations and to fully understand why bad things happen. Why we can't have victory without someone losing, why small children have to suffer terrible sicknesses or abuse, and why good people must be victims of bad people. Imagine what it would be like to carry God's message to people throughout the world, to know him as only an angel can! Wouldn't that be exciting, Samuel?' I then looked into her eyes. I'll never forget her eyes! Oh, how they sparkled, even when she was upset. I smiled and said, 'Maria, if you were an angel, we wouldn't be together.'

"But again, I don't think she was listening because she just went on. 'Samuel, listen to me,' she insisted. 'As an angel, you would have the ability to reach out and touch the stars, spiritually reach out and comfort those people who are in pain and suffering. To be able to look upon the face of God would be the greatest feeling one can only imagine!' After we finished dinner, we sat on the sofa next to the fireplace. We talked about Christmas and a few ideas for the kids at the center, and then we'd tease each other about what Christmas gifts we were going to buy each other. On Christmas Eve, we exchanged one gift before going to bed. We promised when we were married that one small gift would be opened on Christmas Eve and one special gift would be opened Christmas morning after we went to church to celebrate the birth of Christ. But that Christmas Eve, we drank our hot chocolate, and Maria played her flute for me. She always played like an angel. I could listen to her for hours. She even took the time to teach me how to play, but I couldn't ever be as good as she was. Man, could she play!

"Anyway, after she played that night, I stood up and walked toward the window. As I pushed back the curtain to look out at the stars, I saw bright lights flashing across the dark sky. As Maria played, the lights moved as if they were dancing to her music. It was as if she was playing for God and he was responding by lighting up the sky. When she finished, she walked over and stood behind me and put her arms around my waist. I was a lot thinner then, and she whispered in my ear as best she could. She had to stand on her tiptoes to reach my ear. But she said, 'God is showing his shining love to the world. We are all special in his eyes, and you are also special in mine.' We were special to each other. She made my whole world special."

Mr. Pulaski smiled, took a deep breath, and continued, "On Christmas Day, Maria got up early and spent a few hours in the kitchen, getting dinner started before we went to church. I always had to buy the biggest ham you've ever seen!"

Mr. Pulaski stretched out his hands as if he was measuring it, and he seemed to be getting excited as he continued to explain. "And all the trimmings that filled the dining room table from one end to the other. She had to have a whole separate table just for the desserts. She made all kinds of pies; there were apple, pumpkin, and cherry. Then she made banana pudding. We had enough food for the entire town. She loved to have friends share with us the entire day. I felt so good inside when she was happy!

"Then after dark and after everyone went home, she'd ask me to take one last ride to the park and through the town just to see the Christmas lights one last time. The park was her favorite. It took weeks for the entire park to be decorated and just as long to take everything down. Even though it was cold, Maria and I would walk as long as she wanted to. I miss those days, and oh, how I miss my Maria!

"After we returned home, Maria made tea for the two of us, and we settled in for the night. The last thing she did before we closed our eyes from exhaustion was pray, and I'll never forget her special prayer.

"'Lord, bless the children of the world, protect them from harm and sickness. And for the ones who are ill, ease their pain and the pain of those who love them. Lord, please fill the hearts of those who do harm to others with love and kindness. Help them to find peace through knowledge of your Word and love so that they may know you as I do. Give me the wisdom to help others know the peace and serenity of your love . . .'"

Mr. Pulaski opened his eyes and looked up at me after he finished repeating the prayer. "Jimmie, I didn't really understand why she prayed for people who hurt other people, so I asked her. And do you know what she said?"

I shook my head no, and I thought to myself, *How could I? I wasn't even born yet.* But I just sat and listened.

Mr. Pulaski gripped his hands together. He looked at me and said, "She just smiled at me!" Mr. Pulaski tried to imitate her voice. "'Oh, Samuel, don't you know?' 'Of course, I didn't,' I thought to myself, or I wouldn't have asked. But I just shook my head no.

"'The evil ones in this world are the ones that need prayer the most! The only way they'll change is through prayer, so we must pray for them!'"

Mr. Pulaski rubbed the right side of his forehead with his hand, as if he was scratching, and shook his head. "Maria was so much more intelligent than I when it came to religion. I learned a lot from her, and I could have learned a lot more too if . . ."

But he didn't finish. Instead, he turned and looked at the antique clock that sat just above the fireplace on the mantel. It was so old it was a miracle that it still worked.

"Look at the time!" he said. "Where has it gone, and where are my manners? Would you like some lunch, Jimmie?"

Eating wasn't ever a problem for me; that is something I could always do, no matter what time of day it was. "Sure," I answered, "but then I really have to go!"

"Well then, let's grab something quick."

I followed him into the kitchen once again. After pulling out all sorts of lunch meat and some lettuce, tomato, and onion from the refrigerator, we made sandwiches. Mine turned out to be three times bigger than Mr. Pulaski's. And even though he didn't eat potato chips, he kept at least one bag around for me as well as a variety of sodas. It didn't take us long to eat, or I should say it didn't take me long to eat.

"I better be going, Mr. Pulaski! Thanks for lunch though!"

I was almost out the door when I remembered the reason I had come there that morning. "Oh yeah, by the way, Mr. P, would you like to come to our house after church Sunday? Mom's cooking a roast, and she said it would be finished cooking by the time we got back home from church!"

"Sounds good, Jimmie, I'd love to!" Mr. P answered.

"See ya later!" I said as I ran out the door.

I only ran a few feet before I stopped. I could tell the temperature had dropped considerably since that morning, and because the cold was doing its part in helping to prepare our little town for winter, I looked around and then looked at my watch. I thought if I ran fast enough, it would only take a few minutes to check the lake really quick, just to see if it had frozen thick enough to skate on.

Now that it was getting colder, I couldn't wait to start winter sports. I was so excited I turned and started running in the direction of the lake. I only ran a few feet before I began to slow down. *Maybe this isn't a good idea*, I thought. Mom was really counting on me to come home. Feeling a little guilty, I turned again and started back in the direction of home.

Meanwhile, Mr. Pulaski cleaned up the table and put everything away. He slipped his boots on, wrapped his scarf around his neck, and put his coat and hat on.

As he started out the door, the phone rang. He tried to leave without answering it, but he thought it might be important, so he slipped his boots off and quickly picked up the receiver. It was Mom.

"Hi, Mr. Pulaski. Is Jimmie still there?" she asked.

"No, he left fifteen minutes ago. As fast as he runs, he should be home at any time now."

"Thank you very much. You have a nice day," she replied.

"You have a good day as well, Mrs. Jennings."

After hanging up the phone and putting his things back on, Mr. Pulaski walked out the door. He wanted to get to the church before dark so that he could once again make sure it was clean for Sunday morning. There always seemed to be something out of place, so it was customary for Mr. Pulaski to stop and check often.

After his usual stop to feed carrots to the horses, he finally made it to the church. He placed his coat and hat on the rack in the hallway and walked around the church and through the classrooms. There wasn't really much to do except to move some chairs back in their places and turn out the lights in some of the rooms that had been left on. Since it's the largest building in town, it was used by everyone throughout the week: the ladies' club on Tuesdays, Bible study on Wednesdays, boy scouts and girl scouts on Thursdays, both elders' meetings and deacons' meetings on Fridays, and children's programs after school. Mr. Pulaski always worried more about keeping the church clean than anything else.

After he completed his rounds, he returned to the sanctuary to light a single candle for Maria and to say a prayer as always. This time, however, he finished his checks within record time and left for home. He was having trouble fighting his way against the cold wind that caused him to walk a little slower that evening. The clear sky allowed the bright full moon and stars to light the way for him. Although tired, he managed to return home, and once again, the day ended for him with a cup of hot chocolate and the radio playing in front of the fireplace as he sat in his chair.

I, however, spent the afternoon helping Mom and Dad with the Christmas decorations. This year, I had a whole new outlook on this pre-Christmas family event thing. Christmas music was playing. Dad was busy trying to untangle the outside lights, and every time he managed to straighten one set, I plugged them in and replaced the burned-out bulbs. Mom was concentrating on unpacking the various statues, nativity, wall decorations, and a host of many items; even a few that she had forgotten she had. Mom smiled the whole afternoon as she unpacked stuff; there were things that I had made in preschool and elementary school and some that were given to her by friends and relatives, many which were handmade and very fragile.

After we were just about finished, Mom thanked Dad and me for helping, and then she hugged me. "I know you'd rather be with your friends, but I really am glad that you stayed home to help," she said.

I smiled at her. "That's okay, Mom!" I said then continued, "Mr. Pulaski told me another one of his stories this morning. It was about how special Christmas really is, and he made me think how special you and Dad are and the importance of family traditions! And, Mom, do you think we could ride around town sometime before Christmas and look at all the decorations everyone put up? I know it won't take long around here, but I think it'll be fun!"

Dad stopped for a minute and looked a little surprised at me and then at Mom. I think he thought I was nuts.

Mom smiled. "I think that sounds like fun!" she said.

I think Mom was also surprised that I thought of something like that.

There sure was a lot to do that day, but with the combined effort of Mom, Dad, and me, we managed to get the outside decorations and lights up in just a few hours. We even managed to get the inside of the house decorated by suppertime. Actually, we were just finishing up with the last of the inside decorations when Mom turned on the outside lights. After the three of us stood around for a few minutes looking around the inside, we went outside together and stood in the middle of the street to admire everything we had accomplished. As a matter of fact, I thought our home was the best-decorated house on the street, even though several of the other houses hadn't been decorated yet.

By the time we were done admiring our work, it was time for supper. Supper was the last thing on the schedule for the day, and since Mom had her homemade chicken soup simmering for most of the afternoon, it was ready to eat, and so was I. I was thinking about Mom's soup the whole time we were decorating the house. The aroma made it impossible not to think about how good it was going to taste, especially with the homemade dumplings and warm Italian bread.

We washed up and moved the stuff that we didn't use and sat down to eat. I always managed to eat more than my fair share, and that night was no exception. Mom didn't mind because she always made a big pot, knowing that Dad and I both would eat more than our fair share.

Thinking back while eating supper, I thought of everything I had done that day and concluded that it was a fun day. Then after supper, as usual, I helped Mom clear the table and wash the dishes while Dad finished cleaning up the empty boxes and paper from the decorations. Then he returned them to the basement for storage until Christmas was over. The evening ended with prayers and preparation for church in the morning. It truly was a blessed day.

CHAPTER 10

Sunday after Thanksgiving

*I, Jesus, have sent my angel to give you this testimony
for the churches. I am the Root and the Offspring of
David, and the bright Morning Star.*
—Revelation 22:16, New International Version

Mr. Pulaski loved getting to the church early on Sunday mornings, and this one wasn't any different. He liked to arrive as early as possible before the nine o'clock morning Sunday school. He loved talking to the children as they entered the church. Their smiles and excitement in their stories made him smile more than ever. He especially loved to hear all the children's trials and tribulations they had experienced in school throughout the previous week. Even the youngest ones who started kindergarten for the first time, their excitement always seemed to be special to Mr. Pulaski. Most of their more detailed stories were shared during the half-hour break that began at ten o'clock in the morning right after Sunday school and before church service at ten thirty. Not only was this an important time for Mr. Pulaski to tell them his stories, but it was snack time as well, and no one wanted to miss snack time.

Mom always got up earlier than usual on Sunday mornings. Mom made special Sunday breakfasts for Dad and me before we left for church. This morning's breakfast consisted of blueberry pancakes, sausage, toast, orange juice, milk, and coffee for Mom and Dad. She

86

liked to make a big breakfast for us on Sunday mornings because she didn't have to work at the diner. Dad and I managed to get ready for church at the same time; we routinely tried to be the first one down the steps. Sunday mornings just happened to become a competitive sport. I can't even remember when it started. All I remember is one morning, Dad and I came out of our rooms at the same time. He looked at me and smiled. I smiled back and said, "Good morning, Dad!"

Then we heard Mom yell that breakfast was ready, and we raced for the steps. Dad was bigger than I, but I squeezed between the wall and ducked under his arm and down the steps. "I won!" I yelled.

From then on, it was a weekly contest; we even kept score. Dad pulled ahead of me that morning by one point, with an additional point for being seated at the table first.

This competition was followed by a lecture from Mom for both of us. We tried to make being the first one finished with breakfast a sport as well, but that sport was eliminated before it even started by the competition committee, who was Mom. She finished cooking the last of the pancakes and put them on the table. Then we sat down and held hands, prayed, and began to eat breakfast.

While Dad and I finished eating, Mom worked on getting the pot roast ready. She put potatoes and vegetables in with it, except I didn't like the onions much, at least not then anyway. She usually prepared it and let it simmer in a Crock-Pot while we were at church. While she was working that morning in the kitchen, she and my dad began to carry on a conversation as usual about various things. As soon as there was a pause in the conversation, I reminded Mom that Mr. Pulaski was coming over for dinner.

She finished sipping her coffee, and then she answered me. "Yes, I remember, Jimmie!" she said. "I made enough for one more at the table!"

I smiled and thanked her. It was almost time to leave, so we cleared the table. And Dad and I washed the dishes while Mom checked on the roast, potatoes, and vegetables one last time.

As Mr. Pulaski bundled up and left his house, he remembered that the choir was going to start rehearsal for the Christmas pageant right after church, and he remembered that he didn't set up enough chairs in the choir room. Also, he didn't think anyone remembered that that was also the day that the church was to be decorated. The Christmas nativity, animals, and angels had to be set up on the front lawn. Also, plans were to be made for the Christmas Eve play and dinner theater. Mr. Pulaski started to panic. He had no idea at that point how he was going to get all the preparations finished in time for Christmas. As the church became more visible to him, he could see the cross on the steeple shining in the early morning grayish light. With every breath he exhaled, he fogged up his glasses as they slipped down to the end of his nose.

He finally reached the church at the same time as Pastor Foreland was unlocking the front doors.

"Good morning, Samuel!" he said.

"Yes, it is a good morning, and it's a busy one at that! So much to do there's not enough time. I have to get started if I'm going to have everything ready for Christmas!" Samuel said.

Pastor Foreland put up his hand. "Wait a minute, Samuel, slow down. What are you talking about?"

Meanwhile, Samuel quickly removed his coat, scarf, and hat and put them on the rack just inside the door. Pastor Foreland watched as he hung up his coat. Pastor Foreland scratched his head, totally confused as to what was going on.

"No time!" Samuel repeated. "No time at all!"

Pastor Foreland put up his hand again. "Samuel, stop. Take a deep breath and tell me what in God's name are you talking about?"

Samuel began to go down his list. "Decorations, nativity, the tree, shopping for dinner, the children's costumes . . ."

"Samuel, stop please!" Pastor Foreland repeated. "You go through this every year, and you know you always get it done. As a matter of fact, didn't you panic getting ready for Thanksgiving? And didn't everyone pull together to get it done?"

Samuel didn't answer, so Pastor Foreland asked again, "Didn't they?"

Samuel started to protest, but Pastor Foreland repeated, "Didn't they?"

Samuel paused for a minute and answered, "Yes, they did, and yes, it always gets done."

"Okay then, let's get through the morning service first, shall we?" Pastor Foreland smiled and left for his study to rehearse his sermon one last time.

Samuel made his rounds unlocking the rest of the doors to the church. He set the thermostat and turned the lights on.

Samuel finished his rounds just as it was time for the nine o'clock Sunday school classes to begin.

Adult Sunday school class met in the library, and the children gathered in the section of the all-purpose room that was closed off by dividers that could be opened and closed before going to their classrooms. Sunday school and the church service usually lasted an hour. The adults thought they needed more time, but the children, on the other hand, thought they needed less time, except for the half hour before the service when they had coffee and tea, milk, and cookies for the children. Both the adults and children agreed this time should be extended.

As usual, Samuel greeted everyone promptly from eight thirty to nine o'clock in the morning and then again between ten o'clock and ten thirty in the morning. Pastor Foreland always skipped the cookies because he said there wasn't enough time to prepare for the service, but everyone knew it was because Mrs. Foreland wouldn't let him. She said it was because she didn't want to have to buy him new clothes, but it was really because the doctor said he needed to eat healthier at his age. As a matter of fact, Dr. Greg said Pastor Foreland would have to take medication if he wasn't more careful with his diet.

Meanwhile, as everyone else was enjoying the treats before service began, Pastor Foreland put on his robe and said his prayer asking God to both help him with his sermon and to help keep Mr. Peters awake this time through the whole service. He had almost made it last Sunday. Anyway, while Mrs. Post played the organ and everyone was seated, Pastor Foreland took inventory of the new members and visitors. He was glad to see Becky and her parents finally. He had met with them when they were still looking for a place to live.

Then when everyone was seated, it was time for service to begin. Pastor Foreland made his way to the pulpit, smiled, raised his hands, and said, "I thank you, Father, for bringing us together this morning so that we may praise your name and thank you for the many blessings that we have received from your hand."

And everyone responded by saying, "Amen."

Then he looked around for a minute, smiled, and walked down the steps to the first seat in the front row and gave a personal greeting to Mrs. Stark, "Good morning, Mrs. Stark."

Mrs. Stark was eighty-nine years old and always sat in the front row directly in front of Pastor Foreland. Her husband was the pastor of this church a long time ago. He was hired right out of the seminary and stayed until he retired. He only passed away six years before Pastor Foreland arrived and after sixty years of marriage to Mrs. Stark. Pastor Foreland never started his sermon without first giving her a smile and a warm greeting. After all, he felt if anyone was willing to sit right in front of him and listen to every word he said, she deserved to have special attention even if she was hard of hearing.

The first half hour of the service routinely followed the same format: the doxology, three selected songs, collection, Lord's Prayer, Bible reading followed by Pastor Foreland's sermon and ending with another song, and then the benediction.

Pastor Foreland began his sermon. "I'd like everyone to take a minute and think of what Jesus Christ means to you personally. I know all of you are familiar with the Christmas story, and we will be visiting it again this year as we are preparing for Christmas. After all, it won't be long before we are all very busy shopping for presents and new decorations. That means, I hope, as we get caught up in the Christmas spirit, we remain conscious of the commercialization that takes place. Now please take a moment and think what the name Jesus Christ and Christmas really means to you and your families."

Pastor Foreland was the kind of minister who spoke very clearly. He had the ability to draw you in and hold your attention most of the time. Most Sundays, Mom cried before the end of his sermon. The best part about Pastor Foreland was that he never had to look at the time; he almost never went over an hour, and that morning was no exception.

As soon as church was over and everyone was putting on their coats, I was headed out the door. Leaving always took a while because Pastor and Mrs. Foreland greeted every person before they could leave the church; there was no getting around them because there was only one way out of the sanctuary since the other door was mainly used as a fire exit. I tried slipping out once by standing behind Mr. and Mrs. Sikes, but it was embarrassing when he yelled out my name.

"It is nice to see you this morning, Jimmie. Thanks for coming! You have a wonderful day. God bless!"

Then he smiled. He reminded me of Mr. Jones, our school principal, except not as tall. They both had a talent for making you feel guilty for the rest of the day if you did something wrong.

When Mom, Dad, and I finally made it to the door, Pastor Foreland shook Dad and Mom's hand and then asked me if I was going to come back that afternoon to help put up the Christmas decorations. I started to say no, I had other plans. But before I had a chance, Pastor Foreland said, "Sam and Billy are going to be here. I talked to their mothers before they left just a few minutes ago!"

Then Pastor Foreland leaned over and whispered in my ear, "They tried to sneak out, but I called to them just before they went down the steps."

I looked at Mom, and she had that look that gave me a hint as to what the right answer was. In that case, the answer was yes, so I said, "Sure, but Mr. P is coming to have dinner at our house!"

"Good," Pastor Foreland replied. "He will be here too. You can come together."

I smiled or, should I say, I smirked, and then we met Mr. Pulaski at the front door, and we all left together.

It didn't take us long to return home. We went inside. Mom went upstairs, changed, and returned to the kitchen to finish preparing dinner. Dad, however, went straight to the living room to finish his newspaper until Mom had dinner ready. Mr. Pulaski offered to help Mom in the kitchen, but she insisted that he sit with Dad and me in the living room. As he was sitting down, Mr. Pulaski thanked me for volunteering to help with the church decorations that afternoon, and he explained how much fun it was going to be.

"Well," I said, "I didn't think I had a choice, just like I don't have any choice about walking the new girl down the street to school tomorrow morning. Right, Dad?" I was really counting on Dad to change his mind about Mom's decision.

Dad laid his paper down and looked up over his glasses. Mr. Pulaski lifted his head and smiled.

"Oh, that's right. There was a new family in church this morning, wasn't there?"

"Yeah, and I have to walk the new girl to school."

Mr. Pulaski asked, "Isn't her name Becky?"

"Yeah, Becky!" I answered sarcastically.

Then Mr. Pulaski looked at me with his forehead all crunched up. "And let me guess, you're not happy with that, right?"

"Of course not, Mr. P!" I said. "Mom didn't even ask me if I wanted to. She didn't give me a choice!"

"And if your mother would have given you a choice, what would you have said, Jimmie?" That was the easiest question Mr. Pulaski ever asked me.

"I would have said no way!" I replied.

"Well then, that's why she didn't ask you!" Mr. Pulaski smiled, and Dad laughed. "Sometimes life isn't about choices. It's about doing the right thing!"

Dad dropped his head until his chin hit his chest so he could see over his glasses at me.

"But that's not fair!" I had to get that one in, even though I knew I wasn't going to win.

Mr. Pulaski just shook his head. "Jimmie, you're going to find out that a lot of things in life are not fair! And you're also going to find out that there are a lot of things we have to do in our lifetime that we really don't want to do, but like I said, we do them because it's the right thing to do!"

"Okay!" I said. "I get the point!"

I figured I'd better give up before I ended up grounded or something, but Mr. Pulaski wasn't satisfied. He really wanted to make sure I understood, so he went into another one of his life experience stories.

That was one of those times I pretended I wasn't interested. There was no way I was going to let him know that I expected this one. So I leaned back in my chair, rolled my eyes, and listened intently as he began.

"Jimmie, when I met Angela"—I knew Angela was his adopted daughter—"for the first time, she was just a little girl. But it wasn't just a new school that she was going to. It was a new family, a new unfamiliar home, even a whole new life! In just a few minutes, she lost her mother, and it was up to me to help her overcome her fears and to adjust to a traumatic change. Now you have the opportunity to help Becky find new friends and adjust to a new home and surroundings. So why don't you and your friends help make her experience a pleasant one?"

I grinned, an unhappy grin. "Okay, Mr. P, I get the point! I'm still not happy with it, but I get the point!"

Just then, Mom called the three of us in for dinner. We sat down, and Dad held out his hands.

"Why don't we all take turns thinking of something we're thankful for during the past week."

Mr. Pulaski smiled. "I like the idea!" he said. His turn was after mine. "Well, I'm thankful for the kindness of my friends, especially Jimmie."

I smiled and asked Mr. Pulaski if he would like to say the prayer.

"Well, maybe your mom or dad would rather say it."

Mom said in her quiet voice, "Mr. Pulaski, we would be honored if you would say the blessing today!"

We bowed our heads, held hands, and he said his prayer.

"Father, thank you for this nourishment you have provided for us today. As you do every day. Thank you for bringing such good friends into our lives. Thank you for the good and bad times that we face throughout our lives. Help us to learn from our mistakes and to remind one another of your love and sacrifice so that we may enter the kingdom of heaven, and once again, be with those we love and have lost here on earth. Thank you for giving Jimmie the opportunity to show compassion and kindness to Becky as she adapts to her new home and school. Amen."

After the prayer, we began eating. I was all set to dig in, but Mom offered Mr. Pulaski first. He took a small portion and then passed it to Mom. She helped serve me because I had a habit of taking more than I could eat. Even though that only happened a few times, she still didn't trust me, especially with company. As she was serving me, she asked Mr. Pulaski if he was expecting any visitors that Christmas.

He shook his head. "No, I'm afraid not. My son Antonio is unable to get away from his job. He's very busy this time of year."

"What does he do?" Mom asked.

"He's a social director for Social Services. He felt he needed to give something back to an organization that helped him get a good start in life. I'm so proud of him! He's really smart, you know. He completed college in half the time, and he moved up very quickly!"

Dad asked about Angela. "If I remember correctly," he said, "your daughter visited this past summer, right, Samuel?"

Mr. Pulaski had his mouth full. I hate it when people ask you questions when you have your mouth full, but he chewed quickly. He never passed up the opportunity to talk about Antonio or Angela. He could talk about them for hours, I know.

"Yes, John," he said as he swallowed. "Yes, she did, but she really doesn't have any free time either. She has her own family, and she's working very hard! Her husband is a big city lawyer, and she's a paralegal with the firm. But they plan on visiting this summer again. Antonio and Angela call quite frequently, especially on Christmas Day. To be honest, I think they worry about me, Angela more so. Especially because she's been asking me to return home as she calls it and live with her and her family. I don't want to, but I've been thinking that maybe it's time I started to consider it. I've been away for a long time, and I miss them very much!"

Mom looked over at me. My face expressed surprise and worry of losing my best friend. I quickly looked up at Mom and then at Mr. Pulaski, but he didn't say anything for a minute or two. He seemed to have stopped eating and just held his fork.

Mom quickly asked, "You haven't really made a decision yet, have you?"

Mr. Pulaski smiled, and he laughed a little. "Oh no!" he said. "That's a big decision. Besides, I really don't want to intrude on her family. The last thing I want to do is burden her. She's busy enough without having to care for an old man!"

Mom stood up. "Well, Jimmie, I think it's time you and I cleared the table, and we can have dessert and coffee in the family room where it's more comfortable."

Mr. Pulaski pushed his chair back and offered to help clean up. But Mom motioned with her hand as if to say no. "Samuel, you're our guest. Why don't you and John go in the family room, and Jimmie will help me!"

"I will?" I said, surprised.

I was hoping to get out of it, but that happened every time we had someone over for dinner, so I was really kind of expecting it. Mom looked at me without saying a word again.

I thought it would be in my best interest to agree, so I quickly responded, "I mean—sure!"

"Well then, follow me, Samuel!" Dad said as he got up from the table and pushed his chair in.

Mr. Pulaski wiped the corner of his mouth after finishing his drink and pushed his chair in, and the two of them went into the family room.

"Jimmie tells me you've been doing a lot more work around town!"

Mr. Pulaski replied as he sat in the chair located in the corner of the room next to the picture window, "Yes, work is starting to pick up! Winter is here, and there are so many people who need help. Most of the store owners are too busy to notice little things, and I don't mind helping. It's better than sitting at home all day!" Samuel laughed. "I think the way the temperature has been dropping lately, it's going to be a really cold winter this year!"

"Yes," Dad agreed, "it sure does feel like it! Where did the summer go?"

As Mr. Pulaski and Dad were having short discussions about the weather, my involvement in high school that year, high school sports, and how life in general was passing by so quickly, Mom and I were working on the dinner cleanup.

As Mom washed the dishes, I dried. We could hear Mr. Pulaski and Dad talking about how quickly the Christmas season came.

"Mom!" I said. "I think I know what I want to buy you and Dad this year, but I'm still having a hard time figuring out what to get Mr. Pulaski. Do you have any ideas?" I asked.

"Well, let me think for a minute," she said as she handed me a plate to dry. "What does he like to do? You know him better than anyone. You spend a lot of time with him. Did you notice if he has anything in particular that he likes to do?"

I thought for a minute. "Not really. He likes to read, but I wouldn't have any idea what kind of books to buy him!"

Mom handed me another dish to dry.

"Mom," I said.

"Yes!" she answered.

"Do you think he's serious about leaving?"

"Well, I'm not really sure, but usually, when someone makes a comment like that, it may just be a thought at first. But sometimes it grows into a strong possibility. Can you think of why Mr. Pulaski would even consider something like that?"

I thought again. "Not really! I'm worried about him though. He lives in his house all alone, and it seems like I'm the only one that visits him!"

"Well then, there's your answer!"

"I don't understand, Mom! Where's my answer?"

"Maybe he's lonely. He may be thinking that if he moves back with his daughter, he'll have more people around him, and he won't be lonely anymore!"

I thought for another minute and finished the last dish, and then it came to me. "I know exactly what I'm going to get him for Christmas. Thanks, Mom!"

Since it was the last dish, I ran up to my room.

"Don't you want dessert?" Mom yelled just as I went through the kitchen door that led to the hallway and upstairs.

"I don't have time. I have plans to make!" I shouted as I ran upstairs.

Dad looked at Mom as she stood in the hallway. "Where is he going in such a hurry?"

"I don't know. I asked him if he wanted dessert, and he said he didn't have time!"

Dad looked at Mr. Pulaski. "Now that's really strange! Jimmie passing up dessert. It must be something really important!"

Mom brought in coffee and three slices of pie on a serving tray. As she entered the living room, Mr. Pulaski looked up and smiled.

"Is that apple pie?"

"It sure is!" Mom answered as she set the tray down on the coffee table. "Jimmie told me it was your favorite, that and chocolate chip cookies!"

Mr. Pulaski laughed. "Yes, but only yours and my late wife's are the best!" Mr. Pulaski looked around. "I guess Jimmie isn't going to visit with us?"

"I guess not!"

Mr. Pulaski just shook his head. "Ya know that boy is always running, everywhere he goes. Doesn't he ever slow down?"

Dad sipped his coffee. "He does have a lot of energy built up!"

"Jimmie's a good boy. The two of you are very lucky. As a matter of fact, I'm pretty lucky too. He's a good friend to me for one so young."

"Jimmie really likes visiting with you, Samuel. I know he misses his grandparents very much!"

"Well, I'm happy I can fill in for them!"

Mom laughed. "I didn't mean you were old!"

Mr. Pulaski grinned. "Of course, I am, and I don't mind at all!"

After another bite of pie, Dad looked up at Mr. Pulaski. "Your own children are very lucky as well, Samuel. Although we haven't had the opportunity to get to know them, just knowing how you are with Jimmie, they must be wonderful kids!"

Mr. Pulaski smiled. "Yes, they sure are! It was a rough start for Antonio and Angela after we adopted them, more so for Antonio. But with time, they adjusted just fine!"

Mr. Pulaski laughed. "Antonio was a wild one when I first met him, and I wasn't sure he was going to come around. But he did, and I thank God every day for both."

Mom's curiosity got the best of her. She just had to ask. "How did you and your wife decide that Antonio was the one you wanted to adopt? He was the first one, right?"

Dad looked at her, puzzled.

"Well," she said, "I'm sorry, Samuel. But I'm curious as to how people decide on which child they want to adopt!"

"That's all right. I don't mind telling you at all. But we didn't choose them. God did!"

Mom refilled the coffee cups and listened intently to Mr. Pulaski's story about Antonio.

CHAPTER 11

Samuel's Search for Antonio

Suppose one of you has a hundred sheep and loses one of them. Does he not leave the ninety-nine in the open country and go after the lost sheep until he finds it?

—Luke 15:4, New International Version

Mr. Pulaski began explaining that he became a part-time summer counselor at a youth crisis center while looking for full-time employment after arriving in the United States. He was unaware at the time how much he was going to love helping the children who were lonely, abandoned, and in desperate need of someone to love and care for them. He had worked there close to two years before he was offered a full-time position; he explained that he went to school nights and weekends, and upon graduating, he became a caseworker for the center.

"One night, three boys were brought in by Social Services. Two of them had been victims of parents who were drug and alcohol addicts. The third boy, whose name was Antonio, had previously lived with his mother, and she loved him with all her heart and took very good care of him even though it was difficult for her while working a full-time job. They took care of each other since Antonio's father left them just after he was born. When he turned ten years old, his mother became very sick, and Antonio had to literally take care of her. It didn't take long for what little money she had managed to save up to run out, and she died.

"After her funeral, Antonio's father was found, and he agreed to take care of Antonio. But all he really wanted was for Antonio to take care of him. He left Antonio alone most nights and usually didn't come home until morning, and when he did come home, he was usually drunk. Antonio's life changed drastically for the worst. One day, Antonio was at the park, and he met two older boys. They became good friends; at least, that's what Antonio thought. They convinced him that they cared about him more than his father did, which wasn't hard to do at the time. They convinced Antonio that he would be better off with them instead of his father. It wasn't hard to persuade a ten-year-old boy who was in Antonio's situation to run away with someone who promised to take care of him. Unfortunately, these two boys didn't care about him either. They were really looking for a younger boy to help them steal, and because of Antonio's situation: a desire to escape from his father, it didn't take much persuasion. Antonio was much younger and smaller than the other two boys, and I could tell that there was something different about him the instant I met him.

"After working with the three of them the first day, Antonio didn't seem to have the same attitude as the other two. I could tell this little one hadn't been on the streets very long. Every time I looked at him, I wanted desperately to help him start a new life, a good life. It was a challenge trying to get any of them to listen to me. I tried to show them that they could have a better life if they would just let me help. But it was difficult getting them to listen or participate in the counseling sessions. That was the first time I ever became frustrated with children because of their refusal to be helped.

"I tried everything I could think of. I tried talking to them one at a time, and I tried showing them how good life could be. I tried to get them to open up and talk to me. I tried everything. But without being able to build a trusting relationship with them, they were not going to cooperate in any way at all. In fact, they were uncooperative from the first day they arrived. These boys didn't trust anyone no matter who they were or what they said. They were in control of their own lives, and no one was going to tell them any different. But I sensed that there was something different about Antonio. During counseling sessions, he never talked. He just sat in his chair and pretended he wasn't listening. But I knew that he was because every now and then, he glanced up at me. He'd look up at me without lifting his head, only his eyes. During mealtimes, I watched all three of them, hoping to notice something that would give me a sign that I might be getting through to them.

"The next day, it was the same routine except this time during dinner, I was watching them very closely, and I noticed Antonio staring at me. It was like he wanted to say something but was afraid to. I could see it in his eyes, but then all of a sudden, it was like he caught himself, and he quickly turned away before I had a chance to say anything. There was something that was definitely different about him, and I was determined to find out. I just knew Antonio wasn't like the other two boys. It was a feeling I had.

"The next night, the two older boys decided they didn't want to stay at the center any longer. They had been there only a few days, and they ran away. I wasn't sure at the time if Antonio wanted to go with them or not, but I couldn't get him off my mind. I couldn't sleep or eat for the next two nights. All I could think about was Antonio.

"At the end of the day, I returned home, and as always, Maria had a wonderful dinner made. After we prayed and started eating, I didn't really have much to say that night, which was unusual for me. I loved to tell Maria about the children. Maria tried to get me to talk. She asked me how my day was. She asked me if anything exciting happened that day and a lot of other questions that I really didn't hear. She knew something was bothering me, especially because that night, I barely touched my food. Maria took a few bites of her food and waited to see if I was going to say anything to her. She knew I was worried, and she was afraid that something had gone wrong at the center. She was afraid that something might have happened to one of the children. She looked forward to my stories, but I didn't have any to tell that night. I was silent.

"After a few small bites, she wiped her mouth with a napkin and spoke in a soft voice, 'Samuel, you're not eating, and you haven't said a word since we sat down.'

"I looked up, laid my fork down, and began to tell her. 'Maria,' I said, 'three new boys were brought into the center a few days ago, and I tried to get through to them, but I couldn't. I mean I know I wasn't getting through to the older two, but yesterday, I thought for sure I was starting to reach the younger one. His name is Antonio.'

"Maria could tell I was frustrated, especially when I hit my fist on the table when I told her that the boys ran away during the night. What had me concerned though was that I didn't think Antonio really wanted to go with them!

"Maria got up from the table, walked over, and sat down next to me. As she looked up at me, I knew she was worried too. I could hear it in her voice. 'You're going to go look for him, aren't you?'

"'I have to Maria!' I said.

"I was desperate. I told her if she didn't want me to go, I wouldn't. But I didn't even get to finish my sentence.

"Maria knew me so well that she often finished my thoughts. 'If something happens to him, you will never forgive yourself,' she said.

"Then she held my hand and said, 'Samuel, it doesn't matter what or how I feel right now. Of course, I don't want you to go, but if this is what God is leading you to do, then you must.'

"I looked at her. 'There's a lost child out there, and I must lead him home. I have to find him!'

"That night, I helped Maria with the dishes, and then Maria went upstairs and started laying my clothes out for the next day. She knew I was going to get an early start, and she was afraid I wouldn't dress right for the cold. Afterward, she lay in bed and prayed most of the night for me and for Antonio. She prayed that the Lord would keep me safe and that I would find Antonio safe also.

"The next morning, I kissed her as I was leaving. I had to stop by the center first to let Frank know. He was the director at the time. He tried to talk me out of going as did the other counselors. Frank understood though. He didn't agree with me, but he understood that I had to do this. The other counselors told me that I couldn't save them all. They said that I should forget about Antonio, and sooner or later, the police would bring him back. But I just couldn't wait. I had to find him, especially Antonio! I knew the boys came from the south side of the city, and I was confident that I could find him! I had a feeling that they would try to return to the area that they were most familiar with. Frank just shook his head yes as though he really did understand and wished me luck in my effort to find Antonio. He knew it didn't matter anyway what he or the others thought. I was determined find him. Besides, I didn't need luck. I had God with me, and whatever God's will was going to be, I had to accept it.

"I started out. I was worried, but I began my journey early that morning. My fears for Antonio overcame my own feelings of anxiety. I couldn't help but imagine how scared Antonio must have been. As I stepped out onto the sidewalk and into the cool air, I only went a short distance before I stopped and looked up to the sky. I closed my eyes and asked God to lead me in my quest to save a young boy's life. I pulled my collar tightly closed around my neck, took my gloves out of my pockets, and pulled them onto my hands. I looked back at the center one last time and started walking again. I wanted to walk because I thought I would be able to look in store windows and alleyways and even look in trash cans if I had to. I'd even be able to walk up one-way streets. I was determined, and I had no intentions of returning home without him.

"I searched for only a few hours, but it had already seemed for a much longer time, and it was getting late in the day. I had no idea how far I had traveled, but I knew it was quite a long distance, and I was beginning to get tired. I couldn't walk as fast now as I had when I started out because the wind was picking up, and it was hard enough just trying to stay on the sidewalk. I couldn't even keep my head up as I was walking because I had to keep my face down and my hand over my hat to help block the wind. Every few minutes, I had to stop and put my hands in my pockets to try and warm them up a little.

"Then as I began to lift my head up, just to see where I was going, I spotted a young boy eating an apple at a fruit stand farther down the street. I paused to try and focus my eyes. I started walking faster and faster. I was so excited that I started running toward him, and as I approached the stand, I called out, 'Antonio!'

"The young boy turned around, and I started to reach out to him.

"'Thank God!' I said out loud.

"I was so excited, and then I realized it wasn't Antonio at all! I swallowed, choked back my disappointment, and said I was sorry. 'I thought you were someone else,' I said.

"I took a deep breath and paused before continuing my search.

"I stopped everyone on the street that would talk to me. I described Antonio and the other two boys to them and asked if they had seen them. But everyone shook his or her head no, so I continued on. 'Thank you anyway' was my response as I turned and walked away from one right after another.

"I was beginning to wonder if I was really going to find him. I was trying not to get discouraged. I didn't want to stop looking for him. I couldn't. I continued asking store owners, priests, pastors, and rabbis. I asked homeless people, people waiting for buses or taxis, and children. I stopped in bars and asked the bartenders and customers. I was getting so desperate that I even asked a dog, but it only barked at me, and it wasn't friendly either. I didn't know if it would have been easier with a picture or not, but I didn't have one. I was running out of options, and by then it was getting late, and I hadn't eaten since I had left that morning.

"So I went into a restaurant and ordered something to eat. I don't even remember what it was, but I made sure I sat at a table by the front window just in case Antonio passed by. The longer I sat at the table though, I realized that I was losing daylight, and I began to get tired. I leaned on the table and held my head up with my hands until my food came just in case I fell asleep. After I was served, I ate quickly. I asked the waitress for one more cup of coffee, and I described Antonio to her, but she hadn't seen him. Then just before

I began to leave, I asked every one of the customers, the other waitresses and waiters, but no one had seen him.

"As I pushed the door open, an older gentleman stopped me. 'Excuse me, sir,' he said. 'Did I hear you say that you're with the home on the north side of town?'

"'Yes!' I answered.

"He looked up at me and smiled. 'Would that home be an old farmhouse?'

"I answered, 'Yes,' again.

"Then he said, 'I thought they would have torn that old house down by now!'

"'No, it's still there!' I said. The roof leaks. The pipes need to be replaced. It needs to be rewired, and if we don't find the money to replace the furnace soon, it will either blow up the building or just give out, and we won't have heat for the winter. But it's still there!'

"The old gentleman began to laugh. 'Please sit down for a minute with me,' he asked.

"I hesitated for a minute. 'I really can't. I don't have much time left of daylight to look for him!'

"'Please,' he said. 'Please just for a minute!'

"I took my hat off and sat back down. 'I can't stay long. I have to look for Antonio before it gets dark.'

"The elderly man looked at me. 'That home has been there as long as I can remember. It used to have a beautiful apple orchard, acres and acres of beautiful rolling green pastures, you know.'

"'Well, they're all gone now. It's a crisis home for boys. There are so many boys that don't have homes, and they need to be cared for. They need to be given a chance to have a life, and I hope we can continue to help them for a little while longer anyway.'

"I noticed that the man's eyes lit up as I talked about the center. It seems he knew a lot about that area, and I wanted to listen to him talk."

Samuel deepened his voice and tried to sound like him, but no one knew how the old man sounded then, so Samuel was doing really well as far as Mom and Dad could tell. Samuel went on imitating:

"'A man by the name of Frank Shaw and his wife Lilly owned that farm,' he told me. 'My parents died when I was a young boy, and Frank and his wife gave me a job picking apples.' Then the old man laughed. 'I didn't get paid much then, but they let me have all the apples I could eat! Yes, sir, they treated me like I was their own son. Lilly was a schoolteacher, so she made me study. In the evenings, she sat with me and made sure I learned everything. Mrs. Shaw felt it was best for me to learn at night because Mr. Shaw needed me to help in the orchards during the day.

"'After I worked in the orchards trimming trees, picking apples, and watering when they needed it, I also took care of the horses. It took me a few hours to feed all of them, clean their stalls, and brush them down every afternoon. Mr. Shaw took really good care of his horses. After I grew up, he told me the reason he had me do some chores twice was so I could build up my muscles. He said, "Ya had to be strong to make it in this world."' Then he laughed again. 'It's funny how Mr. Shaw thought ya had to be strong to make it, and Mrs. Shaw said ya had to be smart. She said the world was changing, and if I didn't learn, I'd never survive. So I grew up strong and smart, and I did all right for myself.'

"Amazed at the history of the old place, I said to him, 'Well then, you're more than welcome to come visit if you like. Although the orchards are gone, the building still looks the same. Unfortunately, if we don't get all the problems fixed, I'm afraid it's going to be torn down, and we don't have enough money to build a new one. So if you want to visit, you better do it soon.'

"I stood up, put my hat back on, and thanked him for the history lesson. 'I really need to be going!' I said.

"Then just as I turned to walk out the door, I looked back at him and said, 'By the way, you never told me your name!'

"'John Michaels,' he said. 'My name is John Michaels, and good luck finding Antonio. Samuel, I have faith that you will.'

"I smiled, nodded, and walked out of the restaurant.

"The wind was blowing, and the rain was even colder. I tilted my hat into the wind and the rain and went on. I had to hold it with my hand to keep it from blowing away. Once again, I started looking in every store window. I walked down every alley and asked everyone that would stop, but no one had seen Antonio, or no one would admit that they had seen him. After a few hours, the rain let up. It was dark, and I was very tired. I sat down on a bench at a bus stop. I put my head down and closed my eyes.

"As I was sitting there, I heard a voice ask, 'Are you all right?'

"I looked up. I hadn't noticed when I had sat down that a lady was already sitting on the bench.

"'No, I'm not!' I said. 'I have been looking day and night for a young boy by the name of Antonio. He may be with two other boys, but I'm not sure.'

"The lady paused for a minute, and then she said, 'Well, I did see a young boy run across the street at the center of town, and I don't remember seeing him around here before. He looked like he was in an awfully big hurry. You know where the statue is?'

"I felt a burst of energy fill my entire body. 'When did you see the boy?' I asked. I was so excited.

"'It was yesterday, I'm afraid. Yesterday morning!'

"'Did you notice which way he was going?'

"She looked at me and said, 'I believe it was toward the old mill.'

"I jumped up. 'Thank you, thank you very much. You don't know what this means to me!'

"I began running. I headed in the direction I thought Antonio might be going, praying that I might see him. I continued searching everywhere. I made sure that I was very thorough in checking every possibility where Antonio might be. I spent the rest of the night searching.

"Morning came before I even realized it. I'd never felt as tired as I did that morning. I couldn't go on anymore. The wind was picking up again, and the clouds seemed to get darker and darker as the morning went on. I couldn't see the sun anymore, and I began to think about Maria and how worried she must have been. The feeling in my toes was gone, and I stopped once again to rub my hands together, trying to warm them up. I even tried putting them in my pockets, hoping to get them just warm enough to be able to move them without hurting. I shook my head and started to cry. I tried.

I really tried, and I just couldn't go on any longer! I closed my eyes, tilted my head back, and prayed one last time.

"'Lord, my strength is gone. I'm tired, cold, and hungry. I have no choice, Lord, and I've done all that I can. It's time to go home.'"

> *For the Son of Man came to seek and to save what was lost.*
> —Luke 19:10, New International Version

CHAPTER 12

The Chase

*But whoever causes the downfall of one of these little
ones who believe in Me—it would be better for him
if a heavy millstone were hung around his neck and
he were drowned in the depths of the sea!*
—Matthew 18:6, New International Version

"Giving up wasn't easy. I really thought I could find Antonio. I really
wanted to save him from growing up on the streets! Most of those
kids don't survive very long, and the ones that do usually end up in
jail. While Antonio's friends were sleeping, he ran away in the middle
of the night. I know he was scared of being alone, but he realized
what they were doing, so he ran as fast as he could. He wanted to
get as far away from them as possible before they woke up. His heart
was beating so fast he wasn't sure if it was racing from fear of getting
caught or fear of being alone. He was desperate to make it back to the
shelter. Even though he had only been with us for a few days, he felt
safe with us. My suspicions were right. He did want to talk to me. It
was just that he was afraid of what the other boys would do if he did.
Antonio knew I cared about him, so he ran all night, hoping he was
going in the right direction toward the center. It wasn't until morning
before the other boys realized he was gone. When they woke up, they
also figured he was headed in our direction. They knew Antonio was
going to try to come back to the center because he had tried to talk

them into returning with him. Antonio was smart enough to keep out of open areas. He kept hiding along the way to rest for fear of what they might do to him if they found him.

"Unfortunately though, by hiding, I couldn't find him either. The first time he hid, he crawled in behind a couple of trash cans in an attempt to keep warm. He heard noises, bottles breaking, two homeless men fighting over a bottle that one of them supposedly found in one of the trash cans. He was afraid to look though. He could hear people yelling at each other, and the shadows around him were so frightening he stayed curled up in a ball and kept his eyes closed and his hands over his ears. He didn't want to see or hear what was going on. Besides, he was terribly afraid that he might be found. He hid as long as he could, but after a while, he knew he had to take a chance and run. So he took a deep breath and jumped up and ran again.

"He was almost out of the alley when all of a sudden, the two boys stepped out from around the corner right in front of him. It was as if they knew he was there all along, and they were waiting for him to come out.

"'Where are you going, Antonio?' they asked, laughing.

"Antonio pushed one of them with all his strength into the other and ran past them before they could get up. But as he was looking back to see if they were following him, he ran into the street, and he could hear cars' squealing tires in an effort to avoid hitting him. He panicked and ran into the center of the street. He hid behind the statue that stood in the center of the intersection on the opposite side, once again hoping they couldn't see him. Antonio could hear them yelling for him. They were calling out, 'Antonio, where are you? Come on, we're your friends. We'll take care of you! Come back! Come on, Antonio. We need to stick together. We're brothers!'

"But he didn't answer back. Antonio felt paralyzed. He panicked and yelled back, 'Leave me alone! Don't you understand? Just leave me alone!'

"Then he peeked around the corner and saw them split up. Afraid they would see him, he stood with his back pressed against the base of the statue as if he was actually a part of the statue. His fists were clenched so tightly his knuckles turned white. His head was tilted back, and he had his eyes closed. He even held his breath. While standing at the base of the statue, he planned out his next move in hopes of escaping the two other boys.

"The road split and curved around the statue on both sides. The road was a one way, so the traffic was stopped for a moment on both sides of the statue, waiting for the red light to change. Antonio could hear the men on the trash truck talking to each other right next to him.

"Then he took a deep breath and darted out across the street. But he didn't know that the light turned green at the same time, and the traffic began moving again. The trash truck pulled out just as he was in front of it, and it barely missed him as he moved quickly to one side out of its way. Antonio had no idea which way to go from there. So once again, he started running in the direction that he thought was right.

"By then, he was exhausted and needed to rest again, so he went into the clothing store on the corner and hid in the back. He knelt behind a clothes rack where he could see the door. Then after a few minutes, he stood up and walked cautiously back out onto the sidewalk and looked up and down. Then he hid in the middle of a crowd of people walking down the sidewalk. After a few blocks, he thought he was safe. He thought for sure the other boys must have given up looking for him. After all, it had been a long time.

"He kept walking. By then, it was starting to get dark again, and he needed to rest. He sat down on the sidewalk and leaned against the building in a corner by the steps. Antonio was so tired and cold at this point that he closed his eyes and leaned against the wall and began thinking of his mother. Realizing he was falling asleep, he forced his eyes open by rubbing them and trying to focus. He saw a produce stand across the street with fresh vegetables and fruits. He hadn't eaten in days and was very hungry, but he didn't have any money. Then he remembered what I had said during one of the sessions. He remembered I told them that honesty always worked for me and that it would work for them too. So he walked across the street toward the stand, making sure he looked for traffic this time.

"As he approached the stand, his first instinct was to grab the first thing he saw and run. After all, that's what his friends had taught him. They called it 'street survival.' But instead, Antonio walked up to the man with tears in his eyes and said, 'Excuse me, sir.'

"The man turned around and looked down at him without saying a word. Antonio was scared, but he continued, 'I have no money, sir, but I am very hungry. May I please have something to eat, and I promise I will return someday with the money that I owe you. I promise!'

"The man was as tall as he was heavy and overshadowed Antonio tremendously. He didn't look very happy either. He stared down at Antonio for a minute with his hands on his hips, which wasn't very easy to do by the size of him. Then he said, 'If I give everything away to everyone who told me they didn't have any money, I would not be in business.'

"Antonio looked down at his feet and turned to walk away. 'Maybe the boys were right, and I was wrong,' he thought. But then, the man began to smile and called Antonio back.

"'Wait, I wasn't finished. What I was going to say is that you are the first one who ever told me that you would pay me back.' As he was laughing, he said, 'I doubt I'll ever see you again, but my little lost friend, what would you like? Pick anything you want, but if I were you, I'd pick the biggest apple I could find.'

"Antonio smiled and did just what the man suggested, and then he thanked him and promised again to return with the money someday as he walked away.

"Antonio began walking more and more slowly as he ate his apple. He was still very tired and cold. He began looking for shelter for the night as he walked. He was afraid to go into the alleys again, but he knew he couldn't stay on the sidewalk. Besides, it looked like it was going to start raining again. After a few more minutes of walking, he spotted an all-night Laundromat. The lights inside weren't very bright, and for the moment, there wasn't anyone in it. As he walked in, he looked around for a place to hide. It was a rather large Laundromat and warm, so he walked to the very back of the room. He found a washing machine in the very back corner that was out of order, so he squeezed in behind it, and there he found his refuge out of sight for the night.

"Exhausted, it didn't take long before he fell asleep. His dreams that night were of his mother holding him and singing him to sleep. Then all of a sudden, he was startled by loud thunder and clashes of lightning, but as he imagined his mother's soft soothing voice in his mind, he felt safe for the first time since before she passed away, and he quickly fell back to sleep.

"Morning came quickly, and he woke up to find the sky dark and rain still falling heavily outside the window. Antonio peeked around the washer that he was hiding behind to make sure no one was around to see him, and then he stood up. He had no idea what he was going to do or where he was going to go next. He still wasn't sure he was going in the right direction either. Antonio stood by the window looking out, and then all of a sudden, he jumped back behind the wall away from the window and out of sight. The two boys who were searching for him were across the street. Panicking, Antonio ran to the back of the building and found a door to the outside. He pushed it open and ran once again as fast as his legs could carry him. He ran as long as he could before be stopping out of breath.

"He was soaking wet from head to toe. The rain was running down his face so fast it was impossible for him to wipe it away so he could see. Antonio ran out of breath once again and finally stopped. He only walked a few blocks before he found a building with a canopy over the entrance. He sat down and tried to pull his wet coat over his head to keep his ears warm and to wait for the storm to end. By then, it was midmorning, and he was sure he had been able to get far enough away that the other two couldn't find him.

"The apple that he had eaten was good, but it wasn't enough, and he was still cold and hungry. Antonio regretted leaving the center and not talking with me. If he had only listened, he wouldn't be on the street feeling as he did. By then, Antonio wanted so desperately to find his way back. He thought if he could only make it back to the center, everything would be all right. He knew now more than ever that I would have taken care of him! But now, he thought, it was too late. He had had his chance, and he made the wrong choice, and there was nowhere for him to go.

"The wind got stronger, and the rain came down faster and colder. And after a while, the canopy that he was under wasn't doing any good because the wind was blowing the rain in on him. He curled up in the corner as much as he could with his back to the rain, but that didn't do any good either. Antonio wasn't going to go on any farther. He thought he had reached his end. And then he remembered that I also had told them that if there ever came a point when he didn't know what to do, he should pray, and God would show him the way. So Antonio closed his eyes and prayed the best prayer he could for a boy his age. I couldn't figure out what to do next either, so I started praying with all my heart. Then I opened my eyes just in time to see two boys running around the street corner just ahead of me. It appeared as though they were looking for something or someone, and then I recognized the two boys. They were the two that were with Antonio. I moved quickly out of sight so they couldn't see me.

"As soon as they disappeared around the corner, I ran after them. Since I didn't know at that time that Antonio had run away from them, I was hoping that they might lead me to him. So I hurried to catch up to them, and by the time I turned the corner, I saw them again. They had found Antonio sitting under the canopy to the entrance of the building where he stopped. One was on one side of him and the other on the other side. The bigger of the two was trying to pick Antonio up by his arms. They were yelling at him and calling him very bad names. I became angry and started shouting as I ran toward them. 'Get away from him!' I yelled. 'Leave him alone!' I ran faster and faster. Almost out of breath, I yelled one last time, 'Get away from him!'

"Antonio looked up and saw me coming in like a fighter jet ready to strike at its target. 'Mr. Pulaski!' he shouted. 'Help, Mr. Pulaski!'

"I was surprised that I still had it in me because I jumped over the four-foot stone wall on the side of the steps and pushed the boys away from him. As they fell back against the wall, I pulled Antonio toward me and held him close and as tight as I could.

"As the boys stood up and began to lunge toward Antonio again, I raised my hand at them and shouted, 'He's under the Lord's protection now and mine. Leave him alone!'

"The two boys looked at me. One of them had his hand up. But I was so angry they must have seen the fire in my eyes because they looked at each other, and one of them said, 'He's more trouble than he's worth. Let's get out of here!'

"As they left, I held Antonio close to me. 'Let's go home!' I said.

"We were cold, wet, and shivering from the rain. But I was never happier. I couldn't help but smile as I looked up to the sky. I was too exhausted to speak, so we walked very slowly back to the center.

"Frank must have been looking for us out the window because as soon as we were within sight of the building, he ran out to meet us. He was so excited when he saw us coming he forgot to put his coat on. Needless to say, he was quite cold, and by the time we got inside, he was as soaked as we were."

> *See that you do not look down on one of these little ones, for I tell you that their angels in heaven always see the face of My Father in heaven.*
> —Matthew 18:10, New International Version

> *And goes home. Then he calls his friends and neighbors together and says, "Rejoice with me; I have found my lost sheep."*
> —Luke 15:6, New International Version

CHAPTER 13

Samuel and Maria's New Son

*I call on you O God, for you will answer me; give
ear to me and hear my prayer.*
—Psalm 17:6, New International Version

Mr. Pulaski finished telling his story to Mom and Dad, and Mom
was in tears by the time he reached the end. Dad was doing a pretty
good job of not crying, although I think he wanted to. I was in my
room for the first part of the story, but when I came out to use the
bathroom, I was on the steps when I heard Mom ask Mr. Pulaski
what happened when they returned to the center.

"Well," he said, "if I can have one more cup of your wonderful
coffee, I'll tell you."

Mom didn't hesitate for another minute. She poured the coffee,
and Mr. Pulaski began to tell the rest of the story.

"As I was saying, it was a cold walk back to the center. The
other two boys took off running, but they were both picked up by
the police for stealing and put in a correctional facility. However,
Antonio and I got inside, and I made sure he was given some clean,
dry clothes, and we were both exhausted to the point that we almost
collapsed. Frank took care of Antonio. He had some food brought

out, but I was too tired to eat. Antonio was too hungry to sleep, but I can tell you after he ate, he was asleep within minutes.

"In the meantime, Maria came and picked me up, and we went home. I crawled in bed. By the time I woke up, I didn't even realize how long I slept. I didn't even remember what day it was. Anyway, after I was well rested, I returned to the center, and Antonio and I spent a lot of time together during the next week.

"Then one morning, Frank asked me to come into his office to talk. I knew it couldn't be good because Frank never looked more serious than he did that minute. I followed him into the office, and he sat in his chair behind his desk. He folded his hands together and looked straight at me. 'Samuel, we have a problem!'

"I looked at him without saying a word.

"He took a deep breath, 'We're finished. The center is going to be closed by the end of the month! The building is being closed because we just can't afford to fix it!'

"'What about the children?' I asked. 'That's why we have until the end of the month, so we can find alternative locations for them or foster care.'

"I didn't know what to do. I left Frank's office and went to my office and closed the door.

"I must have been in there for three or four hours when I heard the buzzer ring. I didn't get up right away. I waited to see if someone else was going to answer it, but they didn't. I heard the buzzer the second time, so I got up, went to the door, and opened it.

"A man was standing on the porch with a big piece of paper rolled up under his arm and a hard hat on. 'Mr. Pulaski?' he asked.

"I nodded my head and said, 'Yes. Can I help you?'

"'No, sir, you can't. But I can help you!'

"Just then, Frank came to the door. 'What's going on?' When he saw the gentleman standing on the porch, he started to panic. 'We were told we have until the end of the month!'

"'Oh no, sir, I'm not here to condemn the building. I'm here to repair it!'

"'What!' I said, for lack of anything else to say.

"'Yes, sir!' he said.

"Then within a few minutes, trucks started pulling up outside along the curb.

"'Wait a minute!' I said.

"'No, sir, we don't have time . . . If we're to be finished by the end of the month, we can't wait even a second longer. We really need to get started now!'

"Then he walked past me. Three men followed right behind him, and they began taking measurements and talking about moving walls and redoing rooms and how many men it was going to take and all kinds of things that needed to be done.

"Again, I interrupted and asked, 'Exactly what is going on here?'

"'We received a phone call from a gentleman two days ago,' he said. 'He was with a law firm that represented the Michaels estate, and during a recent audit, they discovered an oversight. It seems there was a safe deposit box that was never opened during the original settlement of the estate. Well, to make a long story short, it was opened recently, and a paper was discovered that contained instructions for this building to be restored if it ever reached the point of disrepair. So the bank representative said that he wanted us to come out right away and find out what you wanted done. He said he wanted everything fixed, and the instructions were to keep as much as the old house as possible. So here we are, and I took the liberty of putting some plans together since time is short.'

"He handed me the plans and continued looking around. Then he looked at me and said, 'You know what's really strange is that it specified that all repairs were to be finished by the end of this exact month.'

"He said the bank had been instructed to spare no expense. 'There are more than enough funds to repair it and to make all the repairs and to add a conservatory and a library. As a matter of fact, there's enough to keep it up and running for many, many years.'

"I thought I was dreaming. I had no idea what or how this had happened.

"Frank looked at me, confused. 'What happened, Samuel? Did you talk to anyone while you were out?'

"I looked at Frank. 'No! I didn't talk to anyone except to ask if they had seen Antonio. I was too busy looking for him!'"

Mr. Pulaski began to shake his finger, and he had one eye closed as he said, "Then I remembered. I told Frank 'I remember talking to an elderly gentleman at the coffee shop where I stopped to eat. He said his name was . . .' I thought for a minute. 'John Michaels. His name was John Michaels. He said he grew up here. It was a farmhouse originally owned by a man named Shaw. I invited him to visit if he wanted to.'

"Frank looked at me. He was as white as a sheet. 'I want to show you something, Samuel. Come with me,' he said.

"So I followed him out and to the side of the house where there was a stone marker by a tree. I looked at it, and I couldn't believe my eyes. It read "John Michaels, 1849."

"'Samuel, John Michaels died in 1849! His family planted this tree in his memory!' Frank remarked.

"Frank and I just looked at each other.

"It took a few weeks for the workers to remodel the entire building. They worked around us because we had nowhere else to go. They were even able to add a room or two without disturbing the original appearance of the house. It turns out that the Shaws had left the house to Mr. Michaels, and he loved that house so much that he made sure that there would be enough money to preserve it.

"Well, a few months passed, and Antonio was placed with a foster family. They were good people. I handpicked them myself because I knew Antonio was special and I wanted him to be happy. They enrolled him in school, and he attended church on Sundays with them, and he even became active in the youth group. For the next year, Antonio visited me on Saturdays and helped me around the center now and then. He liked spending time with me, and I liked spending time with him, although I couldn't understand why he'd rather spend time with me instead of boys his own age. I didn't mind having Antonio around. He was a good boy, and I was thankful God had sent him to us.

"Our friendship grew over the next year. He respected me, and I respected him. Although he wasn't very good at it, he liked to go fishing. I remember on the way home from the lake one late afternoon, Antonio bragged about how his stringer was filled with so many fish it was almost too heavy for him to carry. And mine? Well, we really don't need to talk about mine. Anyway, after arriving home, Maria was standing on the porch with her hand over her mouth laughing at me as I carried my fish into the house.

"Maria became quite found of him. She was happy we were able to help him after his ordeal, and we truly enjoyed his company. One Saturday night, we finished eating supper, and it was time for me to take him back to his foster home. As he was getting his things together, I kept talking about how much fun I had had that day with him and that I couldn't wait until his next visit. But he didn't say much. As a matter of fact, he didn't say anything at all the entire time we were eating supper. Maria looked at me and said that she and I had to talk for a minute, and she asked me to go into the kitchen with her. I smiled at Antonio across the table as we got up and excused ourselves. To tell you the truth, I thought I was in trouble for something, and I tried to think of what it could be as I followed her into the kitchen. It wasn't easy to think of what I may have forgotten to do or what I may have done that I wasn't supposed to do in a very short period of time, but I couldn't think of anything."

Dad grinned as if he knew exactly what Mr. Pulaski meant.

Then Mr. Pulaski continued, "Once in the kitchen, Maria said to me, 'Samuel, something is bothering Antonio, and I think you two had better talk before you take him home.'

"'How do you know that?' I asked. 'Maybe he's just tired. We were pretty busy today!'

"Maria looked me straight in the eyes. 'No!' she said. 'It's more than that. I can feel it. Talk to him!'

"I wasn't sure what it could have been, but I said, 'Okay, I'll talk to him!'

"I knew better than to go against her intuition. It was like she knew things. So I returned to the table, finished eating, and walked with Antonio out onto the porch.

"'Supper was pretty good, wasn't it, Antonio?' I said.

"Antonio looked down at the ground as we stood leaning on the railing. 'Sure was!'

"Then neither of us said anything else for a few minutes.

"'Antonio!' I said. 'Exactly what's going on?'

"Antonio shrugged his shoulders, and without looking at me, he said, 'What do you mean?'

"I leaned over a little more toward him so I could see his eyes. 'You were pretty quiet at supper!'

"Antonio looked at me. 'Just tired, I guess.'

"'Nah, I don't think so. I think something is bothering you, and I'd like to know what it is before I drive you back home. Antonio, we're friends, and I told you that you could talk to me anytime about anything. And I know that something is bothering you.'

"Antonio gazed up at me with a puzzled look on his face.

"'Okay,' I said, 'so I don't know when something is bothering you, but Maria knows. So give me a break, okay?'

"Antonio smiled, and then he said, 'Mr. Pulaski, do you like me?'

"I looked at him. 'Of course, I do, Antonio. Why would you even ask me that?'

"Then he looked down at the ground again. 'Do you like me enough to adopt me?'

"I was in shock! I didn't know what to say, and I wasn't expecting that at all! I was a little choked up. 'Is that what's bothering you?'

"I was stalling for time. But Antonio looked right at me. 'You don't have to if you don't want to. I'll still come out and help you, Mr. Pulaski, and we can still be friends and—'

"Before he could say another word, I grabbed him and pulled him close to me. I couldn't hold back the tears in my eyes. 'I would be honored to have you as my son,' I said.

"I hugged him with all my strength that moment, and then I looked into his eyes with pride and excitement. 'Let's go talk to Maria.'

"Then just as we turned around to go back into the house, we saw Maria. 'Yes!' Maria said, crying.

"I had no idea she was standing just inside the doorway, listening to us. She smiled at us, and then she said to me, 'Why do you think I sent you two outside to talk, Samuel? I needed an answer too!'

"After Maria cried and the three of us hugged, we began making plans."

Mr. Pulaski just shook his head and said, "There was so much to do!"

> *O LORD Almighty, God of Israel, you have revealed this to your servant, saying, "I will build a house for you." So your servant has found courage to offer you this prayer.*
> —2 Samuel 7:27, New International Version

CHAPTER 14

Sunday Afternoon— Decorating the Church

*Suddenly a great company of the heavenly host
appeared with the angel, praising God and Saying,
"Glory to God in the highest, and on earth peace to
men on whom his favor rests.*
—Luke 2:13–14, New International Version

Mr. Pulaski finished his story, and then he sat quietly for a minute with a smile on his face as he held back the tears from reliving a very special time in his life.

Mom sat quietly with tears in her eyes, and then she spoke softly, "I'm sorry if I upset you, Samuel!"

Mr. Pulaski shook his head. "No, you didn't upset me. I just haven't thought about that time in my life in a long time, and it's good to bring back memories like that."

Mom wiped her tears and thanked Mr. Pulaski for his story. "You're very welcome, and now I believe it's time we get to the church and start decorating!"

Dad stood up and stretched. "I believe you're right!" he said as he walked over to the steps to call me down.

But I had come down earlier for something. I didn't even remember what it was because after I heard Mr. Pulaski telling his stories, I sat down to listen and forgot what I was doing. Anyway, Mom, Dad, and Mr. Pulaski were putting on their coats. But I was much faster than they were. I was ready to go in seconds, and when Dad opened the door for Mom, I ducked around all three of them and ran out to the car before they had even closed the front door. Mr. Pulaski, Mom, and Dad looked at one another as Mr. Pulaski held the door for Mom.

As we reached the church parking lot, we could see that there were a few cars already there. I was the first one out of the car and into the church as usual.

"It looks like they started without us!" Mr. Pulaski said as he approached the door.

But in no time at all, more cars pulled in, and everyone went straight to work.

The children decorated the classrooms and the bottom of the Christmas tree that stood at the top of the steps leading down to the banquet hall. Then the adults finished the top half of the tree. Mr. Pulaski set up the tall ladder and carried the large wreath to the top of the stained-glass window behind the pulpit while others placed the smaller wreaths that held a single electric candle in the center on each windowsill on each side of the church. Some of the older children placed large red bows on each of the pews along the center aisle. The elders of the church set up the nativity scene on the front lawn.

After a short time, Mr. Smith came in and made the announcement that it was finished. "Come on out, everyone!" he yelled excitedly. "It's all set up. It's almost dark too, so you'll be able to see how nice it looks all lit up!"

Everyone finished what they were doing inside, and Mr. Pulaski stood at the back of the church and looked all around. The church was beautiful; everyone could tell it had his approval by the way he was smiling.

"Mr. Pulaski!" a small voice called out.

Mr. Pulaski turned around; it was little Katy.

"Aren't you going to come outside and see the nativity?"

Mr. Pulaski smiled and winked at her. "I sure am!" he said.

Katy smiled and walked over to him and took his hand as they walked out together.

Katy was so excited, and in so much of a hurry, it was almost as if she was dragging Mr. Pulaski out the door. Her excitement and anticipation was very much of a young girl who was at the high point of her Christmas season excitement and anticipation. Mr. Pulaski could barely keep pace with her. She was hurrying so much that he was starting to lose grip of her hand. Katy squeezed his hand tighter so as not to slip away.

"Why don't you go ahead of me? I'll catch up with you outside!" he said.

"No, I want us to see it together. We're almost there. Just a little bit farther, Mr. P! Come on, hurry, everyone is already out there!"

Mr. Pulaski picked up his pace a little bit.

"Don't turn around yet, Mr. P!" Katy yelled, "Not until we're there!"

When they finally reached the curb of the street, Katy yelled with excitement that only a child could display, "Okay, when I count to three, let's turn around together. Okay!"

They stood side by side.

"Close your eyes, Mr. P!" Katy said as she began counting slowly. "One . . . two . . . three!"

Still holding hands, they opened their eyes at the same time. Mr. Pulaski just stood there in awe of the sight before his eyes. Katy gasped with big eyes staring at the front of the church, just taking in the beauty.

The nativity was centered on the lawn. Above the manger were two angels that appeared to be suspended in midair. A horse, a camel, a donkey, and a sheep were strategically placed around Mary, Joseph, and Baby Jesus. The wise men were approaching the manger with their gifts of myrrh, frankincense, and oils. A star glistened as it rested over the manger. A host of angels were off in the distance around the entire nativity. And the light from the bell tower above the church brought an even bigger smile to Mr. Pulaski's face.

Katy just stared. "I like the outside of the church best, don't you?" She looked up at Mr. Pulaski as he looked down at her, still holding his hand.

"Yes, Katy, I like the outside of the church best too!"

They both looked one last time.

"Now let's go in and have some cookies and hot chocolate," she said, not letting go of his hand.

They walked back into the church, but this time, Katy walked a little slower, and I know Mr. Pulaski was very grateful.

Mr. Pulaski and Katy went through the line and picked out their favorite cookies. Katy picked up a cup of hot chocolate and sat at the table with her friends. Mr. Pulaski picked up his cup of hot chocolate and was met by Mom as he turned to find some place to sit as well.

"The church looks wonderful, Samuel!" she said.

"Yes, it does. Everyone did a great job, especially the children," he remarked.

Mom nodded her head yes, and then she said, "Thank you for sharing your story about your son Antonio earlier. It was amazing what he went through, and I think I know why you like going to the hospital and visiting with the children. You miss the center, don't you?"

Mr. Pulaski smiled and nodded yes. "I'd like to go back some-day and visit."

Mom looked at him with a smile and said, "Mr. Michaels must have been a very wealthy man and very kind to help you like that!"

Mr. Pulaski looked down at his cup of hot chocolate for a few seconds, and then he looked at Mom again. "I was so excited that day! When Frank put his hand on my shoulder and looked me in the eye and told me that Mr. Michaels died over one hundred years ago, I just couldn't believe that he was the man I talked to in the restaurant! Then when he showed me his picture. I believed God had sent him to help us," Mr. Pulaski said.

Mom smiled again. "That's wonderful, Samuel. Not everyone gets to experience a miracle!"

Mom sighed, "Well, it's getting late, and Jimmie has school tomorrow. So we'd better call it a night. Besides, it looks like just about everyone has left. Would you like us to drop you off at home?"

"No, thanks!" Mr. Pulaski replied. "I want to make sure every-thing is cleaned up here, and it's a nice night. The stars are shining, and I like to walk home and enjoy the night air. Tell Jimmie I'll see him tomorrow please."

Mom picked up her coat as Mr. Pulaski went into the kitchen. Dad and I were already at the door. Actually, I was already starting to fall asleep standing up.

Mr. Pulaski locked the door behind us as we left, and he made his rounds that night once again as usual before he left. I'm sure he put every chair back in its place, picked up every piece of lint off the floor on his way out that night, and turned off every light. I must admit I had a great time that day. I almost wish it didn't end, and not just because I had school the next day either.

> *Let the heavens rejoice, let the earth be glad; let the*
> *sea resound, and all that is in it;*
>   —Psalm 96:11, New International Version

PART 2

New Friendships, Sickness, Prayers, and Competition

INTRODUCTION
TO PART 2

He has scattered abroad his gifts to the poor, his
righteousness endures forever; his horn [Horn here
symbolizes dignity.] will be lifted high in honor.
—Psalm 112:9, New International Version

I hope you enjoyed part 1. Before we go on to part 2, please take a minute and try to remember a time in your past when something just didn't seem possible and you couldn't explain why or how everything in that particular situation worked out. For example, one Christmas, my wife and I weren't doing very well financially, and we were worried that we wouldn't be able to afford our traditional Christmas dinner. The local church had provided us with some gifts for our three children, but we weren't sure where the money was going to come from to purchase food. We could have possibly been okay with a few potatoes, bread, and a few other things. But Christmas dinner was always special. It was a tradition in our home to have ham, potatoes, vegetables, and other foods that were special to that time of year.

Well, it was a few days before Christmas. It was late afternoon on a Saturday, and the doorbell rang. I was in the kitchen, and my wife was upstairs, I think—I'm not sure as it was so long ago. But I remember that our eight-year-old son answered the door, and as I came around the corner from the kitchen, I asked him who it was because it was only seconds, and they were gone. My son showed me a fifty-dollar bill and said a man handed it to him and said to give it to his mom and dad. I was overwhelmed by the generosity of this individual. I quickly ran to the door and opened it, but no one was there. I looked up and down the street, but I didn't see a car out front, and no one was in sight. It was only seconds from the time the door closed before I opened it, so if that person was on foot, there wasn't enough time for anyone to get in a car and leave that quickly or run fast enough to disappear. Besides, there wasn't any sound of a car starting, and our dog always alerted us when someone approached the house that he didn't know. I had no idea who that person was, but it didn't matter because whoever it was, he was sent by God. And to me, he was truly an angel. I believed that with all my heart because no one knew that we were in need of help at that time.

Ever since then, my wife and I do our best to take care of others who need help. We do it without their knowledge because the reward is so much greater for us to see the tears and smiles on their faces than if we were to walk up to them and say, "Hi, we would like you to have this." Without knowing who came to their aid, we pray that they too believe that our gift is also a gift from God.

Here's another thought, but it's in the form of a poem and deals with the birth and death of a life. I wrote this poem for my wife when she found out that her nephew was in a bad motorcycle accident, and she wasn't sure if he was going to live. Thanks to prayer and our belief in God, he survived. He has a long way to go before he regains his full potential, but he survived, and we praise God for his progress. However, at the time I wrote this poem for her, my intent was that it would bring her comfort no matter what the outcome was going to be. Now I pray that it brings you comfort as well.

Life of a Rose

A caregiver plants a rose and waits with anticipation
to see its beauty, to smell its fragrance, to stand in awe of
its brilliant deep-red color.
As it grows, the caregiver takes great pride in its nourishment and care.
The rose starts to bud, and then when the time comes and
it finally begins to open,

the caregiver stands and smiles as if it's about to open right before his eyes.
The anticipation grows within him. Then one day, the rose opens its petals wide
as if it's displaying its gracious, unquestionable beauty to the caregiver.
The caregiver watches intently. He closes his eyes as he takes in the wonderful fragrance
that he was so desperately anticipating. Throughout its life, the caregiver continues to provide its needed nourishment and loving touch to sustain its everlasting beauty.

As time passes, the beauty of the rose astounds its caregiver, and its fragrance fills the room.
The rose opens and stretches out each and every one of its petals until it can't stretch any farther.
The caregiver continues desperately to offer a loving touch and all the kindness he has to the rose,
but one day without notice, it drops its first petal, and its fragrance begins to fade.
Even though its petals are soft, as they lightly float to the floor, only he can hear the sound it makes as it lands.
The caregiver cringes with unbelief that this is a sign that its life is coming to an end.
No matter what he does, one petal after another softly falls to earth.
The caregiver looks on and takes in its precious fragrance one last time,
and the rose dies as slowly as it grew and bloomed.

The caregiver smiles with a breaking heart
as his miracle comes to an end but only to begin another.
Long after his precious gift visually disappears from his sight,
the caregiver solemnly remembers the beautiful life he shared.
He remembers the happiness it brought into his life,

and he cherishes every memory of the lost vision that once stood before him
in all its beauty, splendor, and wonder. And one day, another begins to take its place.

As with the rose, the Father in heaven cherishes the life of each and every one of his children on earth.
As with a child, a baby is born, and through the passing years, he grows and blossoms with the Father's love.
Then one day, the child reaches his life's end here on earth, but by the grace of our Lord and Savior, a new life is born on earth,
and the old begins a new everlasting life, a life that is more wonderful than anyone can imagine.

Glory be to the Caregiver of life, our Father in heaven, our Lord and Savior Jesus Christ.

As with my introduction to part 1, I have one last thought, a question actually: Why do we teach our children competition at such young ages? During the past few years, there have been so many parental confrontations at little league games that behavior laws had to be enforced. Our children need to understand that, yes, this is a competitive world when it comes to employment, reaching class ranking in colleges, and many other areas. But can't parents be taught that at a young age, it's about skill? I mean learning the game and being the best they can be, not to win but to be the best they can be at whatever they do, whether it's a spelling bee or it's a football game. I could be wrong, but I think professional team scouts look for ability as well as the player's interaction with the team. For instance, a quarterback on a football team is interviewed and tells the public that he or she couldn't have done it without the entire team. Even in a running competition, our youngest son was on the high school track team, and even though he was very good, he always shook hands with the other runners. And he encouraged them to do well, even if it was only to finish the race. Perhaps it was because he was confident that he was going to beat them, but knowing my son as I do, I know he encouraged everyone to do well because he cared. I can say he didn't get upset when he lost, but it was a disappointment in him and not anger with the other runners.

> *When he heard this, Jesus said, "This sickness will not end in death. No, it is for God's glory so that God's Son may be glorified through it."*
> —John 11:4, New International Version

Time to start part 2! See you at part 3!

CHAPTER 15

Monday Morning—
Jimmie Returns to School

May the LORD now show you kindness and faith-
fulness, and I too will show you the same favor
because you have done this.
—2 Samuel 2:6, New International Version

The alarm went off; I must have jumped three feet in the air without opening my eyes. I reached up and felt around until my hand found the clock; I managed to turn it off without looking. After a few minutes, I forced myself to sit up, rubbed my eyes, and hung my head down, wanting very much to go back to sleep. As I sat on the edge of the bed, I thought it was a bad dream. At least, I was hoping it was a bad dream. Then all of a sudden, I remembered. *Oh no, this is the day I have to walk Becky to school.* I slapped myself in the forehead. *This is not going to be a good day!* I thought. That's all it took, and I was fully awake. In a very short time, I was up and dressed. Most of my clothes were on the floor. I looked around, trying to remember which ones were the clean ones. Mom washed my clothes and brought them into my room with the intention that I would put them away, but it seemed that they never got into the closet. Anyway, after I got dressed, I ran down the steps as fast as I could.

I could smell Mom's breakfast all the way upstairs. Dad was already sitting at the table, reading the morning paper, and drinking his first cup of coffee while Mom was putting his breakfast on the table.

"Jimmie, you'll have to serve yourself. But hurry, you're running late!"

She looked at her watch. "Look at the time! I have to run too. Susan is alone. Janie called in sick. I really need to go."

Susan was one of the waitresses at the diner, and she always gave me one of those big sugar cookies they kept on the counter by the register.

Mom yelled at me again, "Hurry, Jimmie, you don't have much time left. I told Becky's mother that you would be at their house by seven thirty."

"Yeah, thanks again, Mom!" I couldn't help myself from answering sarcastically.

"You're very welcome!" she answered.

Apparently, being sarcastic didn't make any impact on her. "You treat her nicely too!" She just had to say that.

Dad leaned over and whispered, "If you treat her nicely, maybe she'll be your date for the Christmas party at the church."

I could feel my forehead wrinkle up as I frowned. That was almost enough to make me not want to eat breakfast. "Thanks for being there for me, Dad!" I said.

"You're welcome, Jimmie!" he answered. He and Mom are so much alike. Apparently, being sarcastic with him didn't work either.

Dad placed his breakfast dishes in the sink, grabbed his coat, and started out the door. "Oh, please tell your mother that I'll probably be late tonight."

"What's new?" I answered. "I think it would be better if you just told her when you weren't going to be late!"

I jumped up, put my dishes in the sink, grabbed my coat out of the closet, and ran out the door.

Becky's house was first on my way to school, then Sam's house, and last Billy's. I made it to Becky's house, but I had a little difficulty getting my legs to go up the sidewalk to the door. It was like they were refusing to move. I stood on the sidewalk and whispered to myself, "Thanks again, Mom!" And then I forced my legs to walk very slowly up to the door.

I reached up and was about to ring the doorbell when the door opened. It was Becky's father; he was on his way out to work. He came out of the house and stood on the porch. "I guess you're Jimmie!"

He didn't look old enough to have a daughter of Becky's age. Even though they were in church on Sunday, I really hadn't noticed anything about Becky or her parents.

"I guess you're Becky's father!" I said, not trying to sound sarcastically. Well, maybe I didn't really try that hard. I continued smiling.

Mr. Litchner's smile disappeared, and so did mine.

"Thank you for walking to school with Becky and showing her around!" he said as he started down the driveway to his car.

Then he looked up at me again—I think.

"You're welcome!" I yelled back. And I then added in a low voice, "I think!"

The door opened a second time, and Becky came out. "Hi, Jimmie. My mother told me Sunday that you were going to stop by for me!"

"So did mine!" I answered, but I don't think she understood my humor.

As we walked, I really didn't have anything to say, and all she could think of was "You really didn't have to. It's not like I never went to a new school before!"

"It wasn't my idea, believe me!"

But after saying that, I heard Mom telling me to be nice to her. *Oops!* I thought. I really didn't know what to say next, so I just simply explained, "Sam's house is just around the corner. He's never ready on time. And neither is Billy, but he lives a lot closer to the school."

That was the end of the conversation between us until we reached Sam's house.

Becky was only one inch shorter than me, with dark brown hair that hung over her shoulders and brown eyes. She was dressed in a tan coat with a white fur collar and cuffs around her wrists. Neither one of us said another word; we just walked until we reached Sam's house.

As we approached the front sidewalk, Sam was closing the door as he came out to meet us. I looked at him, not saying a word.

"What!" he exclaimed.

"You're never ready on time!" I said, surprised at his quickness that morning.

"So I fell asleep early last night. I'm not as tired as I usually am. Come on, let's go!"

As the three of us continued walking toward Billy's house, Sam introduced himself, "Hi, Becky. I'm Sam."

"Yeah, I know!" she said.

We continued on until we reached Billy's house. He too was ready and waiting on the porch. The three of us came around the corner, and there he stood. I just shook my head.

Billy came down the steps to meet us. "Hi, I'm Billy!"

Becky and I looked at each other, and then I looked at Billy.

"What is it with you two? You're never on time. Neither one of you. What's goin' on?"

Becky smiled as she looked at me. "Let's go. I have to stop in at the office and get my locker number and schedule."

So the four of us continued on, and once we reached the school, we escorted Becky to the office and approached the counter.

Mrs. Todd came up to greet us. She never smiled first thing in the morning; actually, I don't think she smiled in the afternoon either. Mrs. Todd had almost all gray hair and might have been a prison guard at one time. At least, that's what we thought, but no one was brave enough to ask her. She looked down at us from behind the counter. I think she was really hired to scare all of us so we wouldn't want to be sent to the office. It wasn't the principal that everyone was afraid to face; it was Mrs. Todd.

"What can I do for you four?" she said.

"I'm Becky Litchner."

"Oh yes! Well, Becky, we're glad to have you at our school," Mrs. Todd said. Then she looked at me, Sam, and Billy. "And what do you three want?"

I started to explain, but Sam interrupted.

"We're helping her find her way around!" he said, smiling.

"I see!" Mrs. Todd said as she was looking up Becky's locker number. Then she looked at us again. "Well, I'm sure she appreciates your assistance, but I think at this point, she only needs one of you. And since I see she has the same class schedule as Jimmie, I think he can escort her for the rest of the day."

Sam's and Billy's smiles turned into discouragement as they stood there. I think they were waiting for her to change her mind.

"We'll meet you in the cafeteria at lunchtime!" I yelled as they walked out of the office door.

Mrs. Todd looked down at Becky again. "Now then, Becky, here is your schedule, your locker number, and combination. And again, welcome to our school. If you have any questions, I'm sure Jimmie can answer them."

"Thanks, Mrs. Todd," Becky said.

Becky and I then walked out of the office and headed to our first class of the day.

We managed to make it through the morning, and lunchtime arrived quickly. As promised, Sam and Billy were waiting at the entrance to the cafeteria for us. I pointed out to Becky that we go through the lunch line first, but there were two entrances: one for pizza, hamburgers, hot dogs, hoagies, and fries and the other line with the special of the day. And also, that both lines had a salad bar located at the end. Then I continued to point out that the drink machines were against the wall between the two exits and that there was another cooler that contained pints of white and chocolate milk sitting next to the ice cream freezer. Now that Becky was well-instructed on the cafeteria layout, Sam, Billy, and I decided to go with the pizza. And Becky chose the egg salad sandwich and juice.

As we sat down alongside the wall next to a window, I looked at her tray and then at ours. "Is that all you're going to eat?" I asked.

"Yes! Why?"

"You're going to starve!" I said as we began to eat.

"It's getting colder. Hopefully, the lake will freeze by this weekend," Billy said as he was setting his tray down.

"What happens this weekend?" Becky asked.

"The whole town ice skates at night, and we play ice hockey after school," Sam answered.

"That sounds like fun!" she said.

"It is!" I replied. "It's a tradition every year."

We finished our lunch and left for our next class.

Just like the morning, the afternoon went quickly, and after school, we walked home. Becky was the last one, and then I stopped at Mr. Pulaski's house as usual. I knocked on his door, and Mr. Pulaski answered.

"Hi, Jimmie. How was school today and your first day with your new friend?"

I took my coat off as I answered, "She's not my new friend! Mom arranged for me to help her with her first day at school. I did, and now she's on her own!"

Mr. Pulaski didn't say a word. He just sat in his chair next to the fireplace and glanced over at me a few times as he was drinking some milk and grabbing some store-bought cookies off a plate on the coffee table. In the middle of eating one, he looked over at me a second time.

"Okay, Mr. P, here's what happened. I stopped at her house. She came out. We walked to Sam's and Billy's, and the four of us went to school. I walked with her to her classes. We ate lunch, and now she knows her way around. End of story! I did what Mom asked me to do. Now she's on her own!"

Mr. Pulaski raised his eyebrows. "Apparently, you accomplished your mission, and now it's done, right?"

"Right!" I said.

"I want to thank you again for helping with the church yesterday. With everyone's help, we finished pretty quick."

"Okay, Mr. P, I have a feeling you think I'm wrong, and somehow I get the feeling that you think I should do more for Becky!"

Mr. Pulaski smiled. "Sounds like to me that you think you should do more for Becky."

"Why do you say that?" I asked.

"Well, because I didn't say anything. I was talking about the church!"

"I hate it when you do that, Mr. P!" I protested. I could tell that I was feeling a little restless.

"Do what, Jimmie?"

"You know what! I think you want to say something. You think I should be friends with Becky, don't you?" I again protested.

"What I think doesn't matter. You have to make that decision for yourself, but let me tell you a story."

"I knew it! Okay, Mr. P, I'm listening."

Mr. Pulaski began his story about a frightened little girl that he met a long time ago named Angela. As with all Mr. P's stories, I knew that there was going to be a lesson when he finished. There always was. But this time, I wasn't going to give in. No way was I going to let him make me feel guilty and change my mind; it just wasn't going to happen.

CHAPTER 16

Samuel Meets Angela

At that time the disciples came to Jesus and asked, "Who is the greatest in the kingdom of heaven?" He called a little child and had him stand among them. And he said: "I tell you the truth, unless you change and become like little children, you will never enter the kingdom of heaven. Therefore, whoever humbles himself like this child is the greatest in the kingdom of heaven. And whoever welcomes a little child like this in my name welcomes me."
—Matthew 18:1–5, New International Version

"Unable to sleep, I went into the center a little earlier than usual. I thought since I was awake, I might as well get some filing done that I had been neglecting for some time. I hated filing, so I'd wait until the pile was so big that I didn't have any more room on my desk. When I walked through the front door around seven, I stood in front of the coat rack hanging up my jacket, and out of the corner of my eye, I saw a little girl. She couldn't have been more than eight or nine years old, and she was sitting on the bench in the corner of the entranceway. I glanced over at her just to make sure I wasn't hallucinating, and she was staring at me while she held tightly on to a blanket and a small doll. She looked frightened, so I smiled and asked her what her name was, but she just stared at me with very large brown eyes. As a matter of fact, I didn't remember ever seeing eyes like hers before, except when I met Maria.

"Then I heard a voice behind me say, 'It's Angela!'

"I turned and looked toward the hallway. The lights hadn't been turned on yet, so it was still dark at the time.

"As I was standing up, I saw a tall lady coming toward us. I knew Frank was in his office, but he never turned on the lights when he came in except for in his office. He thought that he could save money if he only turned them on when he had to.

"Anyway, she said it again, 'Her name is Angela!'

"I nodded my head and looked at Angela. 'Hi, Angela. My name is Samuel Pulaski, and right now I'm just a little confused.'

"I looked at Angela's mother. 'Did Frank ask you to wait here?'

"'No,' she said. 'When we got here, the door was unlocked, so we came in. I hope it's all right. It's a little cool outside, and I didn't want Angela to get sick. I hope you don't mind!'

"'Oh no, I don't mind at all!' I replied.

"Then she asked if we could talk some place private.

"'Sure!' I answered. 'Let's go in the room around the corner to your right.'

"She told Angela to stay on the bench for a few minutes, and we would be right back.

"As soon as we went in and I closed the door, she started crying. 'I need to find someone to take care of my daughter!'

"'If you want to leave her with the day care center, we have to fill out some paperwork first.'

"She shook her head no. I looked at her, puzzled, and handed her a tissue. She looked back at me. 'I need to find someone to take care of her. I can't do it anymore because I'm dying.'

"I wasn't sure I had heard her right. 'Excuse me?' I said.

"She took a deep breath. 'I don't have much time left, and I need to make sure Angela is safe. You have to help me please!'

"'Why don't you start from the beginning? First of all, what's your name?' I asked.

"'Mary!' she replied.

"'Okay, Mary, start at the beginning and tell me what this is all about.'

"'I was only sixteen when I had Angela. I did everything I could to support her. I thought about putting her up for adoption, but after I held her in my arms, she was so beautiful, and I couldn't take my eyes off her. I loved her from the moment she was born. I tried so hard to take care of her!'

"'What about her father?' I asked.

"'Her father died last year from a drug overdose. I didn't even know he was taking drugs, but then I didn't see him much after I told him I was pregnant. The police found him in an alley one night, and they found my name on the back of a picture in his wallet. I had some money saved up, but it didn't last long. I got a job cleaning the health clinic at night, so I could bring Angela with me. One night, I didn't realize someone had thrown a needle in the trash can, and when I was taking the trash out, I got stuck. I'm dying, and I need to make sure Angela is taken care of. She's a wonderful little girl. Please help me!' she pleaded.

"I asked her about other relatives: her parents, aunts, uncles, brothers, or sisters.

"'I'm an only child, and to be honest, I wouldn't trust anyone but my parents to take care of her. But my mother died a short time ago, and my father is much too old to take care of her by himself.'

"Angela's mother begged me to find her a home, so I promised her that I'd take care of her and that she didn't have anything to worry about. I would personally find her a good home.

"We went back out to Angela. Mary picked her up and held her tight and then set her back down on the bench. She knelt in front of her, took a locket from around her neck, and put it around Angela. Then she kissed her, held her one more time, and whispered in her ear softly, 'I will always love you with all my heart. Remember that.'

"Then she ran out the door crying, and that's the last time Angela or I ever saw her.

"Angela wrapped her arms around my neck, and she cried. I picked her up and held her on my lap until she fell asleep. She was so tired. After a few minutes, I carried her into my office and quietly laid her down on the couch. I closed the door a little bit and started filling out some forms. Her mother didn't want to give me any information, so I had to consider Angela abandoned. After I finished, I sat at my desk and just stared at her. After about thirty minutes or so, I leaned back. I guess the noise from my old chair woke her up. She had no expression on her face. She just stared back at me. So I smiled, and for the next couple of minutes, we stared at each other. I wasn't quite sure what was going to happen next since I had never had this happen to me before. Eventually, she grinned just a little, so I considered it a smile. 'Now we're making progress,' I thought. But then, not thinking, I quickly stood up, and when I did, she jumped and pulled the blanket up around her neck.

"'I didn't mean to scare you!' I said.

"I sat back down, and unable to think of anything else to say, I asked her if she wanted to go shopping.

"I guess I was still in shock. I had never had a parent bring me a child before like this. I didn't know little girls very well either, but for some reason, I assumed that they loved to go shopping. She nodded her head yes.

"'Well then,' I said, 'that's just what we are going to do. We are going shopping for some new clothes. I'm a little hungry. Would you like to get something to eat too?' Angela nodded yes again. We grabbed a quick bite to eat for breakfast, and then we took our time as she picked out dresses, pants, shirts, everything she liked. I don't think we missed one store in the city before stopping for lunch.

"When we entered the restaurant, we were seated at a window where we could see the mountains. It was late afternoon, and the sun was just above the peaks surrounded by white puffy clouds. I pointed out the clouds to her while we were waiting. One cloud looked like a butterfly. The waitress came over and asked Angela what she wanted to eat, but Angela just looked up at her and then at me. I smiled at her and winked.

"'Angela doesn't feel like talking right now, so we will have a big cheeseburger with extra pickles, french fries, and a chocolate milk shake.'

"As the waitress started to walk away, I yelled, 'Oh, and for dessert, we'll have the biggest ice cream cone you can find because Angela here is a very special girl!'

"We just sat and looked at each other and exchanged smiles. With every smile, I knew she was going to be all right. I knew she wouldn't be able to eat everything I ordered, but I didn't care. As we ate, I told her all about Maria. She even looked like Maria because they had the same colored eyes and long dark hair.

"After we finished, I realized it was getting late, and we needed to return to the center. I didn't even tell Frank we were leaving. Actually, I didn't even tell him I was there in the first place. I guess it was because I know he wouldn't have let me take her out of the center. I had a habit of upsetting him a lot. I never was one for rules when it came to the children. I just followed my instinct.

"As I drove from store to store, I kept thinking about Antonio and how happy we were as a family and everything we had gone through. Then I started thinking about Angela and how she'd have to stay at the center until we could find her a home. The rooms at the center were decorated for children, but she'd have to be alone at night for the first time without her mother, and I wasn't going to let that happen.

"When we returned, I pulled into the parking lot, jumped out, and quickly opened Angela's door. I looked at her as I was unhooking her seat belt, and then I thought of an idea, a pretty good one at that. We walked back into the center, and I took her straight into Frank's office.

"He was working at his desk, and without looking up, he just said, 'No!'

"'You don't even know what I was going to say, Frank!' I said.

"'Yes, I do, and the answer is no!'

"'Frank, this is Angela!'

"He smiled at her. 'Hello, Angela!' he said in a quiet, calming voice.

"Then he looked at me and his smile disappeared, 'No, Samuel!' he repeated.

"'Frank, I want Angela to stay at my house tonight!'

"He looked at me for a few seconds. 'I'm doing fine today, Samuel. Nice of you to ask, and that's not possible!'

"'Why isn't it?'

"'It's against the rules. You know that!' he said sharply.

"'Why is it against the rules?'

"He threw his pencil down on his desk and glared at me. 'Samuel, if you took every child home, we would be out of a job!'

"'So what! If I take every child home, you can work for me! I promise! Besides, I don't want to take every child home with me, just this one . . . today!' I protested.

"Standing in front of his desk, I just looked at him. I leaned over and whispered to Angela, 'Angela, now's the time to smile really big.'

"'Come on, Frank. She's a frightened and scared little girl.'

"I leaned over again and whispered in her ear, 'Now stop smiling and look frightened!'

"Frank looked down at his desk and held his hands over his head. 'What will Maria say when you show up with her?'

"'She'll be okay with it!' I said.

"He looked up over his glasses at me. 'Are you sure of that?'

"I shrugged my shoulders and answered, 'I'm almost sure.'

"He laughed and looked at Angela. 'Angela, would you like to stay with Mr. Pulaski tonight?'

"Angela looked up at me at the same time as I was looking down at her. She smiled, then looked at Frank as she was nodding her head yes.

"'Okay! I'll probably lose my job or go to jail. But if I lose my job, I can live with you, right, Samuel? And if I go to jail, Maria has to bake me pies, and you have to deliver them,' Frank replied.

"I grabbed her little hand. 'Let's go, Angela, before he changes his mind,' I said.

"We hurried to get her things together, and then we ran to the car together. Maria had just taken dinner out of the oven when we arrived home. She heard the car pulling into the driveway and yelled to Antonio to wash his hands and get ready for dinner. It took me a little longer than usual to get into the house because of Angela's things. There was so much to carry. Maria looked out of the kitchen window, but because of the angle of the driveway, she could only see me.

"Antonio, however, could see us both from the upstairs window. 'Mom! Who's with him?' Antonio yelled.

"Maria walked closer to the window, but I was already opening the door.

"'I'm home!' I yelled. 'And I brought home a friend with me for dinner!' Still yelling, I added, 'I hope . . .'—by now Maria was standing by the door—'you don't mind,' this time in a softer voice.

"Angela reached up and took my hand.

"'This is Maria and Antonio,' I told her. Then I looked at Maria.

"Maria didn't say a word; she raised her eyebrows and smiled at Angela. I waited for a response from her, but she said hello to Angela and then looked at me again.

"'Frank said I could bring her home with me! Antonio, take Angela into the other room please for a few minutes.'

"But Angela wouldn't let go of my hand. Maria looked at her and back at me. Then she smiled at Angela and asked, 'Are you hungry, Angela?'

"Angela just looked down at the floor.

"'It's all right. Let's go into the dining room and eat. We'll talk later, right, Samuel?' Maria said.

"I smiled at her. 'We can talk if you're not too tired, Maria. I know how exhausting your day must have been!'

"We sat. We prayed, and we ate. When we were finished, Antonio took Angela outside while I helped Maria with the dishes, and then we talked.

"I told her about Angela's mother and our day together. 'I just couldn't leave her at the center, Maria!'

"'I know, Samuel, and that's what I love about you, your compassion. But you can't bring every child home, and we can't adopt every child either!'

"'Who said anything about adopting her?'

"Maria smiled. 'It's only a matter of time!'

"Maria knew me pretty well, and she was right. It was only a matter of time before Angela became our daughter."

Mr. Pulaski smiled at me, and then he explained his point of the story. "The point is, Jimmie, Becky may not show it, but she's feeling lost. Oh, I'm sure she has changed schools before, and maybe she can handle the new surroundings. But she has no friends yet, and she is in a new town and a new house, so it doesn't matter if she is able to handle it on her own. What matters is that someone takes the time to make her transition easier by helping her get used to her new surroundings."

"Okay, Mr. P, maybe I'll help her for a couple of weeks, and then she's on her own!"

Mr. Pulaski smiled. "That's fine, Jimmie. In a few weeks, she probably won't need you!"

"Well, I have to go now. I have some things I need to do!" I said.

Mr. Pulaski smiled and asked, "Like homework?"

I looked at him as I grabbed my coat. "Oh yeah, that too!" I said, and then I ran out the door.

But let the righteous be glad; let them rejoice before God: yea, let them exceedingly rejoice.
—Psalm 68:3, King James Version

CHAPTER 17

A New Friendship

*Trust in the LORD with all thine heart; and lean
not unto thine own understanding. In all thy ways
acknowledge him, and he shall direct thy paths.*
—Proverbs 3:5–6, New International Version

*I am in pain and distress; may your salvation, O
God protect me.*
—Psalm 69:29, New International Version

The next four days were pretty much the same routine. Becky, Sam,
Billy, and I walked to school every morning. We discovered our likes
and dislikes that were mainly about our parents. Not that we didn't
like our parents, it was all about parents' rules. It turned out that
Becky's parents weren't any different from ours. We didn't like having
a curfew at night. We weren't real fond of going to school and a few
other things that I guess were normal for teenager-and-parent rela-
tionships. We didn't like having to ask to go places or making sure
our parents knew where we were all the time. The biggest complaint
was that the town was too small, and there wasn't as much to do as
there was in the city. This small town, nestled high in the mountains,
was closed off from modern civilization and was customarily closed
up at night, which didn't make it the dream location for any of us.
At least, that was according to the majority of young people of the

town. However, to a large population of adults, this small town was considered to be a dream location to live. Ski resorts, fishing lakes, trout streams, and small country stores; these gave it its reputation as a getaway for some and a hideaway for others. For Becky, it was what she described as a culture shock, and I think that described it pretty well.

The nights were getting colder as the days passed; sometimes the clouds were so heavy that I was surprised that it didn't snow every night. By Friday, I was growing more eager than ever for the lake to freeze. I stopped by the diner where Mom worked and asked her if I could visit Mr. Pulaski on the way home from school. There were so many questions I had to ask him; otherwise, it was going to be very difficult for me to make the arrangements for his Christmas present. After all, there were only three weeks left and so much more for me to do. I was so excited I wanted this to be the best surprise ever for Mr. Pulaski. I really needed to visit him.

Mom didn't answer right away. She was thinking I could tell. Then she asked, "Do you have homework that needs to be done?"

"Only a little. It won't take long, I promise!"

"I guess it'll be all right, but make sure you're home for dinner. Your father will be home at six!"

I ran out the door and yelled back, "Thanks, Mom!"

By the time I reached Mr. Pulaski's house, he was coming back from his visit to town. I yelled to him as he reached the top of the steps, "Hi, Mr. P!"

He turned around. "Well, hi there, Jimmie! How was school today?"

"It was great. It was even better when it was over!" I shouted

Mr. Pulaski laughed. "How is Becky doing? Is she adjusting okay?"

"Yeah, she's doing great too!" I said as I held the door open for him.

We hung up our coats, and Mr. Pulaski headed for the kitchen to make some hot chocolate.

"By the way, Mr. P, I was just wondering where do Antonio and Angela live?"

"Why do you ask?" he answered curiously.

"Oh, just wondering. When you said, you were thinking about moving back with them, I was just wondering how far that would be."

"Oh, I see. Well, they live just outside of Chicago."

"Oh, that's pretty far then, isn't it?"

"Yes, it sure is, Jimmie! Why don't you finish making the hot chocolate while I light the fireplace?"

Mr. Pulaski went into the living room and turned on the radio; it was time for his favorite music program to come on. Then he put some wood in the fireplace. I stood at the stove and stirred the hot chocolate as it was heating up. Mr. Pulaski never used instant stuff: it was always the real thing, or he didn't use it.

As it was reaching just the right temperature, I opened the cupboard and brought out two cups and set them on the table. As I poured the hot chocolate into the cups, I noticed Mr. Pulaski's mail lying on the table. On top were two letters: one from Angela and the other from Antonio. Perfect, I thought. Then I stopped for a minute thinking that it was probably wrong for me to be looking at his mail. But then I thought it wasn't like I was going through his mail and opening it up. All I needed was the addresses, so I grabbed a piece of notepaper off a tablet sitting next to the letters and copied down their names and addresses. I put them in my pocket and carried the cups into the living room.

"I can't stay long, Mr. P. Mom told me to be home by six for dinner."

I was really excited about finding the addresses, but I still felt like I had done something I shouldn't have. Fortunately, since I wasn't doing it for something bad, I could apologize later. I was so excited that I almost burned my mouth trying to drink my hot chocolate too fast.

"It sure is getting cold outside. Do you think the lake is frozen yet, Mr. P?"

Mr. Pulaski looked at me and scratched his head. "I suppose so. It sure has been cold for a while."

I smiled. I was really looking for an excuse to leave, but I couldn't think of one, so I just put my cup down and said, "I should be going now!"

He looked at me. "Well, that certainly was a short visit!"

"I know," I answered, "but I forgot to do something. I'll stop by tomorrow!" I hurriedly grabbed my coat and ran out the door.

"Okay, Jimmie!" I heard him say as I jumped down the steps.

By the time I ran to the corner, I was thinking about the lake and whether or not it was frozen. I slowed down as I was running and eventually stopped and looked at my watch. *I might have some time to check the lake!* I thought to myself. So I turned and began running again but, this time, toward the lake. Within a few minutes, I was at the top of the hill where I could see the lake just over the treetops. It looked great. It looked pretty frozen to me. I ran down the hill as fast as I could. I reached the edge of the lake, picked up a rock, and threw it onto the ice. It slid pretty far out, almost to the middle. *This is great!* I thought. I continued running along the edge. I picked up another rock without slowing down and threw it as I continued running. I wanted to get far enough around the lake to check a few more areas just to be sure. I had one more rock to throw, and I was almost close enough to where I wanted to throw it, but I tripped.

I tried to stop myself from falling, but I couldn't. I fell and hit my head. I couldn't move. I tried, but I couldn't even open my eyes. I began to feel very warm and confused. After a minute or two, I sat up and began brushing my pants off. But something didn't seem right. I looked around, and the lake wasn't frozen anymore, and the snow was gone. The sun was shining brighter than I had ever seen before. It was shining so bright that I could hardly see. I looked all around, and everything seemed different.

Then I looked toward the hill leading down to the lake, and I saw a woman walking toward me. But because the light was so bright, I couldn't see her face. She was calling my name. "Jimmie! Don't move! Stay where you are!"

I had no idea who she was, but I asked her, "What happened?"

"You had an accident. Please don't move!" She sat down next to me and explained that I had fallen and hit my head. She told me that help would be there soon.

"I don't understand!" I looked around. Everything looked wonderful, and I didn't feel like I was hurt at all. I felt fantastic.

Mr. Pulaski was getting ready to eat his supper when the phone rang. "Hello!" he answered.

"Samuel, this is April. Is Jimmie still there?"

"Why no, he left some time ago. Is he not home yet?"

There was silence for a few seconds.

"No, he hasn't come home yet, and I told him to be home by six for dinner!" Her voice was shaking. "Maybe he stopped at a friend's house."

Samuel started to become worried too.

"I called all his friends: Becky, Sam, and Billy. And no one has seen him since they left school. Do you have any idea where he may have gone?"

Mr. Pulaski didn't know what to say.

"This isn't like him, Samuel. I don't know what to do! I called everywhere. I don't know where he is. I don't even know where to start looking for him!" she said apprehensively.

Samuel thought for a minute and answered, "I'll try to think of some places he might have gone!"

She was really scared. "I'm going to call the police and then John."

"All right, April, I'm going to go out looking for him. He should have been home by now!"

Mr. Pulaski hung up and sat down for a minute trying to think where I might have gone, but he couldn't wait. He put his coat and hat on, slipped on his gloves, and left the house with his supper still on the table. It was beginning to get dark. As he walked down the street, he shook his head and prayed. "It's happening all over again, Lord! Please help me find him and please watch over him, and I pray that you send your angels to keep him safe! Please, Father, protect him from harm!"

As Mr. Pulaski continued to walk, he remembered I was eager for the lake to freeze. Mr. Pulaski turned and began walking as fast as he could toward the lake. "That's the only place he could be," he mumbled.

The arthritis in his legs made it difficult to hurry, but he did the best he could. It was getting colder, and the sun was already down

155

behind the mountain peak. He had to hurry because the clouds were moving in and beginning to hide the light from the full moon. He finally reached the top of the hill above the lake. He stopped and looked down. He started calling my name. I could hear him, but I couldn't answer.

"Jimmie! Jimmie!" he kept yelling.

He went a little farther down the hillside and stopped again. He closed his eyes and prayed, "Father, if Jimmie is here, please let me find him. You helped me once before. Now I need you again. Please show me where he is!"

Mr. Pulaski was out of breath and could barely speak. He took a deep breath through his hands and opened his eyes slowly. This time, he took his time and looked from one side of the lake to the other and then a second time. There, at the edge, he saw something; he began walking slowly so he wouldn't trip and fall. Then he started to walk faster and faster as the light from his flashlight was beginning to go dim. He began running and forgot the pain in his legs.

Meanwhile, as Mr. Pulaski was approaching the area where I was lying, the woman that was sitting with me and talking smiled as she said, "Everything is going to be all right now. Someone is coming to help you. It's time for me to go!"

"I don't know who you are, but please don't leave!" I asked.

She smiled at me as she stood up. "Please lie back down, Jimmie, and wait. You're going to be safe now, I promise. Help will be here soon. Now I must go!"

As Mr. Pulaski grew closer, I became clearer to him as I lay on the ground. I could hear him talking and calling me.

"Thank you, Lord! Jimmie! Jimmie, can you hear me?"

I tried to answer him, but I couldn't speak. Mr. Pulaski knelt next to me; he unzipped my coat, and then he placed his hand on my chest. He could tell I was still breathing. Then he placed his hand under my head and saw his glove covered with blood.

I heard him praying again as he looked up into the dark sky. "Please, Father, give me strength. I'm old and weak, and I can't carry him without your help!"

Then he placed his arm under my neck and the other under my legs. He took a deep breath and lifted with all his might. He stood up, turned, and began walking toward the hill. The weight from carrying me made the pain in his legs worse than ever, but he was determined to get to the top of the hill. As he began to breathe harder and harder, he walked faster and faster with every step up the hill. I tried telling him to put me down so I could walk, but he couldn't hear me.

Then another man smiled at me as he was walking next to us. He put his hands under me and helped Mr. Pulaski carry me.

"Who are you?" I asked.

"I'm just someone who is helping your friend."

We finally reached the top of the hill, and Mr. Pulaski sat down on the road and held me in his arms. Then he left, and I heard Mr. Pulaski say, "If I could only reach Mike Fern's farm, he could call for help."

The house was in sight from where we were sitting on the hill. Mr. Pulaski stood up again. He began walking, and then he could see bright lights flashing in the distance, and he fell to the ground, out of breath. "Thank you, Father!" he said as the lights came closer.

It stopped just a few feet away, and I could hear Mom and Dad as they jumped out of the back of the car and ran toward us.

Officer George stood at the car and called on the radio for medical emergency assistance. Then he went to the trunk and brought out a blanket and covered me. "Are you all right, Samuel?" he asked.

Mr. Pulaski looked up and smiled as he tried to catch his breath. "I'm fine. My legs aren't what they used to be, but I'll be all right. You just make sure my friend is taken care of!"

Mom sat next to Mr. Pulaski and rubbed her hand over my face to keep me warm.

A few minutes later, the ambulance did arrive, and Mom and I were taken to the hospital. Dad and Mr. Pulaski followed in Officer George's police car. Upon their arrival, I was rushed into the emergency room immediately. Once again, Mr. Pulaski found himself in the hospital waiting room, but this time, it was with Mom and Dad. He sat in the exact chair he had occupied when he was there with

Mrs. Hanson. Dad sat next to Mom with his arm around her as she leaned against his shoulder.

Mom looked at Mr. Pulaski. She was very tired but managed to smile a little and say, "Thank you so much, Samuel, for finding him! But how did you know he was at the lake?"

"When he was visiting me, he kept talking about the lake and whether or not I thought it was frozen. He was so eager for that lake to freeze. I just thought, being a young boy, he was so excited about skating that that was the only place he could have gone."

Mom smiled again. "We couldn't think of any place else that he would go either, but it looks like you thought of it first! We can't thank you enough!"

Mr. Pulaski smiled back. "You're very welcome, but there is no need to thank me! I know how difficult it is for you to have to sit and wait to find out if he is all right, but I'm sure God is taking care of him. I remember waiting for Antonio when he was in the hospital. Maria and I were nervous wrecks. Waiting for the results isn't easy, especially when it's your own child."

Once again, Mom couldn't resist asking why Antonio was in the hospital, and Mr. Pulaski was very willing to explain.

But let all who take refuge in you be glad; let them ever sing for joy. Spread your protection over them, that those who love your name may rejoice in you.
—Psalm 5:11, New International Version

Then he said to him, rise and go, your faith has made you well.
—Luke 17:19, New International Version

CHAPTER 18

Antonio Goes to the Hospital

Father, the time has come. Glorify your Son that your Son may glorify you. For you granted him authority over all people that he might give eternal life to all those you have given him.
—John 17:2, New International Version

Mr. Pulaski remembered that it was a Sunday morning, and he began explaining to Mom and Dad the events that took place that day.

"Maria, Antonio, and I were eating breakfast. Maria noticed that Antonio was kind of moving his food around on the plate instead of eating it. Maria asked him if he was feeling all right. She felt his head, thinking he might have a fever because there weren't any signs of the flu or anything. It was nearing time for us to leave for church, and Maria had planned for her and me to spend the day shopping for a birthday present for Antonio's seventeenth birthday. But instead, she insisted that we take him to the hospital. Even though he didn't have a fever, she said he didn't look well. Angela had left the day before for a weeklong trip with some friends.

"Maria and I sat in the waiting area at the emergency room while Antonio was in with the doctor. He said he was old enough to go in by himself. At his age, he felt a little embarrassed when one of us went in with him while he was being examined. So Maria and I sat in the waiting room for almost an hour. Maria was getting a little worried, so she approached the counter and asked the nurse if she could tell us why it was taking so long. The nurse indicated that they were waiting for a specialist to arrive. Maria turned around and walked back toward me, and I could see the concern or, should I say worry, on her face. She came back to her seat and sat down. I looked at her and asked her if she was okay, and she told me that they were waiting for a specialist. I became worried as well, but I tried not to show it.

"We sat for close to another hour before Maria jumped up and approached the nurse's counter again. This time, she insisted that they tell her a little more information. While they were talking, the doctor came out from the examination room and asked us to accompany her to the room where Antonio was being examined. Maria grabbed my hand. I could see tears forming in her eyes.

"As we walked into the doctor's office, she closed the door, leaned back against the wall, and asked us to sit down. She looked down at the floor with her arms crossed. 'We found a large tumor. I'm having tests run, and the results won't be back for a while, but I believe Antonio has cancer. And by the size of the tumor, we need to perform surgery as soon as possible. He's going to need to stay here for the night, and I'll schedule him for surgery first thing in the morning. Whether it's cancerous or not, we still need to remove it. But by morning, I'll have the results, and then we'll know for sure.'

"Maria and I just sat there. We didn't know what to say. I looked up at the doctor and asked, 'Is he going to be all right?' I could feel my eyes tearing up, but I held them back as best I could. I had to.

"'We'll know everything tomorrow morning after I receive the results. One of you can stay with him in his room!'

"I knew that there wasn't any way Maria would have been able to be alone at the house, so I told her she could stay, and I would be back in the morning. But as I said this, the doctor spoke again, 'My guess is that it is, so I just want to prepare you.'

"Maria stayed in his room for the night, and I returned home.

"The next morning, I returned to the hospital before Antonio went in for his surgery. As with any hospital, we were given all kinds of papers to sign, and the doctor said that more than likely, the surgery was going to take approximately four hours. Maria and I kissed him on the forehead and sat in the waiting room counting the minutes or, should I say, hours.

"After four hours passed and no one came to announce that the surgery was over, Maria began to inquire from the nurse how much longer it would be. The nurse said that the tumor was bigger than they had expected, and it was going to be a while longer, and she assured us that the surgery was going well. Maria and I did our best to wait patiently.

"As Maria leaned against me with her head on my shoulder, I couldn't stop thinking about the time I spent days looking for Antonio. I had wanted so desperately to find him. Maria and I talked about that day while we waited. After we finished that conversation, I said, 'Remember the day Antonio fell out of old Mrs. Reed's tree, and we thought he had broken his arm?'

"Maria looked up at me and smiled. 'Yeah, but he didn't want me to know, so he didn't say anything for two days!' Maria began to laugh as she said, 'After you came home from the doctor's with him and we were eating dinner, you told him it was a good thing the ground stopped his fall.'

"Maria closed her eyes as her laughter turned to tears. I thought how easily we take life for granted.

"Every day, millions of people go to work and return home at the end of the day without ever giving the slightest thought of how precious life is, and in a brief wink of an eye, your whole life can change. It feels like the entire world comes crashing down, and nothing else matters but that moment, that second in time, and how badly you want to change what has happened, and you can't.

"Just then, the waiting room door opened, and the doctor came in. She was still removing her gloves as she called us, 'Samuel and Maria!'

"'Yes,' I said as Maria lifted her head up.

"'Antonio is in recovery. He's doing fine, and we're confident that we got it all, but we won't be a hundred percent sure until we can run some more tests. We should be able to start tomorrow after he gets some rest. He'll have to stay with us for a week or so, but it's all right if one of you stays with him.'

"Since he was going to be in recovery for a while, the doctor made arrangements for us to sit with him. Then after a while longer, we kissed him on the forehead again and went up to his room to wait for him. Maria sat by the window looking toward the sky. Then she bowed her head and prayed that Antonio would survive this terrible disease. As she prayed, I stood facing her with my hands in hers and closed my eyes as she prayed.

"'Father, I have always been a faithful servant to you. You and I have talked many times, Lord. You have always sent your angels to protect me. Now I ask that you send your angels to protect Antonio, not to take him home yet, Lord, but to help him survive. He is a very special child, and I know that you have special plans for him, so I ask that you allow us as his parents to guide and teach him to be your loyal servant here on earth. Please, Father, I ask that you let us have him for a little while longer. If you decide that it is his time, then we thank you for the precious moments we have had together and the joy that he has brought to our lives. But our hearts will miss him terribly, Lord, so please take this illness from his body and make him healthy again. We thank you for your love and many blessings always. Amen.'

"We both stood by the window for a few minutes longer and held each other. Antonio was brought back to his room. He was still a little sleepy, but he looked up at us and smiled. The doctor said that he needed to rest, so we kissed him again, and Maria walked me to the elevator.

"She loved him as much as I did, and as much as I wanted to stay with him, I knew I had to return to work the next day. I kissed Maria and told her I would be back in the morning as early as I could before going to work. The elevator opened. I told Maria that I loved her, and I returned home.

"It was lonely without the two of them. I didn't get much sleep that night, so I spent most of the night staring out the window as I lay in bed until the sun came up. I dressed for work and stopped at the hospital as I promised. I walked in with an armful of flowers that

I had bought at the grocery store on my way. I stood outside his door before I walked in. I had to prepare myself as best I could. I took a deep breath and let it out slow and then walked in smiling. I wanted Antonio to know that everything was going to be all right, even if I wasn't sure myself.

"I spent some time talking to him and Maria before leaving for work. We talked mostly about whatever he wanted to. I stayed as long as I could, and then as I drove out of the parking lot, I couldn't hold the tears back any longer. I had to pull over to the side of the road. I was successful while I was with Antonio, but I couldn't hold the tears inside any longer.

"I finally arrived at work, but as soon as I walked in the door, Frank was standing in the doorway waiting for me.

"'What are you doing here, Samuel?' he asked.

"Before I could say a word, he continued, 'Go home or go to the hospital. You need to be with your family! You won't be very much help for me today anyway. You know that!'

"'What about the children?' I asked.

"'Don't worry about them. They'll be all right for a couple of days. We have other counselors here. I want you to go home!'

"I started to ask again, 'What about—'

"But Frank interrupted me. 'What about nothing? I'll take care of everything. Please go home and take care of your family! I'll tell the other children that you will be out for a couple of days, and they'll understand. Give my love to Maria and tell Antonio that we are all praying for him. Now leave!'

"Then he literally pushed me out the door.

"I drove back to the hospital a little faster than I should have, and Maria was surprised when I walked back in the room. She looked at me with a puzzled expression on her face. But then she smiled at me. I could tell she knew exactly what had happened. She said, 'Frank made you leave, didn't he?'

"I nodded my head yes and smiled at her. I turned my head to Antonio and walked over to the side of his bed. I picked up his hand and just held it. He looked at me, smiled, and said, 'I love you, Dad!'

"I can tell you, there was no holding back the tears this time. I began crying. 'I love you too, son!'

"Maria stood up, walked over to me, and hugged me.

"That evening, Maria and I drove to the airport to pick up Angela. Her plane arrived three hours late, but when she saw us, she ran, dodging every passenger that stood between her and us. She began telling us stories about her trip while we were picking up her luggage. Then she stopped. 'Where's Antonio?' she asked.

"We had just walked through the doors to the outside, and she asked again but a little louder, 'Where is Antonio?'

"I told her that we would discuss it in the car. But Angela insisted. 'No! I'm not going any farther until you tell me. Something is wrong. He would be here if everything was all right. Tell me where he is!' She began to panic.

"'He's in the hospital,' I said. 'He's all right. Please just calm down, and I'll tell you everything in the car.'

"I opened the door for her as she got in. While I loaded her luggage in the trunk, I was trying to think of how I was going to tell her.

"By the time I had loaded everything, Maria had already gotten into the car, so I got in, put my seat belt on, and started the car.

"'Antonio had surgery a couple of days ago for a tumor. He has cancer.'

"This was the first time Angela had ever gotten angry with us. She'd been upset before, but never angry. She became very loud. 'Why didn't you call me and let me know?'

"'Angela,' I said, 'there wasn't anything you could have done, and we felt it was best not to ruin your trip. Besides, there wasn't any way we could have brought you home that fast!'

"But she was so upset. She began crying, and she yelled at us, 'You should have let me know! Why didn't you let me know?'

"'I'm very sorry, Angela, if you feel we made the wrong decision, but we must do what we think is best for you. Right or wrong, it was our decision to make!'

"Angela was quiet for a minute, and then she said, 'I'm sorry! But please take me to the hospital. I want to see him!'

"Maria asked her if she wanted to go home first and put her things in the house, but she insisted.

"'No, please just take me to the hospital!'

"Maria looked at me, and I agreed. 'Okay, I understand,' I said, and I drove her to see Antonio.

"Angela and Antonio were very close. Although she never took her mother's locket from around her neck, Antonio and she were truly brother and sister. That night as soon as we arrived at the hospital, she got out before I stopped the car. Angela ran up the hallway into his room. She startled him as she pushed the door open, but she didn't care. She wrapped her arms around him and cried. After she spent the evening with him, she and I went home. We sat up and talked until she fell asleep from exhaustion. I kissed her and covered her up with a blanket as she slept in the chair. The next day, Angela and I returned to the hospital. Maria and I went to get some coffee while Angela read to Antonio.

"As we walked over to a table, we saw was a man sitting alone. He looked up, smiled, and said, 'Hello, are you here for a visit, or are you a patient?'

"'No, we're visiting our son.'

"'Oh, how is he?' the man asked.

"'Well, he has a lot of tests to go through, but the doctor said he should be able to go home in a few days.'

"'That's good,' he replied. Then he smiled and asked why Antonio was in the hospital.

"'He has cancer,' I said.

"The gentleman smiled. 'Don't you mean he had cancer?'

"'I'd like to say that, but we won't know until they do more tests.'

"He smiled and said reassuringly, 'I'm sure he will be just fine. You prayed for him, right?'

"'Of course, we did, day and night.'

"He looked at me. 'Then I'm sure he will be okay. I just have a feeling it's not his time.'

"I finished my coffee. 'I guess we'd better go back up. We don't want to be gone very long.'

"We stood up, and I thanked him for his confidence, and then I told him that I hoped he was right because Antonio was a very special young man and he brought great happiness to our lives. Maria did the best she could to smile.

"It was four more days before Antonio was released from the hospital. We rearranged everything in the house so he would be able to get to everything he needed without any difficulty. It wasn't going to be easy keeping our anger and frustration from showing. We knew he was going to be going through chemotherapy for the next year, but we also knew God would be there every step of the way.

"Maria and I accompanied Antonio to his chemo every Friday for the following twelve months and to every doctor's visit. He liked to joke with the nurses every time we went in. I think the nurses grew to expect it. As a matter of fact, I think they looked forward to it. Anyway, during our last visit with the doctor, we were told that the cancer was totally gone. The doctor told Antonio that God must have had a very special plan for him because he survived. She had another boy who was the same age as Antonio that was not as fortunate.

"We never stopped thanking God for protecting him, and although our lives returned to normal, we never stopped thinking how blessed we were to have Antonio as our son and for him surviving his cancer. We knew he was special when he came to be our son, but we didn't know how special until then."

Mr. Pulaski's story helped to pass the time for Mom and Dad, at least for a little while.

And then Mom stood up and walked toward the doorway. "Why are they taking so long?"

She looked down the hallway hoping that someone was bringing some news. A few more passes back and forth across the room and she turned around and began walking toward the doorway again as the doctor called to her.

"April!"

She turned around as the doctor approached her. "The doctor's here, John!" she called.

Dad was leaning against the wall in his chair; he opened his eyes and stood up at the same time as Mr. Pulaski.

The doctor smiled. "Jimmie is going to be okay. There doesn't seem to be any internal swelling, but you need to know that he hit his head pretty hard, so it's going to take a few days before we'll know for sure if it's going to affect his vision or not. I want to keep him here overnight so that we can monitor him just as a precaution. I don't want to send him home just yet. One of you can stay with him, and tomorrow if he's doing well and he can eat, we'll send him home, okay?"

Mom put her hands up to her eyes, took a deep breath, and said, "Thank you, Doctor, and thank you so much!"

The doctor smiled and nodded. "They'll be taking him up to his room shortly. You can visit him for just a few minutes, and then he needs to get some rest. The nurses will be checking his vital signs every hour throughout the night. With a head injury, especially one like his, he has to be monitored very closely."

Mom, Dad, and Mr. Pulaski went up to my assigned room and waited for me to be brought up. When I finally arrived, I was barely awake. Mom kissed me on my forehead with tears running down her cheek. "Thank God you're going to be all right!"

The doctor smiled and placed her hand on Mom's arm. "Keep in mind, I said he should be okay. Everything looks good right now, but we really won't know for at least twenty-four hours, all right?"

Mom smiled back as she wiped her tears and nodded her head.

Mr. Pulaski walked over and stood next to me; he looked down with both hands holding his hat in front of him. "Jimmie, my young friend"—I opened my eyes as far as I could; at least, I think I opened my eyes and looked up at him—"you brought back memories to me. Don't ever do that again please. Those memories I don't need to repeat!" He looked at me again and smiled. "I will see you tomorrow, my friend." Mr. Pulaski walked out into the hallway to wait for Dad to say good-bye.

Dad held Mom and kissed her. "If you need me for anything, call me right away." She nodded her head, and Dad leaned over and kissed me on the forehead. "I love you, son, but we are going to talk about this when you're better!"

I sure wasn't looking forward to that. The chances of me being grounded for a while were pretty good.

Dad and Mr. Pulaski left the hospital. After they got in the car, Dad thanked Mr. Pulaski again for finding me. He started the car and looked over at Mr. Pulaski again. "I'm sorry you spent the evening looking for Jimmie, and I'm sorry you had to go through what you did, but if you didn't—"

"That's okay," Samuel interrupted. "I would do anything for Jimmie. You are very lucky parents to have a son like him. He's a good boy!"

Dad smiled. "Thanks, but he can be a handful at times!"

"All young boys can be a handful. It's just that some can be more of a handful than others," Mr. Pulaski replied.

Dad smiled again, and they laughed as they left for home.

Once they arrived at Mr. Pulaski's house, Mr. Pulaski got out and waved good-bye to Dad as he drove away.

Mr. Pulaski's legs hurt him very much that night, but he didn't want Dad to see how much pain he was in, so he waited for him to turn the corner before attempting to walk up the steps to his house. It was difficult for Mr. Pulaski. He had to hang on to the railing and pull himself up the steps. Once he managed to get into the house, he took his coat and hat off and fell into his chair. He was so exhausted that he kicked his shoes off, put his head back, and fell asleep. Although it wasn't as comfortable as his bed, he didn't move for the rest of the night.

> *Yet the news about him spread all the more, so that crowds of people came to hear him and to be healed of their sicknesses.*
> —Luke 5:15, New International Version

CHAPTER 19

Saturday—Jimmie Returns Home from the Hospital

When the sun was setting, the people brought to Jesus all who had various kinds of sickness, and laying his hands on each one, he healed them.
—Luke 4:40, New International Version

It was early in the morning when the nurse came in and woke me up as she took my blood pressure, temperature, and checked my bandages. Even though they woke me up regularly through the night to do these things, I wasn't happy that they kept asking me the same questions every time. But this time, I could see Mom sitting in a chair next to my bed. She opened her eyes and smiled at me.

"Hi, Mom," at least, I thought that's what I said, but I was so tired I wasn't sure. "When did you get here?" I mumbled.

The nurse smiled as she stuck a thermometer in my mouth and then said, "Your mother has been here all night. As a matter of fact, she never moved from that chair!"

Then she looked over at Mom while she did whatever else nurses have to do that isn't any fun for the patient anyway. "Boy, are you going to be sore when you try to get up!"

Mom rubbed her eyes and yawned. "I guess I'm about to find out on the scale of one to ten exactly how sore I'm going to be because I'm getting up right now!"

As she leaned forward, the nurse scrunched up her forehead as if she was able to feel Mom's pain. "Would you like some help standing up?"

"No, thanks!" Mom said. "I think I'll be all right once I start moving around, unless you want to give me a shot of whatever it is you gave my son for his pain."

"I can't do that!" the nurse answered, laughing.

After Mom slowly stood up and stretched, she leaned over and kissed me on my forehead again. "How are you feeling this morning?"

"I'd like to know that myself!" the nurse said cheerfully.

Mom turned and looked at her.

The nurse shrugged her shoulders. "I have to put it in his chart! So on that same scale from one to ten, how are you feeling this morning?"

My throat was a little dry as I swallowed. "I feel like a truck ran over my head!"

"I didn't say on a scale from being hit by a bicycle to a truck. I said on a scale from one to ten!" she replied. She had a pen in hand, ready to write.

"Since you put it that way, make it an eight point five!"

"That works for me! By the way, you're allowed to have clear liquids, gelatin, or something along that line. So what would you like for breakfast this morning?"

I thought for a minute. "I will take some gelatin?"

"Good choice. I see that that is what is on the menu this morning! The doctor will be in sometime later, and then maybe she'll let you eat something else. But in the meantime, I'll be right back with your gelatin."

After the nurse left, Mom gently put her hand on my head, leaned over, and looked me in the eyes—I mean eye; I couldn't really open my other eye very well. "You scared all of us so much, Jimmie!"

"I'm sorry, Mom! I just wanted to check the lake really quick! I wasn't going to go out on it. I only wanted to throw rocks out to see if it was frozen enough for skating. I began running, and the next thing I knew, I woke up in here. I had a dream though. I dreamt that the lake wasn't frozen anymore, and it was warm. Then I saw a bright light, and this lady came over and sat with me. She told me not to get up, and then we talked, but I can't remember what about. I do remember that the light was so bright that I couldn't see her face very well! She told me that everything was going to be all right and that she was going to stay with me until help arrived. I can't really remember much, but I remember after we talked, she told me to lie back down and close my eyes.

"Then she left, and I felt someone pick me up. I couldn't open my eyes, but I heard a man telling me that he was going to get me to the hospital. He carried me for a while. Then I managed to open my eyes just long enough to see that there were two men carrying me: one of them looked like Mr. P., and the other was younger, but he had blond hair and was dressed in a white shirt and pants."

Mom looked at me, rubbed my forehead with her hand, and said, "The only one that carried you up the hill was Mr. Pulaski. He would have carried you all the way to Mr. Fern's farm if we hadn't arrived when we did!"

I was really confused. "I saw Mr. Pulaski and another man. I really did! They both carried me up the hill. He was as tall as Mr. Pulaski, and I know he had blond hair, and he was dressed in white! He even looked at me and said that I should stay calm and not to worry, everything was going to be just fine. Then I heard the police car coming, but I couldn't open my eyes again."

"Well, from now on, you are to stick to our rules! You are not to go anywhere near the lake by yourself. Do you understand?"

I closed my eyes and nodded my head yes.

Mom left to get something to drink when the nurse came in with a pitcher of ice water for me, and the doctor came in right behind her.

"I understand you did okay through the night," he said. Then he took the bandage off my head. "It looks a lot better this morning than it did last night. That's for sure! Let's see if you can keep some breakfast down, and if you can, we'll let you go home. I'll be back in a few hours."

By then, Mom had come back into the room. The doctor walked out with the nurse while giving her instructions for my possible release.

A few minutes later, there was a knock on the door. "Is it all right for me to come in?"

I looked over and saw Mr. Pulaski standing in the doorway with Dad.

"Hi, Dad. Hi, Mr. Pulaski!"

Mr. Pulaski walked over to one side of my bed, and Dad walked over to the other side; Dad leaned over and kissed me on the forehead. I had had enough kissing on the forehead by that time, but I didn't want to say anything.

"Has the doctor been in yet?"

"Yes, indeed!" Mom said.

"I can go home in a few hours!"

Mom corrected me. "He said if you kept your breakfast down, he might let you go home in a few hours!"

Dad looked at Mom. "That's great!"

I looked at Mr. Pulaski. "Thanks for finding me, Mr. P, and helping me."

"You're welcome, Jimmie, but I would appreciate it if we didn't have to do this again!"

"Don't worry, Mom already yelled at me, and I promise I'll never do it again!"

Just as my breakfast arrived, so did Sam and Billy.

"Hi, guys!" I said with a smile.

Sam smiled back. "You mean guys and girl!"

Becky came in behind them with a big smile. "Hi, Jimmie. How are you feeling?" She had some flowers in her hand. "I didn't know if I was supposed to bring flowers for a guy or not, but I didn't care."

The nurse set my breakfast down and turned around. "Okay, it's getting a little crowded in here."

Mom stood up. "I'll go down the hall to the waiting room and let your friends visit for a while!"

Mom leaned over my forehead, and I just had to stop her. "Mom, I think the kissing the forehead can stop now. I mean I love you too, but please, between you and Dad, my forehead is getting wrinkled."

Dad stood up too. "I'm going to go with your mother, Jimmie. We'll be back in a little while, and maybe we'll go down to the cafeteria and get some breakfast ourselves."

"Okay, Dad!"

Mr. Pulaski followed Mom and Dad out the door. "I could use some coffee myself. Do you mind if I join you?"

"I don't mind at all, Samuel. Let's go. I'll even buy!" Dad replied.

After they left the room, Becky asked me how my head was. "Does it hurt a lot?"

"Not really, at least not right now. It did before, but I'm on some kind of medication that helps. I just can't wait to go home."

Sam looked at my breakfast. "Are you really going to eat that?"

I leaned forward a little bit and frowned. "I don't have any choice. If I don't, I can't go home!"

Billy smiled. "It doesn't look that bad!"

Sam looked at him. "This is coming from a guy who will eat anything and everything, no matter what!"

We all laughed.

"You know, Jimmie, if you would have called us, we would have gone to the lake with you. We can't wait until the lake freezes either," Billy said.

"I know, but it wasn't going to take me long, and then I was going home. But from now on, I'll make sure I call you guys first!"

"Okay, well, we have to go. Becky's mother is waiting for us in the parking lot. She would have come up, but she said she wasn't presentable. See ya later!"

Sam and Billy walked out the door.

Again, Becky followed behind them, and as she reached the doorway, she turned around. "I'm really glad you're okay, Jimmie." Then she smiled as she walked out.

It didn't take me long to finish eating, and it really wasn't very good. I pushed my tray out of the way and turned the television on as I anxiously waited for the doctor to return to announce that I was ready to go home.

After a half hour or so, Mom, Dad, and Mr. Pulaski returned.

"Your friends left already?" Dad asked.

"Yeah, Becky's mother was waiting for them in the parking lot. They just wanted to see how I was."

Dad smiled. "It was nice that Becky came too!"

"Yeah, Dad, it was nice! After all, I guess we're friends now. I guess she's okay!"

Dad smiled at Mom.

"I said we're friends, Dad, just friends!" I repeated.

It was getting close to noontime when the doctor finally returned to check on me. He took off the bandage and looked at my head again. "It's looking pretty good, Jimmie, and you were able to keep your breakfast down?"

"Yes!" I said sarcastically. "Can I please go home now?"

"Don't you want to eat lunch before you go?" the doctor asked.

"No! I mean, that's okay, I'll eat at home!"

"Don't you like our food?" he asked.

"Yeah, it's great, just like Mom makes!"

Mom's eyes opened really wide as she looked at me.

"I'm just kidding, Mom, but can I go now?"

The doctor checked my blood pressure and temperature again, listened to my heart, and breathing. "Yes, Jimmie, you can go now. But you take care of yourself, and no more visits to the lake without someone with you!"

Mom thanked the doctor as he left the room.

It didn't take me long to get dressed. Mom asked if I needed help.

"No, thanks, Mom. I think I can manage. It wasn't long, and I was ready and on my way out when all of a sudden, I heard something.

"Hold it right there, mister!"

I turned around.

"You can't just walk out of here. I have to give you a ride, so come on and sit down. It'll be fun!" The nurse was standing behind a wheelchair, smiling. I walked over and sat down, but I wasn't smiling, and then we were on our way.

Once we were outside, Dad went to get the car. He pulled up to the curb, and we got in. I was very happy to be leaving the hospital. We stopped at Mr. Pulaski's house first and dropped him off, and then we continued home. When we pulled up in the driveway and I began to get out of the car, Mom hurried to get out first, and she literally ran around the car to help me. I was really happy to be home, but I wasn't happy that all I was allowed to do the rest of the day was lie on the sofa in the living room, and every time I made the slightest move, Mom asked me where I was going.

Dad left for work as soon as I was settled since he missed so much time visiting me at the hospital; he wanted to try and make up some time. I think we were all glad that the day had come to an end. Mom said since the next day was Sunday, we were going to go to church, and that's all we were going to do. She insisted that we were going to stay home for the rest of the day, and when Mom makes a decision, no one argues with her, not even Dad.

CHAPTER 20

Sunday—Twenty Days before Christmas

*To Him be glory in the church and in Christ Jesus
throughout all generations, for ever and ever! Amen.*
—Ephesians 3:21, New International Version

Mr. Pulaski arrived at the church as usual before anyone else; he walked up the four short steps to the sidewalk leading up to the front door of the church. As he reached for the handle, he paused. With one hand in his pocket, he took a deep breath of wintry cold air, stepped back, and stared at the outside of the church. *It looked so wonderful,* he thought, *if Christmas would only last all year!* He had these thoughts as he opened the front door. Once inside, he turned the lights on and adjusted the thermostat. The last thing he wanted to hear was Mrs. Sanders complaining that it was too cold and how she had to keep her coat on all morning and how terribly uncomfortable she was. And when Mrs. Sanders was uncomfortable, then Mr. Sanders was uncomfortable because he'd have to listen to her complain for the rest of the day, which resulted in Mr. Pulaski getting a phone call letting him know how unhappy they both were. Pastor Foreland arrived an hour earlier that morning as well. Actually, it was just after Mr. Pulaski unlocked the door.

Pastor Foreland admitted to Mr. Pulaski that he didn't go over his sermon the night before, so he thought it might be a good idea to go through it that morning before standing in front of everyone and being embarrassed from making mistakes. As he hung his coat up, he asked, "How are you feeling this morning, Samuel? Mrs. Jennings called me yesterday about Jimmie's accident, so I stopped by last night after dinner to check on him. I would have visited him at the hospital had I known sooner, but sometimes people forget to let me know when things happen!"

"Well, everything happened so fast!" Mr. Pulaski explained. "We thanked God he didn't do any permanent damage."

Pastor Foreland looked down at Mr. Pulaski and commented, "Actually, it's a miracle that he didn't. From what I understand, Samuel, you're the one who found him and saved his life. I was told that because of the injury and the cold weather, if you hadn't found him when you did, he could have died."

Mr. Pulaski smiled. "It was God who saved him, and I'm thankful that Jimmie's going to be fine!"

The doors opened, and the ushers arrived to welcome everyone.

Pastor Foreland looked around. "Well, it looks like people are starting to come in. Excuse me for a few minutes. If I don't go into my office before someone sees me, I'll never get the chance to look over my sermon before I have to give it."

Mr. Pulaski turned and began greeting everyone as they entered the church. It wasn't long before the church filled up. After all, it was the Christmas season, and attendance always goes up that time of year. Mr. Pulaski looked around as the organist started to play and shook his head as if in disbelief that there were so many people there. *No one ever told me that God was seasonal*, he thought to himself. A few minutes later, Pastor Foreland entered on cue by the organist and took his place at the pulpit. He raised his hands to signal everyone to stand up, and they all sang the first song. Pastor Foreland referred to it as a motivational song. At the end, he greeted everyone with his warm smile and cheerful voice giving thanks to God.

As he delivered his sermon, everyone listened, or at least, mostly everyone listened. Some paid attention more intently than others, and there were the regular few who most likely were thinking about other things and didn't hear a word he said at all. They were the members of the congregation who smiled and shook Pastor Foreland's hand on the way out and commented on how wonderful his sermon was.

Mr. Pulaski had no doubt that the young parents were most likely thinking about what they were going to buy their young children for Christmas presents, but he couldn't really blame them; he still finds himself thinking sometimes how nice it would be if Antonio and Angela were to visit him for Christmas, or he finds himself thinking of Maria. He doesn't mean to, but sometimes he just can't help himself; his mind just wanders.

After the service, everyone followed the Sunday routine of refreshments and conversation with one another. Mr. Pulaski spent time with the children as they all crowed around him to hear one of his stories while their parents stood and watched. Sometimes Mr. Pulaski went on so long that parents had to interrupt him. When that happened, he made it a point to finish whatever story he was telling the following Sunday. Pastor Foreland was always pleased because that meant that they wanted to come back even if it was to hear Mr. Pulaski's story and not his sermon.

After everyone left, Mr. Pulaski cleaned up what was left by the children and the bulletins that remained in the pews from the parents who forgot to take them with them or from the children dropping them on the floor. Then he left the church after making one last check.

Mr. Pulaski stopped by our house to see how I was doing and to find out if we needed anything. It was normally a twenty-minute walk to our house from the church, but it usually took Mr. Pulaski a little longer because of the stiffness in his legs. When he finally reached our house, he rang the doorbell, and Mom answered.

Mom was surprised when she opened the door because she wasn't expecting anyone. "Hi, Samuel. How are you?"

"I'm fine, Mrs. Jennings. I just wanted to stop by and see how Jimmie was doing and to find out if there was anything I can help with. We missed you at church this morning!"

"Please come in. Everything is just fine! We thought it would be best if we kept Jimmie home this morning. He wants to go to school tomorrow, but I'm not sure he should, and he and I were just discussing it!"

As Mr. Pulaski took off his coat, I yelled from the living room, "I'm fine! There's no reason why I can't go to school tomorrow!"

Mr. Pulaski walked into the living room. "I'm very surprised, Jimmie. I thought you would be happy that you didn't have to go to school!"

"I know, Mr. P!" I said. "It surprises me too, but as cold as it's been, I know the lake is frozen. I don't want to miss the first practice!"

Mom rubbed her forehead. "Jimmie, I don't think you are going to be skating anytime soon. That's all we need is for you to fall and hit your head again. You need to give it some time!"

I was pretty upset. "I have a helmet, Mom. I promise I'll wear it! I promise, and I won't skate hard. I'll be goalie or something for a while!"

Mom just shook her head and said, "We see the doctor tomorrow, and we'll see what he says, but I know he won't want you to skate this soon either!"

I leaned my head back and closed my eyes.

"Well, Jimmie, I'm glad to see you're doing okay. I just wanted to check on you, so make sure you do whatever you have to get well, okay?"

"Okay, Mr. P!" I answered as Mom was walking him to the door.

"If there is anything you need, please call me!" Mr. Pulaski said.

Mom smiled and then added, "We will, Samuel, and thank you again for everything!"

Mr. Pulaski left, and Mom closed the door.

The wind was starting to pick up just enough to once again make it difficult for him to walk. When he arrived home, he made a cup of tea, lit the fireplace, and read the Sunday newspaper. He finished his tea and closed his eyes; it was difficult for him to keep his eyes open, and with the warmth of the fire, it wasn't long before he fell asleep.

As his eyes closed, he could hear the wind blowing against the house and the wind chimes clanging in the breeze. He drifted off to sleep, and in moments, his dreams were of two small children laughing as they played in the backyard. He heard the sounds of Antonio and Angela laughing as he helped them build a snowman. He remembered Antonio, Angela, and himself lifting the big heavy ball of snow up to the top of the other two as they finished building the snowman. Antonio and Angela weren't tall enough, so the two of them stood on the tips of their toes, and Mr. Pulaski pretended to struggle as well. Then Maria came running out of the house with a carrot for the nose and coal from the basement for the eyes and mouth, and she carried one of Mr. Pulaski's hats that he customarily shared all winter with their newly built friend.

Samuel's sleep was close to coming to an end as he rolled over. He tried not to wake up; he didn't want to let go of this moment. If it was up to him, he would remain in this dream of the past forever, but it just wasn't possible. He opened his eyes, stretched, and sat in his chair as the fire was dying down. *Maybe it is time to return home*, he thought. Where he could visit Maria and spend every day with his Angela and Antonio and his grandchildren. He missed them so very much.

CHAPTER 21

Jimmie Returns to School After All

Honor your father and your mother, so that you may live long in the land the LORD your God is giving you.
—Exodus 20:12, New International Version

Monday morning arrived with the sound of an alarm. It was the type that had a very annoying buzz that always made me jump two feet in the air when it went off. My head was still hurting a little, but I managed to get up and get ready for school on time. I wasn't as fast as usual, but I finished last-minute grooming, and I tried on a few different hats hoping to hide the bandages around my head. As I stared in the mirror, I put my hat on with the visor pointing up in the air, and then I tried it on with the visor pointing to the right and then to the left. I tried on every hat I had. There were five different baseball hats, one trucking hat, one of Dad's work hats, and three that I had no idea where they came from. I tried them on pointing in every direction until I found just the right one. Actually, I think I decided it was the right one because I was getting tired of trying them on. Anyway, I ran down the steps and into the kitchen because by then, I was running late.

But all of a sudden, Mom stopped me abruptly. "Just where do you think you're going, young man?" she said, and with a very stern voice, I might add.

I wasn't expecting her to be standing by the kitchen table. I looked up and noticed very quickly that she wasn't smiling. I looked over at Dad, once again looking for a little male support, but he slouched down in his chair as if he was hiding behind his coffee cup so that Mom couldn't see him. Hiding wasn't one of Dad's best qualities either.

"I'm going to school. It's Monday!"

I was hoping she didn't notice the bandages with my hat on, and I was in midstride heading toward the refrigerator for the milk when she continued her train of thought. Again, I tried to distract her, so before she could say anything, I tried talking about her.

"So are you working all day today, Mom?" I said while eating breakfast. But it didn't work.

"I don't remember your father or me giving you permission to go to school this morning!

As a matter of fact, the last thing I remember is telling you that you needed to rest for a few days. Remember the doctor's instructions?"

"Mom," I blurted out! "I'm feeling fine! I need to go to school. I have things I need to do before Christmas, and time is running out for me to get them done!"

"What is so important that it can't wait?"

I hated it when she asked questions because I knew that the odds of thinking of something convincing were against me.

"I'm working on Mr. P's Christmas present, and there are a lot of people I need to talk to! Please, Mom! I promise if I start feeling sick or anything, I'll call you!"

Mom calmed down a little bit. I could tell by her voice that I had a slight chance of convincing her. "Jimmie, I'm not sure about this!"

Then she paused, but only for a second. "But if you really want to go, I want you to call me at lunchtime and then before you leave to come home! Do I make myself clear?"

182

I couldn't believe I won. "Okay, Mom! I promise I'll call you at lunchtime and before I come home! Would you please write a note so that I can wear my hat all day?"

Mom wrote the note as I requested. I finished pouring the milk on my cereal, and then I sat down next to Dad at the table.

Dad looked over at Mom while asking me if I wanted him to drop me off at school on his way to work.

I looked at Mom with a smile. "Sure, that way, you can make sure I get there okay!"

Since he was only offering to make Mom feel better, I thought I'd take advantage of this situation and get the most out of it. "Oh, by the way, can we stop and pick up Becky, Sam, and Billy too?"

"Sure, why not!" he agreed, and then we finished our breakfast and grabbed our coats as we hurried out the door.

Dad leaned over and kissed Mom before we left. "He'll be fine!" he said.

Mom looked at him. "I hope so!" she whispered.

After we left, Mom cleaned up the table and left for work. I knew she was going to be looking at the clock until it was time for me to return home.

We stopped at Becky's house first. She was really surprised when she opened the door and saw me standing on her porch. "What are you doing here? I thought you had to stay home for a few days!"

"I'm fine!" I said. "Besides, I have a lot to do this week."

We got in the car and then stopped at Sam's house. Sam had the same reaction as Becky when he came to the door, then Billy.

"Hey, Jimmie, what are you doing—"

I cut him off before he finished. "If one more person says anything about me staying home or resting for a few days, I'm going to yell! I'm fine, and I'm not going to stay at home and rest. Got it?"

"Okay! Okay! Let's go!" Billy said after my outburst of frustration.

We all got in the car, and Dad dropped us off in front of the school.

All four of us walked into the office while I handed Mrs. Todd my note for the hat.

"Well, hi, Jimmie! I didn't expect to see you back so soon!" Mrs. Todd smiled with surprise in her voice.

"I'm fine. Can I go to my class now?" I answered.

"Sure. Have a good day!"

"He's in a bad mood," Becky said as we walked out.

"I'm not in a bad mood!" I said.

Sam and Billy closed their lockers after getting their morning books out and left for class. Becky and I finished getting our books out and left for our first period class also. Neither one of us said another word to each other until lunchtime.

I was the first one to sit down at the table. Billy and Sam stood in front of me, holding their trays. They looked at each other, and then Billy asked, "Are we sitting together today, or do you want to be alone?"

I looked up at them both. "I'm sorry, guys," I said. "It's just that I can't wait to get out on the ice! I know it's ready. I just know it!"

Becky sat down next to me and across from Sam and Billy.

Just before the bell rang signifying the end of lunch period, Mrs. Todd made an announcement. "May I have everyone's attention please. I'm happy to announce that Officer Frank called and informed us that he checked the lake, officially, Jimmie, and it is frozen enough to skate on . . ."

"I knew it!" I yelled out loud as she finished.

"However, Jimmie . . . no one is allowed on the ice alone. You must be with a friend or a parent. Anyone caught on the ice alone will be escorted off the lake and fined! Thank you!"

"So are you going to the lake tonight, Jimmie?" Billy asked.

"I can't. I've been waiting for this, but I can't. I have some things I've got to do, and I don't think my mom will let me. She didn't even want me to come to school today! Besides, I'm trying to get Mr. Pulaski's Christmas present finished."

"What're ya doing? Making it?" Sam asked curiously.

"Well, sort of!" I answered. "I don't want to say anything until I have it ready. It may not work out."

"Well, I don't think I'm going to be able to go either!" Becky replied. "My mom has plans for us this evening."

Billy and Sam stopped walking.

"I thought you said you never skated before!" Billy said, surprised.

"I said, I'd never skated on a lake before. We had skating rings in the city!" Becky argued.

"Oh, well, we don't just skate. We play hockey!" Sam explained.

"Well, it shouldn't be that hard to learn!"

I could tell she was starting to get a little frustrated by the sound of her voice.

Sam looked at her with squinted eyes and sarcasm. "Girls don't play ice hockey. They figure skate!"

"I don't think you should have said that, Sam!" I warned.

Becky put her hands on her hips. "Who made that rule?"

Now she was getting a little more than frustrated, but Sam did make a valid point.

"We never had a girl play hockey before!"

Becky had an answer for that too; but somehow, I had thought she would.

"Well, Sam, I guess there's a first time for everything, isn't there?"

I think Becky was being a little sarcastic with her answer too.

Sam looked at me. "Come on, Jimmie! You have to come! It's the first night we can play!"

"Okay, Billy, maybe for a little while, but I honestly don't think my mom is going to let me!"

The afternoon bell was about to ring, so we left for our afternoon classes. As we separated and walked out of the lunchroom, Billy gave me his overall evaluation of our discussion. "I think that went well."

I just looked at him and rolled my eyes.

The afternoon seemed to go by quickly, and before we knew it, the bell rang signifying the end of the day. Then on my way out, I realized I had forgotten to call Mom at lunchtime, so I hurried into the office.

"Mrs. Todd, can I use the office phone to call my mother?" I yelled as I burst into the office.

"Well, that's not a good way to enter the office, Jimmie!" she advised. "But I guess you can since you forgot to call her at lunchtime."

I looked up at her as I was dialing the phone. She smiled at me, but I knew it wasn't sincere.

"Oh, she called when she didn't hear from you. She told me that you were supposed to call her as you were going to lunch!"

"Yeah, I forgot."

"Anyway," she continued, "I told her you were doing fine and not to worry."

"Thanks, Mrs. Todd," I said as I heard Mom pick up the phone.

"Mom, I'm on my way home. I know I was supposed to call, I forgot. I'm sorry. I'm on my way now. Yes, Mom, I'll be careful. Bye."

"See you tomorrow, Mrs. Todd, and thanks!"

I picked up my book bag off the floor and ran out to catch up to Sam, Billy, and Becky as they were outside the main entrance waiting for me on the steps.

On our way home, we continued to discuss girls and boys playing ice hockey. This argument, mainly between Sam and Becky, continued until we reached Billy's house.

"Well, maybe Jimmie can get you to understand how this works. It really isn't hard. Boys play hockey. Girls figure skate and watch boys play ice hockey!"

Billy went inside. I was surprised at Sam because he hadn't said a word during the whole argument earlier.

Becky and I continued walking. Sam didn't really pursue this issue as much as he did earlier. After Sam left, Becky asked, "Why are they so immature?"

I hesitated to answer since I agreed with them on this point. I didn't say anything, but she was right too. There is a first time for everything. However, I was a little more open to new things than Sam or Billy. Maybe it was because of Mr. Pulaski's influence that I was exposed to all the time.

"Look, Becky, maybe if you give them some time to get used to the idea . . . We never had a girl want to play ice hockey with us before!"

By the time we reached her house, she had calmed down a little and smiled. "Well, I guess I'll see you tomorrow."

"Guess so!" I said as I began to walk backward toward home.

My home wasn't very far from Becky's house. I ran in the back door, and as I was passing through the kitchen, I noticed a note from Mom standing up in the center of the kitchen table. It was instructions on placing dinner in the oven so that it would warm up before Dad came home. I looked at the time. Mom wasn't due home for another hour. That was just enough time to make some phone calls that I felt were important in arranging for Mr. Pulaski's Christmas present. Dad was to be home approximately at the same time as Mom, so I followed her instructions and set the timer on the stove. Then I put the casserole in the oven. I sat down at the table and began making a few phone calls.

Timing was perfect: by the time I had made my last phone call, both Mom and Dad arrived home as the timer on the stove started buzzing. I turned it off and hurried to set the table. By the time Mom and Dad hung up their coats and washed their hands, I had the table set and dinner on the table waiting to eat.

"Well, this is a surprise!" Mom commented.

"What's a surprise, Mom?" I asked.

"I forgot to tell you to set the table in my note, and you did it anyway!"

We sat down; Dad said the blessing, and we began eating.

"I made some phone calls while I was waiting for dinner to be done. I never thought that Mr. P's Christmas present was going to be so much work! I was wondering, Mom, if maybe you might have some time to help me."

"I suppose I can. What do you need me to do?"

As we ate, I talked about some ideas I had and explained why I needed Mom's help.

I helped Mom clean up the table and dishes, and then I went to my room to study for a while before going to bed. It was too late for me to go to the lake; besides, I really wasn't feeling well, and I didn't want to say anything to Mom. I fell asleep as soon as I lay back on my bed.

During the next couple of days, I hardly had time to visit Mr. Pulaski except for some really short visits on Wednesday and Thursday after school. But the main purpose of my visits was strictly to obtain information that would help in getting more information, without him realizing what I was doing. With school and trying to get Mr. Pulaski's Christmas present finished, the week went by really fast.

It was Thursday already, and as I approached Mr. Pulaski's house, I could see him walking up the steps to go in the front door. He must have been returning from his visit in town again.

"Mr. P!" I yelled.

He slowly turned around. "Well, hi, Jimmie. How was school today?"

"It was okay, I guess. Did I tell you that a couple of days ago, Mrs. Todd announced that Officer Frank said the lake was frozen enough to skate on?"

"I believe you did. As a matter of fact, I believe you told me Wednesday when you came to visit me!"

"Oh yeah," I said as I rubbed my head. "With so much on my mind, I didn't remember. So are you going to go to the lake tomorrow night? It's Friday, ya know." I was so excited.

"Yes, I know, and yes, I will be at the lake! It's a tradition, isn't it?" he said. Mr. Pulaski sat down in his chair, leaned back, and closed his eyes.

"Are you all right, Mr. P?" I asked.

"I'm fine, Jimmie. I'm just a little tired. This cold weather tires me out quickly, and I think it's going to snow again. I can feel it in the air. You know, I was remembering the first time I arrived in this town as I was walking this afternoon. It was twenty-five years ago!"

"Wow, Mr. P! You've been here a long time!"

Sometimes I say things without thinking, but he laughed a little.

"It seems like it was such a short time though, but you're right, twenty-five years is a long time ago."

I asked him a few more questions that I thought were important and that I needed answers to, and then I left for home.

CHAPTER 22

Competition

A cheerful heart is good medicine, but a crushed spirit dries up the bones.
—Proverbs 17:20, New International Version

Friday morning had come, and I was scheduled to visit the doctor for a checkup. Actually, to put it in words that seemed to strike humor in the minds of my friends, I was to have my head examined. I remember very well the reaction when I told Sam and Billy: as a matter of fact, the two of them couldn't understand why Mom hadn't had it done sooner. I wasn't amused at all, but even Becky laughed.

Mom picked me up at school right at nine o'clock that morning since my appointment was scheduled for fifteen minutes after ten. I was amazed that for the first time, the doctor was able to see me at my scheduled time.

"Well, Jimmie, how are you feeling?" he asked as he looked through my chart.

"On a scale from one to ten?" I asked.

"No, just in general. Are you experiencing any headaches, nausea, blurred vision, anything at all that would be out of the ordinary?"

"No, not that I know of!"

After a thorough examination literally from my head to my toes, Dr. Ramsey cleared me to resume my normal activities, which to me meant skating. Then while looking at me, he continued to give

189

my mother clear instructions. "When it comes to skating, I want him to continue to wear proper gear." Then he spoke directly to me, "As a matter of fact, all of you should be wearing protective gear when you're playing hockey. Are there any questions as to my instructions?"

I jumped down off the examining table without answering.

Dr. Ramsey always required an answer, so he repeated himself, but with fewer words. "Okay, Jimmie?" He wasn't going to let me leave his office without agreeing. He looked at me over his glasses as he waited for a reply.

So I gave him one. "Okay, what?" I said, but that wasn't the answer he was looking for.

So he repeated his instructions again, but with a little more detail so there wasn't any misunderstanding on my part. "Okay that you and your friends will wear the proper gear while playing hockey!" He wasn't smiling.

So at that point, I thought it would be in my best interest to agree to his terms. "Okay, we'll wear gear!"

"Can we go now, Mom?"

"Yes, we can go now. Thanks, Dr. Ramsey," she replied.

As Mom and I walked out of the office, I could tell Mom she wasn't happy.

"That was very rude, Jimmie!"

"I'm sorry, Mom!"

But she wasn't happy with that answer either. "That doesn't sound sincere to me at all! Get in the car," she instructed. "I'll take you back to school, and we'll discuss your behavior this evening at supper."

I didn't say another word all the way back to school, and neither did Mom. I didn't even say good-bye when I got out of the car; I just went straight to the office and signed in.

I walked into my next class just before the bell rang. "Hi, guys!"

"How did it go at the doctor's office?" Billy asked.

"Great, I'm cleared to play hockey, but there's one thing we have to do from now on." The three of them just looked at me. "We have to wear hockey gear!"

"Why? We never did before," Sam said, confused.

I didn't feel like going in to any lengthy explanation, so I came up with the best answer I could at the time. "Look, if I have to, then so do you. I'm not going to be the only one on the ice with pads, gloves, and all the stuff on. Besides, you don't want to take a chance of having the same thing happen to you that happened to me, do you?"

"Okay, Jimmie. I don't like it, but okay, we'll get some pads! So does that mean that you're going to the lake tonight since you didn't show up the last time like you were supposed to?" Sam asked.

"Yeah, I am. And I couldn't help it. I told you I didn't think my mom was going to let me go until I saw the doctor!"

Just then, the bell rang, and we had to hurry before our teachers closed the doors.

It's hard to concentrate on a Friday afternoon when you're a teenager waiting for class to end so you can concentrate on more important things like your weekend. By the time the three fifteen afternoon bell rang signifying the end of the day, I couldn't wait to get to the lake.

Not wanting to waste any time, we hurried out the door. First, we went to Billy's house, then Sam's, and then Becky's.

"See ya at the lake, Jimmie!" Becky said as she opened the door.

I stopped just as I was getting ready to run home. "What! Becky, you're not serious about playing hockey, are you?"

"I sure am!" she said. "See ya there!"

As she went inside, I shook my head. This was going to be very interesting, I thought to myself as I took off running to my own house.

Upon arriving home, I burst in the door and ran up the steps into my room. I then proceeded to pick up my skates and hockey stick as I dropped my book bag on the floor right where I stood and then ran back down the steps and out the door. Then I remembered that I needed to put on the rest of the uniform, so I turned around and ran back into the house and up the stairs to my room.

I made it to the lake in record time, but when I arrived, Billy and Sam were already on the ice. I quickly put my skates on and flew out onto the ice as if my feet were on fire to meet them. Right before we started the first game, all three of us agreed that we had to win two out of three games, and in the case of a tie, we would play a tiebreaker. Because there were only three of us and we only had one net, we each agreed that we had to take a turn being goalie.

As we were getting ready to start the first game, I heard some-one yell. I looked up; then Billy heard it.

"What's wrong?" Sam asked as he looked at us. Sam turned around and protested, "Oh no, she's not playing, Jimmie. No way is she going to play hockey with us!"

"Hi, Becky," I said.

"Hi, guys! I'll have my skates on in a minute," she said. Then she continued, "Sorry I'm late. Mom ran me down to the sporting goods store, and since I never played hockey before, I didn't have any equipment. Dad's not going to be happy when he finds out, but Mom said he'd only be upset for a little while. He can never stay mad at me for very long."

Sam was not happy to see Becky. "Becky, you're not—"

I interrupted, "Going to do well when you first start, but you'll get the hang of it."

Becky stood there for a minute. "You really don't want me to play, do you, Sam?" she asked.

Sam just continued to protest as he replied, "Girls don't play hockey. They just don't!"

Becky looked at Billy. "What about you, Billy?" she asked.

"Heck, I don't care! If she plays, the teams will be even!"

But Sam was stubborn and had no intentions on giving in. "No, they won't! How would they? She doesn't know how to play. Besides, we don't even know if she really knows how to skate!"

Everyone was quiet.

"Okay," Becky said, "I'll make a deal with you, Sam. I'll race you! Jimmie, you skate out as far as you can, and Sam and I will race out to where you're standing and back to Billy! If I beat you, Sam, I play. If I don't, I'll go home, and I won't bother you again. Deal?"

Sam looked at Becky for a minute. "All right, deal, but we race with hockey sticks, and we push the puck all the way!" he answered.

"Wait a minute, Sam!" I said.

"It's a deal!" Becky agreed.

"Becky . . ." I started to say.

But before I could say anything more, she simply said, "It's okay, Jimmie!"

So I skated out onto the lake at a good distance while Billy stood in place.

"On your mark, get set . . ." Billy yelled.

Becky held her stick behind the puck while Sam leaned over with his stick behind his puck as if it was the last thirty seconds in the game and he needed one point to win.

Then Billy gave the final word. "Go!" he shouted.

Sam and Becky took off. Sam took the lead right from the start, but Becky wasn't far behind him. Not having any experience with a hockey stick and a puck, she was doing a pretty good job keeping up. Sam stayed in the lead all the way out to where I was standing and then circled me first with Becky right behind him. Then Billy held his hands out to his sides so they could hit his hand as they came in; that way, he would know who was first.

Sam was still in the lead, and Becky was staying close as they picked up speed. Sam was clearly out front of Becky and coming in first. All of a sudden, Sam tripped and fell. He had run over a stick frozen in the ice and lost his balance, dropping his stick as he fell and sliding face first into Billy. Becky was able to reach out and hit Billy's hand just as Sam slid into his legs, knocking him down. Becky raised her hands in triumph as Sam and Billy were regaining their balance.

As they were standing up, Becky turned around in time to see me as I skated in behind them. "I believe I won!" she exclaimed.

As he was brushing himself off, Sam proceeded to say, "What!"

Then Becky blurted out, "How did you win?"

"I tagged Billy first!" Sam protested.

"You weren't standing. You were sliding, and that doesn't count," Becky answered. Then she continued, "When you race someone, you have to finish standing up!"

"That wasn't one of the rules!" Sam said as he tried to argue with logic.

But I had had enough. We were wasting time, so I decided to just finish the argument by stating the obvious, "Sam, you lost. Becky won. Get over it!" I said this as I skated over to him, then picked up his hockey stick, and handed it to him. "Come on, let's get started, or we won't have enough time to play even one game!"

Without saying a word, he took his stick from me, and we began the game.

We had just enough time to play one game because we briefly helped Becky learn some quick moves. We had fun though; even Sam agreed that it was fun. We then changed into our boots and started for home. We knew from experience if we were late getting home for dinner, none of us would be allowed to come back for the weekend night skating. We all agreed to return sometime around seven that evening. On our way home, we all told Becky how much fun we had for the first time skating that winter and how we never could wait until summer was over to do it. Then when we came to the cross-roads, we split and went our own directions.

I had to hurry the rest of the way home in order to make it on time. Besides, as upset as Mom was with me, there was no way I was going to be late for supper. It was already five thirty, and Mom said dinner was going to be at six, and she was never late. When she says, dinner is going to be ready, she means everyone is sitting at the table and not a minute later.

I entered through the back door just as she was putting the mashed potatoes and gravy on the table. I washed my hands at the kitchen sink and sat down at the table.

Dad could tell I was out of breath. "Had to run again?" he asked.

"Yeah, but I made it!" I replied.

"Barely," Mom said as she sat down. Then she held her hands out to each side, and we all held hands to pray.

After the blessing, I told Mom and Dad about the plan to go back to the lake at seven. "You and Dad should come too," I said. "Everyone is going to be there."

"I'm afraid I have to get up early to open the diner for breakfast, and your father has an early morning too!" she said.

"Okay, but it's all right if I go, isn't it?" I asked.

"I'm not sure, Jimmie!" she replied.

I knew with that statement that she hadn't forgotten about the doctor's visit, and therefore, I quickly proceeded to say, "Mom, I'm really sorry for the way I acted, and I promise I'll apologize to Doc Ramsey. So please can I go back to the lake tonight?"

"Okay, Jimmie, but you need to be home by ten."

"Ten!" I said in disagreement. "That only gives me three hours!"

"I think that's plenty of time, don't you, dear?" Mom said as she looked at Dad.

Dad swallowed, and before he could answer, I started to plead my case for a later time. "It's the first night, and I don't have school tomorrow, and Mr. Pulaski will probably be there too!"

"Well, I guess I don't see any reason why you couldn't stay out until eleven!" Dad then said.

"Eleven!" I protested again.

"Eleven!" Dad repeated. "We can go back to ten if eleven isn't good enough!" he continued.

I agreed, "No, eleven's fine. That's a good time. I'll leave the lake at eleven."

"Jimmie," Dad said, "I mean I want you home by eleven!"

"Okay!" I answered. I figured I'd better not push my luck because Mom hadn't told Dad about Dr. Ramsey yet, and I figured I better leave before that conversation took place. So I asked, "Can I go now?"

"Yes, but make sure you dress warmly!"

I was already on my way out the door and barely heard Mom's comment.

"I don't know what is going on with him lately!" she said as she was picking up the rest of the plates to wash.

Dad laughed. "He's just a young teenager with a lot of energy and a crush on a young girl."

"What!" Mom didn't think it was so funny.

"He may not know it yet, but he will. Just give it time. I'll help you with the dishes, and then I'm going in the living room to read the paper."

PART 3

A New Home, Christmas
Plans Begin:

The Beginning of a Cold
Winter's Journey and Trying
to Find a Renewed Faith

INTRODUCTION
TO PART 3

Faithfulness springs forth from the earth, and righteousness looks down from heaven.
—Psalm 85:11, New International Version

There are people who travel most of their lives and sometimes think how nice it would be to stop traveling and stay in one place. I am amazed when I talk to people and find out that they know everyone and everything there is to know about the area they live in. They know when the farmers around the area bought their first cow or horse. They know when the Joneses sold their farm fifty years ago to the Smiths and when the Smiths passed it on to their children and then sold the ten acres to the state for a new road. It's amazing the information you find out from people who never left the area they were born and raised in.

On the other hand, you have the people who never left their town and wished they did. They talk to someone like me who moved every three years and experienced a whole new life each time. The education that our children received because they had the opportunity to see new things and experience new environments every three years was great, but then they didn't have the opportunity to have best friends that they grew up with. You know, friends whom they started kindergarten and graduated with, then perhaps went to college, and returned home to be married to a high school sweetheart and build a business, had children, and at times talked to their friends about their childhood and the memories that they experienced together.

Which of these worlds is better? I'm not sure, and I don't think I'll ever figure it out. I do, however, know that no matter where we were, we established traditions for our children every Thanksgiving, Christmas, New Year, and Easter. It doesn't matter where you live; it's the traditions that are carried on from year to year that binds a family together.

With this in mind, here I go with the second thought—friendship. Every time we moved to a new location, our children had to start over with making new friends. As they grew older, making new friends became harder. The reason for this was because most of the kids already had established friendships, and it was a little more difficult for them to move into a new friendship circle. Fortunately, since we always lived in a military community, the other children were aware of what it was like to make new friends, and acceptance of new group members wasn't as difficult as at nonmilitary communities.

Now let me move on to my third thought—faith. With every move, we had to have faith that everything would turn out just fine. Faith that our children would find new friends and faith that they wouldn't have any difficulty adjusting to a new school, new town, and even a new home. Faith that we wouldn't have any difficulty either, especially adjusting to a new job. But most of all, faith that I was following what God wanted me to do and not what I wanted to do. I confess though, sometimes I had difficulty making decisions because I was confused. Sometimes I thought that God had abandoned me. But my best friend and wife, Debbie, reminded me, frequently I must add, that everything would work out, and worry wasn't necessary if I just had—faith.

Do you have faith? Do you believe, I mean really believe, in God with all your heart and soul? Because that's what it takes, my friend—one hundred percent dedicated faith.

CHAPTER 23

Friday Night at the Lake

*If it is encouraging, let him encourage; if it is con-
tributing to the needs of others, let him give gener-
ously; if it is leadership, let him govern diligently; if
it is showing mercy, let him do it cheerfully.*
—Romans 12:8, New International Version

The minute I jumped down off the porch and missed every step,
I began running and didn't stop until reaching the top of the hill
where I could see the entire lake. I could see it from the top of the
hill because the firelight was always so bright it glowed across the ice
from one side to the other. Sometimes, while everyone was skating, I
liked to take a few minutes just to stand and look down the hill and
watch Mr. Pulaski as he was busy making the hot chocolate and hot
dogs and putting wood on the fire to keep it going.

Every weekend during the winter, practically everyone in the
whole town was at the lake, whether they skated or not. That night,
however, as I ran down the hill, I could feel a light snow beginning to
fall against my face. Once I was halfway down, I stopped again but
only for a minute or two so that I could simply watch it snow against
the beautiful scenery.

The trees surrounded the lake with only a brush of white from
the snow falling softly as it covered the trees just as a mother carefully
lays a blanket over her baby while it sleeps. The ice, clear as glass and

just as smooth, held the reflection of the fire's light as it cast shadows of both the trees and the many skaters gliding across it as they met others and raced to prove themselves winners. Some couples held hands wishing that the night would never end, and parents helped their tiny children as they tried to stand for the first time in their brand-new skates and laughing as they struggled to keep their balance while holding hands.

Meanwhile, as these skaters continued to skate, I just took a deep breath and walked the rest of the way down the hill waiting for Mr. Pulaski to call me for our first polish sausage of the winter. As I descended the hill to the lake, I remembered what Mom told me about winter the year before. She said that winter made people slow down and caused them not to be in such a hurry all the time. She said it gave people time to think about their lives and focus on the things that are most important. "Reprioritize" is the word she used. I asked her what it meant once, and she made me look it up so I'd never forget the meaning. Sam and Billy were always my friends, but I believe my best friends were Mom, Dad, and Mr. Pulaski. They never missed a baseball game, track meet, or anything else that I participated in. But I can honestly say I remember it was Mom that sat and watched everything I did no matter what the weather was like or how far she had to travel. She was the one that everyone could hear from the stands, cheering louder than anyone else, whether I was first or last.

Meanwhile, as I approached the lake, I could see Mr. Pulaski standing in the same spot he always stood year after year; he was still right next to the fire. As a matter of fact, Mr. Pulaski made it a point to be at the lake before anyone else so everything would be ready by the time the first person arrived. He brought his camping stove as usual and hot cocoa and hot dogs for everyone. That is, everyone except himself and me. As I pointed out earlier, he always made it tradition to bring two polish sausages. I could feel my smile growing from ear to ear and my mouth watering with anticipation from the minute Mr. Pulaski yelled to me and as I continued to get closer to him.

"Jimmie, come over here! I brought hot dogs for everyone, but I have something special for my little friend."

I always knew he had polish sausages waiting for me, but I played along, and then I'd yell back at him, "What do you have, Mr. P?"

Then he'd say, "For you and me, I bring polish sausages."

I could never stop licking my lips as I watched him put them on a stick and hand me one to cook in the fire. That's probably the reason why my lips were always chapped in the winter. However, before I took to the ice to skate with my friends, the two of us would always sit on a big tree stump as we ate together.

As we drank our hot cocoa and ate, Mr. Pulaski told me stories from when he was a boy in Poland. His stories were always very detailed and long, but I didn't mind. We each took a bite, and then he'd begin his story.

"I was a very young man in my late teens when I came to the United States. With the help of my mother, I managed to save up enough money to pay for my long voyage to America on a freighter, but not enough for food. So my mother talked to the captain and made arrangements for me to work on the ship in exchange for food. She told him that I was a hard worker and could do anything he needed. The captain agreed, and I was on my way to America the next morning. It seemed like we were at sea a very long time. So long that I almost forgot what land looked like. When we finally arrived in the New York Harbor, I found work in a small restaurant, but it didn't pay much. The owner said I could sleep in the storeroom until I had enough money to get a place to live, but I had to go to the mission down the street to bathe. It took a while, but I managed to save up the money I needed. Then I began looking for an apartment.

"I looked for a couple of days, but then one night as I was going to sleep, I began wondering if I really wanted to stay there. Then I realized I came a very long way to America, and I wanted to see more, to do more, and to travel. So I packed what few possessions I had, and I left. I wrote a thank-you note the best I could. I could speak English, but writing I was not so good at! I then left the note at the restaurant and walked to the bus station.

"It was late evening, so I knew they wouldn't see the note until morning. I guess I should not have left like that, but the impulse hit me, and I knew if I didn't go at that exact moment, I would not go at all. Besides, I didn't want the owner to talk me out of leaving. I bought a ticket out of the city and was gone within the hour.

"I thought since I came all the way to America, I should see more than New York City. I had no plans, no idea where I was going. I just wanted to go somewhere. I continued to travel for a few years, finding small jobs so I could earn enough money to buy my next ticket. I continued to move around from one place to another, and then I met Maria."

At this point in the story, Mr. Pulaski took another bite of his sausage, and I finished mine. I was ready to get out on the ice with my friends, but I didn't want to just get up and leave in the middle of his story; besides, I liked to listen to Mr. Pulaski's stories. I wanted to know everything about him that I could learn. For some reason, I was curious to know when he came to live in this small town and why. So I asked, and he responded with all the information I was looking for.

"Well," Mr. Pulaski said as he was thinking, "after Maria died and Antonio and Angela left for college, I decided that I didn't want to stay there anymore. Maria was my whole world, and I just couldn't stay without her! So I sold the house and put the money in a scholarship fund so that the money would be available for the kids that were in the children's home. I did this because I wanted to make sure every one of them would have an opportunity to go to college, and I knew that's what Maria would have wanted too. Anyway, I got off the bus here on October twelfth, and it had been snowing most of the day, but not very hard. I went into the diner, the one where your mother works, and I ordered some supper. It wasn't much: a ham and cheese sandwich and coffee. At least, that's all I wanted, but your mother talked me into a piece of apple pie." Mr. Pulaski laughed a little as he continued to say, "She tried to talk me into ice cream with it, but I was able to resist: the ice cream that is, not the pie.

"While I was eating, I asked her if there was some place in town where I could stay for the night. She said yes and pointed down the street. She said there weren't any fancy motels or anything unless I wanted to go back down the mountain to the interstate. The ski lodge was at the end of town and more convenient, and then there was Mrs. Grady's bed and breakfast. She also said that Mr. Evens had people stay in his barn from time to time, but he didn't know it until morning when he opened the door to let his cows out, and they ran out too!

"So after I finished my dinner, I went to Mrs. Grady's bed and breakfast. I was so tired I fell right to sleep, and I didn't wake up the entire night. In the morning when I did wake up, a little later than usual, I looked out the window. And the snow was so deep it was up to the windows of the cars that were parked on the street, and it was still snowing. I quickly showered, dressed, and hurried outside. It was very cold and quiet, and I certainly was not used to quiet. The snow was coming down so hard I could hardly see where I was going. As I walked toward the diner, I thought I'd get some breakfast because when I came downstairs, Mrs. Grady wasn't around. Due to this reason, I thought I had slept past her breakfast time because she was very strict on the mealtimes.

"Meanwhile, as I opened the door to leave and was trying to walk in the deep snow, I looked around trying to figure out how I was going to get out of this town. When I had gotten off the bus the day before, I had forgotten to check the schedule to see when the next one was leaving. Then I was afraid that with the snowstorm, the bus was most likely not going to be leaving anyway.

"Well, just as I turned the corner, I saw a big truck parked in the middle of the street. The street hadn't been plowed yet, so I thought it might be stuck, and I was going to help push it out. As I was coming around from the side, I could hear voices coming from behind it, so I thought there must be people already trying to push it out of the snow. Then as I made my way around to the back of the truck, there were two women handing out blankets to people. I approached one of them and tried talking to her. I was going to ask what was going on, but she didn't give me a chance.

"As soon as I stood next to her trying to get her attention, she handed me a stack of blankets and told me to take them to the shelter in the church down the street!

"'Excuse me?' I said, confused.

"She repeated herself as if I didn't hear her. 'Take them down to the church for the shelter and hurry!'

"I looked at her and tried to talk to her again! 'But . . .' I said.

"And that's all I got to say because just then she interrupted by saying, 'Hurry, they are waiting for them!' Then she paused, finally took a breath, stared at me, and said, 'You're not from around here, are you? I know everyone in town, and I haven't seen you before!'

"I tried to explain to her again, but she cut me off again! 'Don't worry, it isn't hard to find. Follow George over there!' Then she yelled, 'George, show . . . What's your name?'

"I told her my name was Samuel.

"'George, tell Samuel how to get to the church. People will freeze before you get there!'

"After this, George and I began to make our way down the street.

"'Is she always like that?' I asked.

"'No, not really,' he said. 'That's Betty. She's actually the owner of the diner. She looks out for everyone. She's lived in this town her whole life, and she will probably stay until she dies which, I might add, may not be for another hundred years. She thinks she owns the town and that she's responsible for the whole town.'

"'Why?' I asked.

"George continued, 'Because everyone lets her, and they don't want the responsibility.' Then George laughed as he said, 'And no one in this town is brave enough to tell her differently. She has a good heart, if you're ever in need. Betty's the one that steps up without any questions. She trusts everyone. I guess you could say that she's the heart and soul of this town. Anyway, Samuel, what brings you to this little secluded town where people who are intelligent want to visit but not live?'

"I smiled. 'I don't really know,' I replied. And then I continued, 'I guess I felt it was time to move on from where I was. My wife died a few years ago, and our two children are in college, and I had no reason to stay where I was anymore, I guess.'

"By this time, George and I had arrived at the church and taken the blankets inside. We warmed up for a few minutes and then left to go back for more. The whole day was spent delivering blankets and food to shelters. The snow was falling faster as it got toward evening. We had to walk everywhere. In fact, the only thing on wheels that were moving was the tractors. Some people had snowmobiles, but they too were busy picking people up and taking them to the make-shift shelters and delivering food. They were expecting four to five feet more before it stopped. I had never seen anything like that storm before. I was exhausted by evening. As a matter of fact, everyone was exhausted by the time we were finished. It was late, and I was starving; none of us had stopped to eat the entire day.

"After all the blankets and food were delivered, Betty smiled at me and nodded her head as if to say thank you. Then she said, 'Why don't you take a break and go have some dinner. Go over to the diner and tell them Betty sent you, and they're not to charge you anything if they know what's good for them.'

"'Thank you. You're very kind,' I said, and Betty laughed.

"'No, I'm not. I just want you to keep your strength up just in case we have to make more deliveries.'

"'Okay!' I said. Then I continued, 'But thank you anyway.'"

At this point, Mr. Pulaski just looked at me and stood up to stretch.

"Times sure have changed around here since then. During that time, people helped one another, and for the next few days, neighbor helped neighbor. People went to one house and then, the next, fixed the damage the snow had caused. I just can't believe how much this town has changed over the years. I guess it takes a bad snowstorm to bring people together. It's still a great friendly town, but nothing like it used to be!" Just then Mr. Pulaski sighed as he continued, "If I weren't so old, I'd give some thought to moving on again." Mr. Pulaski tapped me gently on the knee and said, "Let's get another hot cocoa, and I'll tell you a little bit more."

So I stood up, and we walked over to the stove and poured another hot cocoa, and then we walked back to the tree stump.

Just as we got there, Billy yelled to me as he was finishing his cocoa. "Jimmie, are you going to skate or what?"

Mr. Pulaski agreed with Billy that I'd better go skate before it got too late, but I wanted to hear more of his story. I loved to listen to him talk, especially because of his accent. I loved to hear his voice, and his gentleness and caring personality made me feel warm inside even without the hot cocoa.

When we sat back down, Mr. Pulaski looked at the trees covered with snow and pointed to the stars in the darkness. "Jimmie," he said, "do you ever sit and look at the stars?"

"I never really paid much attention to them, Mr. Pulaski!" I replied.

He was quiet for a few seconds and then began, "Well, you should, my friend! Watch them very closely and then watch the star's light as it sparkles against the snow. I close my eyes sometimes and think of them as stars beneath my feet."

I turned and looked at Mr. Pulaski, and he had his eyes closed all right. He had a habit of doing that a lot.

Just then, Sam ran by us. As he turned around backward, still moving, he yelled, "Are you coming or not?"

I yelled back, "Yeah, in a while."

Then Sam replied very loudly, "I have to go home in a while!"

Mr. Pulaski leaned over toward me and in a soft voice said, "Maybe you'd better go. I can finish later if you want me to."

By then, Sam had disappeared in the darkness.

"Well, I guess I'll go skate before they get mad at me," I said. And then I asked Mr. Pulaski, "Can I stop by your house tomorrow?"

"Sure, Jimmie, anytime—you know that!" he replied.

"Okay, Mr. P!" I said.

Just as I stood up, Becky came by, so I introduced her to Mr. Pulaski. He knew who she was from church, but they had never been formally introduced. Afterward, Becky and I both skated out onto the ice to find Billy and Sam. We had a great time that night. Billy, Sam, and Becky didn't argue or fight once. That is, until the end when we were sitting on a bench taking off our skates. We talked about meeting there at the lake the next afternoon, which was Saturday.

Billy asked, "Are we meeting at one o'clock in the afternoon tomorrow?"

"Yes, the meeting sounds good to me, Billy," Sam said. "Hey, Jimmie, are you really going to skate with us tomorrow, or are you going to spend the whole day with old man Pulaski?"

I tried to answer him without sounding angry. "Mr. Pulaski is my friend. Besides, he tells really good stories. You guys really should come with me sometime and listen to him! But to answer your question, yes, I plan on being here tomorrow by one. Okay?"

Billy just looked at Sam and said, "Sounds like fun, but no thanks. Just don't forget your friends. We'll be waiting for you."

"Well, maybe I'll be here waiting for you!" I said.

Sam laughed. "Okay, Jimmie, we'll see, but I think the chances of that happening are ten to one. Besides, I think that you're probably going to be the last one here tomorrow and late."

As I started to leave, Billy yelled at me, "If you're late, you owe all of us a pizza!"

Becky finished changing her skates and ran to catch up to me. "How often do you visit Mr. Pulaski?" she asked.

"I visit him as much as I can. Why? You want to make fun of him too?" I asked sarcastically.

"No, I was just wondering," she answered. And then she continued, "Is he as old as Billy and Sam say he is?"

I started to get a little irritated. "I don't know how old he is. I never asked. And frankly, I don't care. All I know is that he's really nice to me. He tells me stories, true stories, and he helps me figure out stuff."

Then Becky asked, "What kind of stuff?"

"I don't know, just stuff. I can ask him anything, and he helps me to understand things, and I get really mad when they make fun of him. They don't even know him!" I answered.

Becky stopped walking and said, "I'd like to!"

Just then, I stopped and turned around. "You'd like to what?" I said.

She stood there looking at me. "I'd like to get to know him. Can I go with you the next time you're going to see him?" she replied.

I looked at her and answered, "I guess so. I'm going to see him tomorrow. I always stop at his house on Saturday mornings, just to check on him, to make sure he's okay. He lives alone, and his family lives some place in Illinois."

"Okay, what time should I meet you?"

"Meet me where?" I asked.

"Where should I meet you to go to Mr. Pulaski's house?"

"Oh, come by my house around nine tomorrow morning. We'll pass his house on our way to the lake."

"Okay!" she said with a smile.

As we walked the rest of the way home, I told her everything I knew about Mr. Pulaski. I even showed her which house he lived in.

We reached my house first. I started to go in, but for some reason, I stopped and stood on the porch until Becky walked down the street and turned the corner. I didn't know why, but I felt like I had to make sure she made it home okay walking in the dark. Mom and Dad were still sitting up waiting for me, so as soon as I walked in, they went to bed. Dad had to get up early to go to work, and Mom had to be at the diner early again since Saturday was one of the restaurant's busiest days. I still had a lot to do to finish getting things together for Mr. Pulaski's Christmas present. I only had one more weekend left before Christmas.

Do not forsake your friend and the friend of your father, and do not go to your brother's house when disaster strikes you—better a neighbor nearby than a brother far away.
—Proverbs 27:10, New International Version

Give portions to seven, yes to eight, for you do not know what disaster may come upon the land.
—Ecclesiastes 11:2, New International Version

CHAPTER 24

Saturday Jimmie and Becky Visit Mr. Pulaski

Shout for joy, O heavens; rejoice, O earth; burst into song, O mountains! For the LORD comforts his people and will have compassion on his afflicted ones.
—Isaiah 49:13, New International Version

Let the rivers clap their hands, Let the mountains sing together for joy.
—Psalm 98:8, New International Version

The morning sun shone through the window as soon as it peeked over the horizon. I was directly in its path as it shone through the window. I attempted to move over slightly in my bed to escape its awakening brightness and go back to sleep. But it didn't work. Once I woke up, no matter how hard I tried, I couldn't go back to sleep. So I threw the covers off, rolled over to the edge of the bed, and pushed myself up in a sitting position. I was contemplating whether I really wanted to get up or if I wanted to lie back down.

As much as I wanted to lie back down, I forced myself to stand up. I yawned, stretched, and then made my way to the door by sidestepping everything that was on the floor in my path. Mom insisted that my room was a total disaster. As a matter of fact, she said that it should be condemned, and a sign should be placed on the door for people to enter at their own risk. But I was a pro at crossing my bedroom in the dark without ever tripping because everything was strategically placed, and I was able to maneuver around it just fine.

I managed to force myself to the bathroom and showered, brushed my teeth and hair, using different brushes of course, and dressed. I was able to complete this routine within a minimal amount of time. I was kind of proud of myself for being such a fast dresser, but Mom didn't share my enthusiasm. She said she didn't agree that my morning ritual was an art that would help me earn a living when I was older.

By the time I found my way downstairs, Mom and Dad had already left for work. As usual, Mom left me a note that read:

> Have cereal or oatmeal this morning. Dress warm
> if you go out. I'll be home at noon. I love you,
> and don't get into trouble today.
>
> —Mom

This was too much; I was faced with another choice, and too lazy to make instant oatmeal, my choice was cereal.

As I took the last bite, I put my bowl in the sink just as the doorbell rang. I had no idea who would be at the door that early on a Saturday. As I opened it, I saw Becky standing on the porch. "Oh, hi, Becky," I said as I scratched my head and looked at her in wonder. "What are you doing here?"

She looked at me puzzled as she said, "You said I could go with you to Mr. Pulaski's house. You said to be here by nine o'clock, so here I am!"

I thought for a second and responded intelligently as I often did. "Oh yeah, is it nine o'clock already? Well come in. it'll only take me a few minutes to get my stuff." As I was going upstairs to my room, I yelled down, "Did you bring your hockey stuff so we don't have to come back home?"

"I sure did!" she answered.

I grabbed everything I needed and ran back downstairs and threw my coat on, and we headed out the door.

As we walked down the street, I explained a little more about Mr. Pulaski to Becky, which wasn't very much. I also explained what I was going to do for a Christmas present for him. I thought since she was going with me to see him, then maybe he would tell her some things that he wasn't telling me. I needed to know as much as possible. Anyway, by the time we reached his house, the sun had disappeared, and it looked like it was going to snow again.

As we went up the steps, Mr. Pulaski was already opening the door.

"Good morning, Jimmie, and Becky, right?" he said.

Becky smiled as she replied, "Yes. Good morning, Mr. Pulaski."

Then he smiled and invited us in.

Once we were inside, Mr. Pulaski closed the door.

Becky looked around as she was taking off her coat and boots. "Your home is really nice!"

"Thank you!" Mr. Pulaski answered. "Please come in and make yourself comfortable. No matter who visits, my home is theirs!"

We followed Mr. Pulaski into his living room as he continued his conversation, "So, Becky, how do you like our small but friendly town?"

Becky smiled. "It takes some getting used to, that's for sure, Mr. Pulaski!"

He laughed. "Yes, it does! So have you gotten used to the school?"

"Yes, it's the same as any other school I've been to, except it was a little easier finding my way around, thanks to Jimmie."

"Yes, Jimmie is a very helpful young man. We've been friends for a long time, ever since he was in my Sunday school class! I think it was third grade."

I had just picked up a plate of cookies and two glasses of milk and was on my way in from the kitchen when Mr. Pulaski yelled to me, "Wasn't it, Jimmie?"

"Wasn't it what, Mr. P?" I asked since I was concentrating on not spilling the cookies and milk.

"Wasn't it third grade Sunday School when we first met?"

"Yeah, I think so!" I yelled.

Upon arriving in the living room, I handed Becky one of the glasses of milk and placed the cookies on the table.

"Would you like anything, Mr. P?"

"No, thanks, Jimmie, I was just about to put another log on the fire."

Then Becky asked, "Are you going to the hospital today, Mr. P, to visit the children's ward?"

"Yes, I have a few stops to make on the way, starting with the horses. If I don't give them their carrots, they'll be mad at me for weeks!" Mr. Pulaski replied.

Becky laughed. "How do you know when they're mad at you?"

"They won't talk to me. They ignore me. When I stand at the fence and call them, they turn their backs on me and pretend I'm not there! They're pretty smart!"

I decided to change the subject, "Are you going to the lake tonight, Mr. Pulaski?"

"I sure am! I don't think I've missed very many weekends in years," he replied.

"Oh, by the way, Mr. P, next Saturday night is a special performance by the school orchestra, and I was wondering if you would come. It starts at six o'clock in the evening."

Mr. Pulaski stood up, put his hand up to his chin, and looked toward the ceiling for a moment. "Let me think for a minute. If I go to the concert, who is going to start the fire at the lake and make the hot cocoa?"

"You've gotta come, Mr. P! It's a Christmas special, and it's going to be at the Double-D Chateau and Resort. We've been rehearsing for months. Besides, no one will be at the lake. They'll all be at the concert. C'mon, Mr. P, you gotta come! You just gotta!" I said pleadingly.

Mr. Pulaski smiled. "Jimmie, I wouldn't miss it for anything. Of course, I'll come!"

"Great!" I was so excited. Then apologetically, I said, "I didn't mean to yell. It just came out. I have one more question. Since it's actually Christmas Eve, Mom and Dad decided to go earlier and have dinner first, and they said you could come with us."

"I would be honored to have dinner with you and your parents. What time should I be ready?"

"Mom said we'd pick you up at four so that we would have time to eat."

"Then I'll be ready at four, and I'm looking forward to it! Now I'm going to make another cup of tea. Would you two like anything else?"

"No, thank you, I'm fine," Becky answered.

However, I was still hungry. "I sure would like more cookies if you don't mind."

"More cookies it is!" Mr. Pulaski answered as he went into the kitchen.

Just as Mr. Pulaski had reached the kitchen, Becky leaned over toward me and whispered, "I don't remember a school concert!"

"Shhh, I had to think of some way to get Mr. Pulaski to go to dinner with us. I'll explain later."

Just then, Mr. Pulaski came back in with the cookies. "It sure does look like a snowstorm is forming over the mountains. I'd hate to be up there when it does. I remember very well how bad it can get!"

"Is this a story, Mr. P?" I asked.

Mr. Pulaski smiled, lit his pipe, and winked at Becky. "Yes, Jimmie, I believe it is! So here it goes!

"It was a long time ago. As a matter of fact, I believe it was my third winter here if my memory serves me right. At around six in the evening, the snow began falling. It was the kind of snow with big flakes. You know the kind that's so big that when they land on your glove, you can see the detail of each one right before they melt. They just float down because there's no wind, and the air is just the right temperature, but it really doesn't feel cold enough to snow on your face. Well, I finished supper and made a hot cup of tea. The snow looked so wonderful as it was falling that I couldn't help myself. I went outside and stood on the porch for a few minutes.

"As I stood looking at the mountains admiring the beautiful scenery God provided that evening, the wind began blowing just slightly enough to make the snowflakes dance in the air. I finished my cup of tea and was ready to go back in the house when I heard something that sounded like music. I looked around, but all I saw was the snow falling and the trees moving in the gentle breeze. I couldn't figure out where the sound was coming from! So I listened for a few more minutes, and then I didn't hear it anymore, so I went inside. For the next few days, every evening I went out on the porch after supper, I heard the same sound night after night." Mr. Pulaski took a sip of his tea.

By this time, Becky and I were eager to know what it was, so we both happened to ask at the same time, "Did you find out what it was, Mr. P?"

He looked at us with a smile. "Now be patient!" he said. "After a few days passed, I asked around town if anyone else had heard it besides me, but mostly everyone I talked to didn't have any idea what I was talking about, and the ones who thought they had heard it said it was the wind blowing through the snow on the mountains. Their theory was that the wind was being forced through small crevasses in the snow, like when you blow up a balloon and let the air out really slow. Well, it all sounded scientific to me, but I wasn't convinced!"

"Well, what was it, Mr. P?" I asked again.

"I never did find out, Jimmie!" Mr. Pulaski answered.

Becky and I just looked at each other; we didn't know what to say.

Then all of a sudden, Mr. Pulaski smiled as he paused. "Until two years later. Every winter, I heard the same sound. I sat on my front porch and closed my eyes, and I'd pretend that the mountains were singing to me. It was comforting to hear in the still of the night when everything was quiet, and in the darkness, it was very peaceful. By the time the next winter came around, my curiosity got the best of me, and I wanted to find out for myself exactly where this beautiful sound was coming from.

"Well, I can tell you I was in no shape to go mountain climbing! So that following summer, I spent a lot of time at the library reading about winter camping and hiking. I bought snowshoes, a subzero sleeping bag, a cooking kit, below-zero snowsuit, a tent, and everything that the clerk at the sporting goods store told me I needed. I even bought rope and waterproof matches! Oh, and a lighter just in case the matches didn't work. I began going on long summer hikes to prepare myself. Lord knows I needed a lot of conditioning before going up that mountain.

"By the time winter came, I was ready! I packed everything I needed into or on my backpack. I put everything in the car and drove to the base of the mountain. I parked in the parking lot on the east side of Highpoint Park. I chose that side because it had the trail that led farther up the mountain than the other trails. It was four days until Christmas, and I figured I'd be at the top and back down before Christmas Day. I began my journey up the mountain at noon. It was pretty easy going in the beginning, but as I said, the trail went pretty far up, or so I thought. Unfortunately, things weren't as easy as they looked. It wasn't long at all before I reached the point in the trail where it turned and went back down to the park. I stopped and rested for a few minutes. I sat and stared at the sign that read 'End of trail, hike at your own risk.' I almost turned around and went home, but I didn't."

"Mr. P," I interrupted, "you went by yourself?"

"Yes, I did, Jimmie! I know I shouldn't have, but I can tell you I didn't think anyone would want to go up a mountain in December with me, so I didn't even ask. They thought I was crazy to start with, especially the store clerk! Well, now or never, I thought! I stood up, threw my backpack over my shoulder, and looked at the sign one more time. And then I raised my eyes up toward the sky and said, 'Here we go, Lord,' and started singing, 'Put one step in front of the other, and soon you'll be hiking up the mountain.'"

"It was good that no one was around to hear you!"

Mr. Pulaski just laughed. "I suppose so! Anyway, three hours passed, and I was beginning to slow down, not that I was really moving very fast to start with, but I began thinking. What if I do make it to the top but for some reason can't make it back down? I'd feel really stupid if they had to send a search party to find me.

"Then before I realized it, it began to get dark! It doesn't stay light very long in the mountains, and once it starts to get dark, it happens real fast. I dropped my backpack right where I was standing and quickly gathered some firewood, but by then, I had to put my tent up using a flashlight and a lantern for light. After I set up camp, I started a fire and rolled my sleeping bag out in the tent. I rolled the flaps back and just sat looking into the fire, and then I heard the sound again.

"As I listened, I watched the wind flow through the trees. I watched the branches move as they danced in the wind. The wind pulled the trees gently to one side and then the other as if they were taking a bow for a wonderful ballet performance. They looked like giants against the dark clouds that hovered above. As the moon peeked through the passing clouds, the light glistened for short periods of time against the undisturbed snow. The light looked to me like earthbound stars lying on the snow as if I could just reach down and pick them up."

Mr. Pulaski always used his hands when he was trying to make a point. When he mentioned the trees dancing in the wind, he moved like the wind was blowing and he was a tree, and then he stretched his hands out as he was talking and bent over as if he was really picking up stars from the floor. I guess that's what made his stories come alive, the fact that he demonstrated as he told them.

"After the fire went out, I closed the flaps. I was so tired I crawled into my sleeping bag and fell right to sleep. Morning came real fast though it seemed like I had no sooner closed my eyes and I was awake again! I dressed in my sleeping bag because I kept my clothes in the bottom so they would be warm. I had brought a few cans of tinned heat so I could make some coffee in the mornings. They're much faster to start than building a fire, and those little collapsible camp stoves work great!"

"Mr. P," I interrupted again, "what about the sound? Where was it coming from? There are two people here who really want to know!"

Becky laughed.

"Now just hold on, Jimmie!" He motioned with his hands.

"Mr. P, I hope you plan on telling us before we go to college!"

He smiled and began again. "I'm getting to that, Jimmie. Just stay with me here. I don't want to have to start over because I can't remember where I was."

"We don't want you to start over either!" I said.

"Okay then!" Mr. Pulaski remarked as he thought for a minute and then began to continue on with his story once again. "Oh yeah, I made some coffee and started a fire to keep some heat going while I packed up my gear. I drank a few cups of coffee and started hiking again. The sun was warm, but the wind did a good job of keeping it from warming the air up!

"Meanwhile, as I made my way up the mountain, the snow was gradually getting deeper, so I had to put on snowshoes. Just in case you're wondering, they really do make it much easier to walk in snow. I remember how brisk the air was against my face. The only sound was the rustling of the wind blowing through the trees and my snowshoes sliding over the snow. I was still worried though, a little apprehensive you might say, and maybe even a little scared. But after I took a deep breath and smelled the cool air and began thinking of Maria, I pretended that she was with me, and we were walking together." Mr. Pulaski shook his head and chuckled a little.

"You know," he said, "I even talked to her. As a matter of fact, I still do! Anyway, I took a short break for lunch and drank some more hot coffee hoping to warm up a bit. I guess it was about an hour. I always lose track of time, ya know!"

I didn't say anything, but I definitely agreed on that point.

"As I sat leaning against a tree, some squirrels decided to find out who was imposing on their territory. It was quite entertaining and amusing as I watched them run quickly across the snow, and then they stopped and stood for a minute or two staring at me. Then they ran up one tree and down another. One of them was holding a small nut in his cheek. He wasn't in much of a hurry, but the other one kept running away, and then I guess his curiosity got the best of him because he turned around and came back as if he was telling the other one to hurry along because they had things to do.

"After I watched them for a while, I began hiking again. It didn't take long for the clouds to move in. Once they blocked out the sun, it got dark real fast again. I wasn't very good at timing either. I picked up my pace a little faster. It just didn't seem like I was making very much progress, and I was afraid it was going to snow before I could get my tent up!" Mr. Pulaski stopped to sip his tea again and then went on with his story.

"By that time I decided that I didn't have any choice, I had to stop. Night came faster than I wanted it to, and so did the clouds. The sun was entirely blocked out, so once again, I was putting up my tent using a flashlight and lantern for light. By the time I finished setting up, the wind was getting stronger too. That wasn't something I had anticipated either. I knew there was going to be cold winds, darkness, and snow, of course. But I didn't think that the wind was going to be as strong as what I was to face that night. I zipped the front tent flaps as tight as I could, and I sat in my sleeping bag reading with the lantern. The wind was so strong that it almost blew the lantern out even with the tent zipped shut. I looked around to see where the wind might be getting in from, and then I realized I hadn't closed the bottom of the flaps. So as I was reaching over to close them, I thought I heard a voice. I listened and shook my head. I wondered who, besides me, would be crazy enough to be halfway up a mountain in the dark, in the middle of a winter storm. Then I heard it again. I stuck my head out to listen, but I forgot about the snow, and the wind blew it right into my face.

"Then I heard it again.

"'Hello, is anybody there?' asked the voice. 'Can I share your shelter? It's really cold out here, and I'm lost!'

"'Oh boy!' I thought. 'What if this is someone that escaped from prison for murder and was there hiding in the mountains?'

"Then the voice came again. 'I'm really lost, and I promise I didn't escape from prison. Really I didn't!'

"'Great, an escaped convict that can read minds!' I remarked to myself. Then I thought if he was an escaped convict, I didn't think he would be honest and yell, 'Hey, I'm an escaped convict who killed someone, but I won't kill you. I promise!' I thought for a minute, and then I realized that I wasn't going anywhere, and he was coming closer. And if he were someone from prison, he wasn't going to ask. He'd just kill me and move on with his life and my things because no one would find me until spring. Since I didn't think I really had a choice, I yelled back, 'Who are you?' It was the only thing I could think of under the circumstances.

"'My name is Jacob, and I live on the other side of the mountain. Can I please share your tent? It's very cold out here.'

"I opened the tent flap and motioned with my hand for him to come in. 'Hurry!' I yelled. I didn't pray much after Maria died, but I figured my chances would be better with a prayer than relying on hope. Hope never worked for me before, and prayer always worked for Maria, so I figured it was the better of the two choices.

"As he came in, I quickly closed and zipped the flaps to keep the snow out.

"'Thank you!' he said, holding his hands over the small tin of heat. I was using it just to keep the chill off. 'I'm sorry for my intrusion,' he said, 'but the storm came fast, and I became disoriented!'

"'What are you doing so far out in the middle of the mountains?' I asked him.

"'I live on the other side, and I was out hiking when the storm caught me by surprise. And what about you?'

"'Oh, my name is Samuel, and you might say I'm sort of on a quest to reach the top of the mountain for no particular reason, except that most of the people in town think I'm crazy. So I'll just stick with saying that I had a strong ambition to reach the top of this mountain for no particular reason.'

"Jacob smiled, and then he said, 'I believe everything happens for a reason, don't you?'

"I thought for a minute, but I had no idea what he was referring to, so I explained, 'I've been staring at this mountain for a few years from my front porch, and since I had some time on my hands and nothing really important to do, I decided to climb it.'

"Jacob smiled at me. 'Well,' he said, 'since I really don't have anything exciting going on in my life right now either, I'll hike with you for a while. That is if you don't mind of course. It's always more enjoyable when you have someone to talk to. Don't you think so? Besides,' he said with a smile, 'since I know this mountain and I feel somewhat responsible for what happens up here, I'll be your guide for a while, and I promise not to get you lost!'

"We laughed, talked for a little while longer, and then fell asleep. Since he didn't have a sleeping bag, I gave him my snowsuit to put over him for the night even though he was wearing warm clothing. It didn't take long for us both to fall asleep. We were exhausted."

Stopping at this point in his story, Mr. Pulaski looked at the clock over the fireplace in his living room. Then he spoke, "As a matter of fact, I'm a little tired right now, and if I don't get moving into town, I'll never make my rounds. I'll probably fall asleep. Would you two mind if I finish this story later?" Mr. Pulaski yawned, stood up, and stretched.

I couldn't believe how fast the time went by. "Wow! I and Becky have to meet the guys at the lake anyway, and we're going to be late!" I said, assuring him.

Then Becky and I stood up, grabbed our things, and hurried out the door. As we ran down the steps, we both yelled back to Mr. Pulaski, "See ya tonight at the lake!"

Mr. Pulaski waved as the two of us took off running. Mr. Pulaski then closed the door. He yawned again and then coughed a little. He felt a little stiff as well as tired. As he walked back to his chair, he stopped to look at himself in the mirror that hung on the wall in the hallway between his kitchen and living room. A little flushed, he thought, but nothing out of the ordinary. He rubbed his forehead and could feel his eyes closing. He reached over and picked up the telephone that sat on the stand next to his chair and dialed the number to the hospital. He wanted to go, but he wasn't feeling quite right, so he postponed that day's trip. He really wanted to visit the children, but he felt weak. He explained to the nurse and promised to make his next visit extra long. He put another log on the fire and sat down. As he covered himself with the blanket that hung over the back of his chair, he leaned to one side and continued to reminisce about the life-changing days he spent on the mountain.

CHAPTER 25

The Mountain—December 16

Your righteousness is like the mighty mountains,
your justice like the great deep. O LORD, you pre-
serve both man and beast.
—Psalm 36:6, New International Version

Mr. Pulaski remembered the following morning on the mountain when he and Jacob had woken. The sun was shining, and he pushed back the flaps to the tent. In amazement, he rubbed his eyes and looked again. It must have snowed three feet during the night, but with the wind blowing as hard as it did all night long, there must have been close to five feet leaning up against the side of the tent. He used one of his snowshoes to make a path from the tent so that he and Jacob could get out. Then he found his small collapsible shovel and dug the snow away from the tent so he could fold it up for that day's hike. As he and Jacob uncovered the tent stakes and removed them from the ground, Samuel shook his head and said, "We were pretty lucky the wind didn't blow the tent down last night, as strong as it was!"

Now standing up, Jacob answered, "Yeah, God must have had his angels looking after us. That is for sure!"

As he said this, Samuel just stopped and looked at Jacob for a moment but didn't say anything. Then he just continued to fold his tent.

"Don't you believe in angels, Samuel?" Jacob asked as Samuel finished putting his tent away and lit the tinned heat fire to make some coffee.

Samuel then proceeded to answer by saying, "Yes, I believe in angels. I was married to one for ten years! Her name was Maria. I loved her with all my heart and soul. She was my life. Before I met her, every day was the same. Maria made life exciting. I couldn't wait to see her when I woke up in the morning and then at the end of the day when I came home from work. Maria had the kind of eyes that when you looked into them, you could see stars sparkling. I remember the sun used to dance through her dark hair. She was the best thing that ever came into my life."

Trying not to become overwhelmed with emotion, Samuel just poured a cup of coffee for Jacob, took a deep breath, and then poured one for him and continued. "I'm sorry for sounding upset, Jacob. I try really hard not to get upset when I think of Maria, but I can't understand why she died! Maria was always there for me. Whenever I had a bad day or things just didn't go right for me and I was upset, she'd smile and tell me that everything happens for a reason and that God would give me the answers when the time was right. But I'm still waiting for the right time! I'm still waiting for him to tell me why he took her from me!"

Samuel finished packing, threw his backpack over his shoulder, and then extended his hand to Jacob as he said, "I guess I better get moving. I don't have much time left to reach the top of this mountain." Samuel looked at his watch, then continued, "I lost two hours already this morning. Are you going to be all right, Jacob?"

After that, Jacob answered, "Oh, I'll be just fine. But unless I was dreaming last night, just before we fell asleep, I think I asked you if you would allow me to accompany you for a while on your journey. I really have nothing to do the next couple of days, and besides, as I said, I know this mountain pretty well!" Jacob laughed as he continued, "Except when we have a blizzard, that is! Maybe I can help you make up some time!"

Samuel looked down as he thought for a few seconds. "You're right, I guess I don't remember that part of our conversation. I was pretty tired. Well, why not. I do have an extra pair of snowshoes!" As Samuel put his backpack down again and handed his extra snowshoes to Jacob, he replied, "Let's go!"

As they started out, Jacob asked, "What happened to Maria, if you don't mind me asking?"

Samuel replied, "She died from cancer. We went to three different doctors, and they all said that it was too late and that there was nothing they could do. I prayed to God, but there was nothing he could do either. Maria brought warmth and happiness to my life, and then she was taken away from me after ten years. I still don't understand why! I've asked, but God won't answer! She meant everything to me in the entire world! Maria's love was the only happiness I ever knew, and now it's gone. So since then, every day is the same just as it was before she and I met!" Samuel was quiet for a minute and then continued, "I thought climbing this mountain would help in some way, but I'm having second thoughts. Maybe I should go back down and forget the whole thing!"

Jacob could hear the hurt in Samuel's voice. It was apparent that he had never shared his feelings about Maria's death with anyone before and that he had kept his hurt and anger to himself all these years.

Jacob, sensing Samuel's need to share his pain with someone, simply replied, "No, Samuel, I think you made the right choice. Maybe God wanted you to come here so you and he could spend some time together. After all, he is your Father, and you are his child, and I think you and God need to work this out between the two of you. Just tell him how you feel, Samuel. Besides, you may not understand now, but he is ready to listen if you are ready to talk!"

Samuel swallowed and stopped then strongly replied, "No, I was finished talking to God a long time ago!" Samuel's voice became angry as he then added, "I think it's his turn to talk to me and tell me why he took my Maria and left me to raise two young children by myself! Not to mention that these two children have lost their mothers twice. As a matter of fact, it's time he gave me some answers. Don't you think so, Jacob?" After concluding his thoughts, Samuel simply began walking again, and Jacob was left following a step or two behind him.

As he hurried to catch up, he yelled, "Samuel!" Then he proceeded to reach out and put his hand on Samuel's shoulder as he said, "I know you're hurting, and you've been hurting inside for a long time."

Samuel interrupted sarcastically, "That's an understatement." Now becoming a little upset and angry, Samuel continued, "I've tried to do what Maria asked me to do. I tried to understand. I even tried to let it go and continue to have faith in God, but I couldn't then, and I can't now! So I gave up. I need answers, Jacob!" Samuel clenched his fist. "I . . . need . . . answers!" he added. Samuel's voice began to tremble. "I prayed every day for him to let me take her place. I asked him, why Maria? She loved life. I couldn't think of anyone who was as kind and loving as she was, and she loved God with all her heart. It just wasn't fair!"

Just then, Jacob's voice became louder. "Samuel!" he shouted. Samuel quickly turned around to face Jacob as he continued to say, "I know what it's like to watch someone you love go through pain! And I know what it's like to watch someone you love very much die! And I know that you and Maria were very happy together! And I also know that you shared something very special, but you couldn't have spent ten years together and not have learned something from each other! Samuel, I have been on this mountain for a long time, and I have met some very special people. Listen, although we just met, I think God has a special plan for you, so give it time. Just talk to God! Let him know exactly what you are feeling in your heart, and I'm sure you'll feel as though a giant weight has been lifted off your shoulders! I'll stay with you tonight, and I'll walk with you tomorrow for part of the day. But then you must spend some time alone with God because I have to move on, and so do you, Samuel!"

Samuel took a deep breath as his heartbeat began to return to normal. "Okay!" he answered. Then he paused for just a second before he added, "At least, I'll give it some thought, but that's the best I can do right now."

Jacob smiled as he said, "It's a start! Now come on, we better get moving. We need to make up for lost time."

Samuel and Jacob hiked as long as they could, even after the sky got dark. Samuel wasn't sure where he was going, but he trusted Jacob because he didn't seem to be slowing down any. And as far as Samuel was concerned, as long as they were going up, it had to be the right direction.

After some time hiking, they finally stopped, and Jacob helped Samuel put the tent up for the night. Then Samuel lit the tinned heat fire both to take the chill out of the air for a little while and so that it would provide a small amount of light. They spent the next few minutes talking a little bit more about Samuel's life. Samuel explained to Jacob that he liked to walk through town helping the shop owners. He also talked a little bit about Angela and Antonio. As the night went on, Samuel grew so tired that he went to sleep right in the middle of a sentence.

Morning greeted the two of them with bright rays of sunlight streaking across the sky as they bounced off the few white clouds that brushed seamlessly against the blue background. The blue sky shone around them as if it were a backdrop created only to enhance the pureness of the white snow-covered mountain. Samuel was in awe as he emerged from his tent to the point of taking his breath away.

Jacob followed behind, saying, "God sure does create a wonderful sight, doesn't he, Samuel?"

Samuel smiled as he looked up at Jacob squinting because of the brightness of the sunlight. "Don't push it, Jacob!" he said.

Jacob smiled as he turned to start breaking camp.

After they drank coffee and ate a fast nutritional breakfast, they began again hiking toward the top of the mountain. It didn't seem to be as cold as it was the day before, and Samuel wasn't sure if it was actually warmer or if it was because he was becoming used to the cold.

As they hiked, Samuel looked around at the snow-covered trees and a rabbit or two playing tag as they seemed to be jumping from one bush to the other and back. Additionally, off in the distance, three deer ran away as they were startled by the sound of snowshoes gliding once again. As the morning turned into afternoon, the sight of a few more deer running through the trees as if they were being chased captured their attention for the few seconds that they were in sight. It wasn't long before Samuel and Jacob stopped to rest.

As Samuel dropped his backpack, he asked, "Jacob, are you hungry? I think it is lunchtime."

Jacob simply looked at Samuel and replied, "It's time for me to go, Samuel. It's time for us to go our separate ways!"

By now, Samuel was used to Jacob's company and became apprehensive at the thought of continuing alone.

Jacob, as he sensed Samuel's concern, added, "Don't worry, Samuel. You'll be fine! God will be walking with you all the way to the top! Samuel, you will fulfill your destiny!"

Samuel didn't say anything; he just silently looked around and noticed four deer standing at a short distance behind a thicket of leafless bushes. Three of the deer looked like the same ones they had seen earlier. Samuel began to think they were following them.

As Jacob turned to leave, he said, "Samuel, open your heart to God. Let him know exactly how you feel and ask that he take your pain away. I know you've been hurting for a long time, and so does God. It's now time to let it go. You'll never find peace until you do!"

Samuel just stood still and didn't speak a word as Jacob took off his snowshoes and handed them back to him. Understanding what Jacob meant, Samuel simply smiled as he said, "Why don't you keep them? It's hard enough walking with them. Without them, it'll take you forever to get back."

Jacob just smiled and nodded as if to say thank you. He put the snowshoes back on his feet and turned as he began to walk away.

Samuel watched until Jacob was barely out of sight. With a sigh, Samuel turned toward the mountaintop and looked up. He hadn't really noticed how close he was getting until now, and surely, he would be able to make it by tomorrow evening, he thought. Then he glanced in the direction that Jacob had gone, hoping one last time that he may have changed his mind. But by then, Jacob was completely out of sight. Samuel turned back toward the direction of the mountain.

As he listened to the sound of his snowshoes gliding across the hard-packed snow, he began to give some thought to Jacob's words. Every once in a while, he caught himself talking out loud with anger in his voice. "It's not fair . . . She didn't deserve to die . . . She was a good person . . . The best God had ever created . . . She had so much to live for!" The more he thought, the angrier he became. The angrier he grew, the faster he walked.

Samuel shook his head; then all of a sudden, with fists in the air, he screamed and fell to his knees crying as he dropped his backpack from his shoulders and stretched out his arms.

"Lord, I never felt like I belonged anywhere in my entire life until I met Maria!" With a gasp of air and tears rolling down his cheeks, he began speaking softly, "She filled my heart with love, joy, and peace. She loved life!" Samuel closed his eyes with his arms stretched out to his sides and his fists slowly opened. He leaned his head back and prayed for the first time since Maria's death.

"Father, for the past ten years, I have carried this pain in my heart. I ask that you, Lord, take it from me and replace it with love, joy, and peace! I ask that you give me the courage and contentment that I once had. I need you, Father, to put your arms around me this day and give me the wisdom to help others who may be feeling the same pain as I am. Help me to open my eyes once again and help me to be your servant in faith and in love! Father, also please help me find the peace and happiness in my thoughts of Maria and the life that we shared together! Forgive me, Father, forgive me. Amen."

Just moments before Samuel had started praying, Jacob knelt and asked God to help Samuel find the courage to ask forgiveness, to walk beside him, and to help him find the peace he was looking for and the faith that he had lost so many years ago. The instant Samuel finished praying, Jacob looked to the sky, smiled, and said, "Thank you, Father!"

Although Samuel and Jacob were far apart from each other, they both stood up and continued on their separate journeys, Jacob traveling toward home and Samuel toward the top of the mountain in hopes of fulfilling the emptiness in his life.

Just then, Mr. Pulaski awoke from his wonderful dream that occurred during his short nap. He proceeded to look all around, only to realize that he was sitting in his own chair in the comforts of his living room. After dreaming about his adventure on the mountain, he realized he had not fulfilled the task that God had laid before him a long time ago. At least not yet, he thought, but he would soon.

Mr. Pulaski felt better after resting for the afternoon, so he began to get his supplies together for the evening's skating. Since he didn't drive anymore, he either used a wagon or a sleigh to transport everything to the lake. Because of the snow during the past week, he loaded his sleigh with cocoa, cups, a camping stove, and everything else that he needed to serve the community with a fun evening. After all, it was getting late, and he had to hurry if he was going to be ready for everyone's arrival. It was approximately one half mile to the lake from his home, and he enjoyed the exercise. He had plenty of offers from people who wanted to give him a ride, but he always refused. No one really understood why, but they never asked him either.

There was something for everyone at the lake. Some of the older men brought their musical instruments and played in the gazebo at the edge of the lake not far from Mr. Pulaski's fire. Some used to visit the lake only to listen to the music and drink the hot cocoa. Many of the conversations between the elderly were of "the old days" when they were much younger.

Mr. Pulaski loved to listen to the conversations of everyone. He wasn't listening on purpose; it was just that most of the conversations took place around his fire. He particularly enjoyed hearing them talk about how nice it was to be able to warm up by the fire before returning to the ice. Some people mentioned to him that they skipped supper because they knew he was going to be there with his hot dogs. Usually by nine o'clock in the evening, however, most of the skaters were young couples and the four of us: Billy, Sam, Becky, and me. It wasn't long before the crowed left and only the four of us remained along with Mr. Pulaski.

The night ended and everyone left talking as they returned to their homes. Mr. Pulaski always made sure the fire was out and all his supplies were packed up. As usual, his load was much lighter going home than coming, but then he didn't have the hot dogs and cocoa to pull either. That night as I normally did, I helped Mr. Pulaski pull his sleigh back to his home and unload before I went back to my house.

That night, Mr. Pulaski was so tired that I told him to go on to bed, and I finished putting the rest of what was left away. He agreed, and when I had finished putting everything away, I turned out the lights and went home.

> *Listen to what the LORD says: "Stand up, plead your case before the mountains; let the hills hear what you have to say."*
> —Micah 6:1, New International Version

> *In the same way, I tell you, there is rejoicing in the presence of the angels of God over one sinner who repents.*
> —Luke 15:10, New International Version

CHAPTER 26

Sunday, December 17

Let the righteous rejoice in the LORD and take refuge in him; let all the upright in heart praise him!
—Psalm 64:10, New International Version

By the time Mr. Pulaski arrived at the church, Pastor Foreland had already unlocked the front door and a few cars were pulling into the parking lot.

So Mr. Pulaski hurried into the church. As he was hanging up his coat, he was asked a number of times if he felt all right. He quickly answered each time, "Yes, thank you. I'm fine!"

I think I was the only one that could sense that he was a little embarrassed because Mr. Pulaski was never late to church. That Sunday was the last Sunday before Christmas, and he knew from experience that the church was going to fill up quickly.

Mom was up early that morning, and as always, she made Dad and I get up early too. She had also expected the church to fill up early, and she wanted to make sure we were able to get our usual seats. She didn't even make breakfast. She set the cereal boxes on the table. When Dad and I came downstairs, she simply said, "If the two of you want to eat before we leave, then eat fast."

So Dad and I did just that. A quick bowl of cereal and we were out the door. Upon our arrival, we discovered that Mom was right. If we would have been any later than we already were, we would have had to sit all the way in the back of the church in the fold-up seats. And believe me, they were not comfortable chairs.

We weren't at all surprised that some of the people that morning hadn't been in church since Easter. I guess they thought if they came early, it would make up for lost time. Others who we didn't know were vacationing at the ski resorts around the area. Pastor Foreland was pretty happy to see that they took the time out of their vacation to visit the church. You could see how pleased he was when he asked all the visitors to stand and there were more people standing than sitting. As soon as Pastor Foreland had welcomed everyone, the choir began singing, and everyone stood up. I had to turn halfway around so I could watch the choir come down the aisle. Mom was usually the fourth one, but she wasn't feeling well, so she thought it was best not to sit with the choir that morning. She had a great voice, but since she was chosen to sing "Silent Night" and "O Holy Night" solo on Christmas Eve, she didn't want to strain her voice.

Anyway, just as we stood up and the choir came down the aisle, Billy leaned over and whispered in my ear, "It looks like it's going to snow, Jimmie. You better bring a shovel to the lake this afternoon so we can clear the ice!"

I turned and whispered back, "Maybe my dad will bring the small plow down, and we won't have to shovel, like he did last year when the ice was thick enough."

We could see the heavy clouds from the church window. They didn't seem to be very far from the tops of the trees. Snow clouds always had a way of making the day seem like it was much later than it really was. Billy and I whispered back and forth during the announcements and the choir singing. I never listened to Pastor Foreland's announcements anyway. It wasn't that they weren't important; it's just that I figured Mom always knew what was going on, so I didn't have to. Besides, she always talked about it on the way home, so I didn't think I needed to listen twice.

Furthermore, I was concentrating on whether or not we were going to have to clear the snow from the ice and about my plans for the day, which didn't consist of very much except to go home, eat dinner, go to the lake for the afternoon, then return home to eat supper, and then go back to the lake for night skating. I remembered hearing Mom tell Dad on our way to the church that we were going to skip the after-church social hour. This meant that we were going to eat dinner an hour earlier, and that in turn meant I could be at the lake an hour earlier. I guess you could say it was one of those win-win situations Ms. Steels was talking about in school. I wasn't happy that Mom was sick, but I was happy that I was going to go to the lake earlier than usual.

Billy leaned over and whispered in my ear a second time, "Look out the window, Jimmie. It's snowing pretty hard! How soon can you get to the lake? We need to start clearing it as soon as we can just in case your dad can't plow it!"

I opened my mouth to answer him, but Mom was on the other side of me, and just as I leaned toward Billy, I glanced at Mom to see if she was looking at me. Sure enough, she was. She didn't say anything, but there really wasn't any need to. The expression on her face said it all. She was yelling at me to be quiet. She was really good at yelling without saying anything. As a matter of fact, she yelled at me, and then she yelled at Billy. Billy knew she was yelling at him too because his Mom could do the same thing. Dad told me that all moms are good at doing that. He said it's a natural ability that doesn't require any practice.

The service finally ended, and as soon as the choir walked to the back of the church and Pastor Foreland gave the benediction, Billy and I thought we'd take a chance and get out of the church quickly by sneaking through and around all the adults. We really didn't want to stand in line as everyone thanked Pastor Foreland for a wonderful sermon. As many people there were, you'd think it was a convention or something. I really didn't understand at the time what a convention was, but that's what Dad always said. Then Mom would just simply look around to make sure no one could see her, and then she'd pinch Dad right in his side.

Billy and I made it outside without any trouble. We couldn't believe we made it past Pastor Foreland. We were so happy; it was like winning the Olympics or something. The only problem was that we still had to wait for Mom and Dad to go through the line. Mom never missed an opportunity to tell Pastor Foreland what a great service it was.

As we were standing by the car waiting, Billy picked up some snow to throw it at me just as Becky and her parents were walking by.

"See ya at the lake, Jimmie and Billy!" she yelled. Billy just smiled.

"Okay, Becky!" I yelled back.

"Bring a shovel!" Billy yelled.

I looked at him. "What if she doesn't know how to use one?" I asked.

"We can show her!" Dad laughed as he was opening Mom's door.

Billy's parents met up with us, and they followed us out of the parking lot. They decided not to stay after church either, but they let Billy ride home with us as long as we took him straight to his house. That was because he told Mom and Dad once that he was allowed to go to our home, and he really wasn't. Boy, did he get in trouble by his parents and mine.

After we arrived home, Dad made Mom take some medicine and lie down. He told her not to worry about dinner, that he'd heat up the chicken soup that she had made for us the night before, and he'd heat her up some broth.

This is great! I thought because the less time it took to eat, the sooner I could get to the lake. I got out the bowls and spoons while Dad heated up the soup. We sat; we prayed, and we ate, and then I left.

As soon as I arrived at the lake, Billy yelled, "Is your dad going to clear the lake for us?"

I shook my head no. "Mom wasn't feeling well, and Dad is taking care of her. I didn't want to ask. Besides, we could use the exercise!"

"Okay then, you and Becky start on that side. Sam and I will start on this side. And by the way, Jimmie, even Becky beat you here."

Becky and I skated to the other side the best we could through the snow and began clearing the ice. Because the snow was light that afternoon, it didn't take us long to push it with our shovels to the sides.

Becky stopped for a minute to rest. "Do you ever go skiing, Jimmie?"

"Sure, usually in January and February, but I'd rather skate. Mr. Pulaski said I might have a chance at a college scholarship if I could keep my grades up in school. I told him I'd be lucky if I made it through high school."

Just then, I stopped and pointed. "Look over there, Becky. See that road coming down to the boat launch?"

Becky put her hand up just above her eyes to block the snow. "Yeah?"

"Well, Mr. Collins owns the Ice Company, and every year, he donates big blocks of ice and carves them out so that a toboggan fits in the groves. Then he places them next to each other to make a long ramp for speed. After that, we try to put as many people as we can on a toboggan and race down the hill on the ice blocks and out onto the lake. It's really fun, but he doesn't do it until the middle of February."

"Hey!" Billy yelled. "Sam and I would appreciate it if you two would stop talking and help, or we'll never get it cleared!"

I yelled back, "I think you're getting a little carried away, Billy! We only need enough room for us to practice! Everyone in town will be here later with shovels, so let's save some for them to do!"

Then with everyone in agreement to my response, we all stuck our shovels in the snow and picked up our hockey sticks and started practicing before it got too late.

After Becky and I won two out of three games against Billy and Sam, it was time to go home for supper. Sam insisted that they should have been awarded the second game because the hockey puck hit a stick on the ice and went into the goal. He said it wasn't fair, but I simply said that it was an act of God, and you can't argue with God. With this said, Billy smiled and pointed out that if it was an act of God, then that meant we had three on our team, and therefore, it wasn't fair either. We just shook our heads and changed into our boots and headed for home, but only after we agreed to meet again at the lake by six and that Becky was going to stop at my house on her way so that we could walk down together. I didn't mind at the time since she had to pass my house on the way to the lake anyway. Then we all went our separate ways to our homes so we wouldn't be late for supper.

We finished eating, and Becky arrived at my house just as I was closing the front door on my way out. On our way to the lake, we talked about Mr. Pulaski's Christmas present. I said I was glad that everything was coming together. As we reached the top of the hill overlooking the lake, I didn't see the smoke from the fire that Mr. Pulaski should have started by then.

Instantly, I stopped frozen in place.

Becky was in the middle of a sentence when she looked at me and stopped in the middle of her sentence. "What's wrong?"

I stood still, not moving an inch as I looked from one side of the lake to the other. I kept looking for Mr. Pulaski, but I didn't see him anywhere. I ran down the hill to the lake and looked all around and then ran up to Sam and Billy. I was pretty much out of breath. "Where's Mr. Pulaski?"

Sam shrugged his shoulders.

"He wasn't here when we got here!" Billy said.

I looked all around a second time, but he was nowhere in sight. Then I quickly asked everyone else that was also already at the lake, but no one had seen him.

Becky caught up to me and put her arm on my shoulder. "Maybe he's just late!" she said.

"No!" I yelled, franticly looking all around again. "No! Something is wrong. He's never been late, and he's never missed a weekend! I have to go find out where he is!" I yelled again, still franticly scanning the entire lake surroundings.

Just then, I began running back up the hill.

Becky tried running after me. "Wait, Jimmie! I'll go with you!" she yelled.

But I just kept running until I reached his house. I knocked on the door, and then I pounded. "Mr. P, you in there? Mr. P, are you all right?"

Receiving no reply, I quickly ran around to the back door and looked in every window, but I didn't see him anywhere. I left my hockey gear on his porch and ran home as fast as I could.

As soon as I got there, I burst into the door shouting, "Mom, Dad, Mr. Pulaski wasn't at the lake, and he's not at home!"

"Calm down, Jimmie. Calm down. We know where Mr. Pulaski is! He's all right!" Mom answered. "He's at the hospital, and everything is all right!"

"Can we go? I need to go. I need to see him!"

Dad was already getting his coat on. "Come on, Jimmie. I'll take you if it'll make you feel better," Dad said as he tried to get me to calm down.

As we hurried out to the car, I wanted answers to my disbelief. "Why is he at the hospital? What happened? Is he going to be all right?"

Dad just closed his door as he got in. "Yes, Jimmie, we just told you he was all right. The doctor made him go just as a precaution. The doctor thinks he may have pneumonia, and he didn't want to take any chances because of Mr. Pulaski's age! So Doc Ramsey made him go to the hospital. He's going to be just fine!"

I sat there wishing Dad would drive faster. It seemed like time was standing still. It was taking so long to get to the hospital. Then when we finally arrived, I jumped out of the car. Dad hadn't even put the car in park yet before I jumped out. Immediately, I ran in through the hospital doors and up to the front desk. I tried to be calm and polite, but it didn't come out the way Mom would have wanted it to. "Where's Mr. Pulaski?" I said loudly.

"Excuse me?" the nurse asked as she turned around.

I swallowed as I looked up at her. I couldn't believe it, it was Nurse Crouch, from when I was in for my head injury. I always called her Nurse Grouch when she left my room. I know I shouldn't have, but the reality of it all was that Grouch fit her personality better. As a matter of fact, if there was a contest between her and a Doberman, I think I'd have to bet on her to win.

"I'm sorry, Nurse Crouch!" I said, and let me tell you it took a lot for a boy my age to get her name right. Then I said, "My friend

Mr. Pulaski is here, and I need to see him! I mean, I'd like to see him please. He's my best friend!"

Just then, Dad came in behind me.

"I'll check!" she said. And then she continued, "You stay right here and don't get into trouble! I'll be right back!"

Silently standing there, I looked up at Dad. He put his arm around me and pulled me close. "I'm sure he's okay, Jimmie!" he whispered.

Nurse Crouch came back. "He's in room two hundred eight A! Go down the hall to the elevators and go to the second floor then make a right off the elevators."

She was explaining the directions to Dad because I was gone by the time she said 208A. She interrupted her instructions with a very loud, "No running!"

But I knew she couldn't catch me, so it didn't matter at that point. All I wanted to do was to see Mr. Pulaski for myself. It didn't make any difference how many people said he was going to be all right; I had to see for myself.

I found his room without any trouble. I stopped as soon as I got to the edge of the doorway. I swallowed really hard and looked around the corner, just to make sure he was really there. It only took a second for him to see me.

He leaned forward with his glasses on the end of his nose. He was looking at a magazine. "Well, it took you long enough to get here!" he said as he laid his book down on his lap. "What took you so long?" he added as he started laughing, but it turned into coughing.

"Mr. P, are you okay? Why didn't you tell me you weren't feeling well? I would have come to the hospital with you!"

"Well, I haven't been feeling myself lately, but I just thought it was a cold. I was on my way to the lake, and just as I was stopping to feed the horses, I started coughing, and my chest started to hurt. Mr. Jackson was driving by and stopped. He asked me if I was all right. I said my chest hurt, and the next thing I knew, he spun his car around and took off. Two minutes later, the ambulance was pulling up with lights and sirens followed by the police and fire trucks. You'd have thought a house caught on fire. One paramedic opened the back of the ambulance and pulled out the stretcher, and the other started pulling out all this stuff and asking me questions. Then the next thing I knew, I was in the ambulance, and off we went. If I didn't know better, I'd have thought I was being kidnapped," he explained.

I looked at Mr. Pulaski for a second and scrunched up my forehead. "Why didn't he just put you in his car and drive you to the hospital?"

Mr. Pulaski just laughed. "Because he panicked, and you know how Mr. Jackson is when he gets excited . . ." Mr. Pulaski tried not to cough. "You know Mr. Jackson, if there was a bucket of water next to a fire, he'd go call the fire department instead of dumping the bucket of water on it."

"How long are you going to be in here?"

"A day or two I suppose. They haven't really said yet, but I plan on going home as soon as I can. I'm not much for hospitals you know. Never was!"

I tried to encourage him. "Well, I'll come see you tomorrow after school, but you have to get better because Christmas is only seven days away, and you can't miss the school concert Saturday night. It's on Christmas Eve, and it's going to be special this year."

Mr. Pulaski smiled at me and said, "I have no intention on missing your concert, Jimmie. If I have to have them push my bed all the way there, I'll be there. I promise!"

I felt a lot better after seeing Mr. Pulaski that night. Dad and I didn't stay long. Mrs. Crouch wouldn't let us, but it was too late to go back to the lake, and I didn't feel like going even if it wasn't.

After we pulled into the driveway, Mom opened the door for us. I told her what Mr. Pulaski said, and then she told me that Becky came by and asked that I call her when I got home. She wanted to know how he was too. So I called her and filled her in on the details, and by the time I was finished, I was really tired. I got ready for bed and fell asleep as soon as I lay down. I don't think I could have ever been as exhausted as I was that night.

CHAPTER 27

Monday before Christmas Day

*Trust in the LORD with all your heart and lean not
on your own understanding;*
—Proverbs 3:5, New International Version

I was just about to launch the hockey puck into the net and score the winning point when the buzzer went off, and then as I opened my eyes, I realized it was only my alarm clock. I turned over, and instead of turning it off, I hit the button for ten more minutes. I stretched one arm and then the other as I began to think about Mr. Pulaski.

Although I visited him and he seemed to be okay, I was still worried. I remember hearing about people his age getting pneumonia and not recovering. I wish Mom had let me skip school and let me go straight to the hospital after breakfast. I even tried the old "we aren't doing anything this week because everyone is too excited about Christmas vacation" excuse. Then I even confessed that I wasn't really paying any attention in class anyway. I argued every point I possibly could, but she just wouldn't see it the way I did. So I got ready for school.

After I met Becky, Sam, and Billy, we talked about Mr. Pulaski until we reached the front steps of the school, or I should say, I talked about Mr. Pulaski. As we were closing our lockers, Sam asked me if I was going to the lake right after school. Sam already knew the answer before he even asked, but he felt the need to ask anyway.

"I don't think so!" I said. "I'm going to check on Mr. Pulaski, that is if Mom or Dad are able to take me." I was expecting Sam and Billy to get upset with me and was really surprised when they didn't.

The two of them just looked at each other, and then Sam said something I never expected. "We understand, Jimmie!"

I don't think my eyes could have gotten any bigger as I looked at them in amazement. "You do?" I asked.

"Sure!" Billy answered.

Sam looked down at the floor. "Look, I know we make fun of you because you spend so much time with him." Then he looked at Billy. "But it's because sometimes you brush us off like we're second on your list of things to do!"

I looked down at the ground, with my thumbs in my pockets and my hands on my hips. I thought for a minute. With my head tilted to one side, I looked up at them and answered, "I guess you're right! But I don't mean to! It's just that Mr. P is like a grandfather to me! I never really knew my grandparents, and he's always there for me!"

Billy just shook his head. "Okay, but listen, Jimmie, since you're not going to the lake tonight, we'll expect you to go tomorrow night, okay?"

"Okay!" I said, and then the bell rang, and we hurried to our classrooms.

It seemed to take forever for lunch period to come. I couldn't help thinking about my conversation with Mom before I left for school. I knew I was going to be bored all day. If Mom had only listened to me, I would have been a lot happier if she let me spend the day at the hospital with Mr. Pulaski.

A few minutes passed before Becky asked me, "Would it be all right if I went with you?"

I wasn't paying too much attention to her at that point. As a matter of fact, I hardly even noticed she was there as I was concentrating on Mr. Pulaski. I looked at her. "Where?" I said.

Becky leaned across the table as she looked at me sarcastically. "I want to go see Mr. P! You really need to concentrate, Jimmie," she said.

I shrugged my shoulders. "Sure, if you want to!"

Once again, the bell rang, and we cleared our trays and hurried to class. I couldn't wait until our afternoon classes were over. As with the morning, the afternoon seemed like it was taking forever. Then all of a sudden, unexpectedly, the bell rang. I was pretty good at getting out of there fast, but that day, I think I set a record. I threw my books in my locker and ran out the door before I realized that I forgot to wait for Becky, Sam, and Billy. So I slowed down and waited until they caught up with me. "Sorry guys," I said, "I guess I was in a hurry." I really didn't have anything to say on the way home. I was really in a hurry.

"I'll come up to your house as soon as I ask my mom if it's all right to go with you, okay, Jimmie?"

"Sure, Becky," I answered as she went in the house and right before I began running.

I stopped running as soon as I reached the back door of my house. As I walked in, Mom was standing at the stove putting on a pot of water for tea. She had just gotten home from work.

"Will you take me to see Mr. Pulaski at the hospital, Mom? Becky is asking her mom if she can go with us," I pleaded.

Mom filled her cup with hot water. "No need to, Jimmie. He came home today. Reverend Foreland called the diner to let me know. They let him go home, but he had to promise not to leave his house until the doctor thinks he's ready."

I ran into the living room and called Becky to let her know.

After a quick dinner, Becky came to my house, and the two of us went to Mr. Pulaski's house to see him. We walked up to the door, and I rang the doorbell.

"Come in, Jimmie!" he yelled.

I opened the door and stuck my head in.

"Come in, come in and close the door!"

I walked in, and Becky came in behind me. Mr. Pulaski was sitting in his chair by the fireplace with a blanket over his lap drinking a cup of tea.

"Are you doing okay, Mr. P?" I asked.

"I'm doing just fine! How was school today?"

Becky and I sat on the sofa. "It was all right, I guess." I couldn't believe that I couldn't think of anything to say. I never had that trouble before, but for some reason, I just couldn't.

As Becky and I sat with Mr. Pulaski, I was wishing that he would come up with one of his stories. But the three of us sat there for a minute not saying anything, and then I couldn't believe the only thing Becky could think of was to ask if she could she use his bathroom. There's a way to start a conversation.

I thought. Mr. Pulaski smiled. "Sure, Becky, it's down the hall on the right."

Then Mr. Pulaski looked over at me. "Why don't you go to the kitchen and find something to eat. Maybe Becky would like some cocoa!"

"Okay, Mr. P. Would you like me to get anything for you?"

Mr. Pulaski began coughing. "No, thanks, Jimmie," he said, trying to catch his breath. "No, I just need to rest. I'm pretty tired. Why don't you and Becky make yourselves at home. And I apologize if I fall asleep, the medication you know, it makes me a little tired."

"That's okay, Mr. P. I wasn't going to stay long anyway. I just wanted to find out how you're doing!" I answered as I left to go into the kitchen.

In the short time that it took me to go into the kitchen, pour two cups of cocoa for Becky and myself, and return to the living room, Mr. Pulaski had fallen asleep. It seemed like Becky was taking a long time getting back from the bathroom, so I slowly walked over to the hallway and looked toward the bathroom, but the bathroom door was open, and the light was off.

"Becky," I yelled in a whisper, "where are you?"

"I'm in here!" she whispered back.

"In where?" I answered as I started down the hallway.

"In here!" she said again.

I peeked in one room, and then the next, there she was. "What are you doing in here?" I whispered again.

"Look at all this stuff, Jimmie!" she said.

"Come on, Becky, I don't think you're supposed to be in here!"

She grabbed my arm. "Look at this stuff!"

I turned around. She was standing in front of a glass display case. Wow, there were baseball cards of Babe Ruth, Mickey Mantle, and a lot of others. As I looked closer, I noticed that all the cards where autographed too. Even a baseball bat. Then in another glass case, there was a picture of Mr. Pulaski's son Antonio, a baseball glove, a fishing pole, and more trophies. His daughter's picture was in another one along with a flute, music, dance shoes, hair ribbons, and a few other trinkets. And next to it was a picture of Mr. Pulaski and his wife, with letters and some of her hair and a brush and comb.

"We better get out of here, Becky, before he wakes up and catches us. He's never told me about this room. Come on!"

Just as we turned to walk out, I saw another case, but this one had a picture of me in it and all kinds of things, pictures that I had drawn and things that I had made in art class and other stuff that I had given him.

"Come on, Becky, let's go!" I said again. Just as I turned around, hoping that Becky was following me, I heard Mr. Pulaski call me.

"Jimmie, are you still here?"

We hurried out of the room and back to the living room.

By the time we returned, Mr. Pulaski was standing up, fixing his blanket, and then he sat back down.

"Mr. Pulaski?" I said in an asking kind of voice.

"Yes, Jimmie," he answered.

"Mr. P, I'm sorry, but I was wondering . . . I meant I didn't mean to . . . I mean . . ."

Mr. Pulaski interrupted, "You want to know about my room of memories, is that it?"

Becky looked at me. "It's my fault, Mr. P!" She sounded a little worried. "If you want me to go home, I will. I'm really sorry . . ."

Mr. Pulaski put up his hand and said, "That's all right, Becky, no need to explain! As a matter of fact, I enjoy sharing special moments of my life. You would have seen other things like a painting that my wife did, statues that my daughter made, and things from the kids at the center where I worked. I try to keep a little something to remember everyone who touched my life in a special way. Because of them and God, I'm the person that I've become today."

I looked at Mr. Pulaski a little confused. "I don't understand, Mr. P. You have my picture and things I gave you in there too!"

"And why shouldn't I, Jimmie? You touched my life too. Even Becky has touched my life. Even if it's only for a short while, every single person that you come in contact with has an impact on your personality, your emotions, and even your future. Your future is an extension of the present, and the present is an extension of the past. Who you meet and what you do builds on what you will accomplish and who you will become!"

Becky looked at me with raised eyebrows and wrinkled forehead.

"What don't you understand, Becky?" Mr. Pulaski asked as he grinned and tilted his head.

"Well, you mean that Sam, Billy, and Jimmie have an impact on my future?" she asked.

"That's exactly what I mean, Becky. Think for a minute. Think about one specific thing that has happened in your life since you met them."

Becky looked down as she thought. "I guess that would be showing them that I can play ice hockey."

"Okay," Mr. Pulaski answered. "Let's start with the day you met Jimmie and work up to Billy and Sam. What would have happened if Jimmie didn't go to school with you the first day? You probably would have found your way around the school, and you might have met some other friends, but you may not have experienced playing hockey. You might not have experienced Jimmie's friendship."

Becky looked at Mr. Pulaski as she shook her head. "But they didn't really want me to play hockey with them!"

"That may be so, but you did, and you are. And now the four of you are a team! You proved yourself, Becky, and now they accept you. Well, Jimmie does anyway. You may have to give Billy and Sam some more time. Look at it this way, when you go to college, you'll be challenged academically. And after you graduate and start looking for employment, you will be competing with everyone else, old and young, for the same job, and because you proved to yourself that you are as good—"

"Or better . . ." Becky interrupted.

"Or better! You know in your mind and heart that you can win because you have the confidence to prove yourself. And because you do, you won't just stop and accept what people tell you! Becky, you don't know what the future holds for you or Jimmie or Billy or Sam for that matter. Only God knows."

Mr. Pulaski closed his eyes, bowed his head, and then looked up at us again. "God knows which path you both are going to take. God knows which path he wants you to take, but the decision is yours. He isn't going to make it for you. He wants you to ask him for guidance, and sometimes you may think he's telling you which way to go, but you may find out that Satan may have led you the wrong way instead. Satan is very good at what he does, and what he does is deception. Often, we make the wrong decisions and think they're the right ones because we're in a hurry for an answer, and we don't really give God the chance to lead us. But I can tell you from experience, when you make a mistake, God will always forgive you, and he will always give you another chance! Let me give you an example.

"I remember Maria and me getting a call to visit a store that required a membership to join. So the next day, we visited the store. As we entered, we were treated with coffee and cookies and then given a tour. At the end of the tour, we were taken into an office where the sales person asked us a few questions and then told us how much it cost to join. I remember telling them that I wanted to go home and think about it and I would call them the next day to let them know our decision. When Maria and I stood up to leave, we were told that we had to join that night, or we would not be offered the opportunity again. I smiled, nodded, picked up my hat from the coffee table, and then thanked them for their hospitality and explained that we didn't make on-the-spot decisions unless it was a life-or-death situation. And even if it was, we always took time to pray for guidance. Then I thanked them for their time, and we left. That's how Satan works: he takes advantage of us at our weakest moments. God never tells us that we only have one chance."

Mr. Pulaski coughed a few times and cleared his throat. "I don't have all the answers to everything, but I know if you pray every time, you need to make a decision that God will help you. And if you do make a mistake, learn from it. Take the time to listen to other people and evaluate what you hear, especially from older people"—

Mr. Pulaski smiled—"especially ones with a lot of experience. But beware, even old people make mistakes, even ones that you respect. Don't ever take life for granted because it's short. And if you miss an opportunity to share your experiences with others, then one day, you'll regret it because you can't go back in time."

Becky and I looked at each other.

"I know that both of you are young, but when you decide what you want out of life, ask God to help you reach your goal. Don't think you can do it alone because you can't. I learned the hard way to let God lead your life, and whatever happens, it happens for a reason, and you'll find out one day exactly what that reason is! If you rely on God, you will achieve everything you'd ever need out of life, not what you want but what you need!"

Mr. Pulaski smiled at us both and then looked back at Becky. "Now that my sermon is over, bring me a picture, Becky, and I'll have a special place in my room of memories for you too!"

Becky smiled. "Thank you, Mr. Pulaski. I guess you made an impact on my life and my future this evening."

The three of us laughed, and Becky said, "I guess I better get home since it's a school night."

Mr. Pulaski smiled as we got up and put our coats on. I opened the inside door for Becky to go out first, but she stopped just before opening the storm door and turned around.

"Thank you, Mr. P. Now I know why Jimmie likes coming here!"

"Bye, Mr. P. See you tomorrow. You take care of yourself!" I said as I was leaving.

Becky and I talked as I walked her home. After she went inside, I just stood on the sidewalk in front of her house. I didn't know why at the time, but I didn't want to leave, so I continued staring at the front of her house for a few minutes. I even felt myself smiling, and for the life of me, I couldn't figure out why.

> *In all thy ways acknowledge him, and he shall direct thy paths.*
> —Proverbs 3:6, King James Version

CHAPTER 28

Tuesday—Five Days before Christmas

And they that be wise shall shine as the brightness of the firmament; and they that turn many to righteousness as the stars forever and ever.
—Daniel 12:3, King James Version

Mr. Pulaski didn't have as much trouble sleeping through the night as he had previous nights; the medication Dr. Ramsey prescribed helped him get the rest he needed. He was a little drowsy when he woke up in the morning, but he didn't have anything to do since he was restricted from leaving the house. It was kind of funny to know that you're never too old to be on restriction.

It wasn't easy for him to be missing out on his daily visits to the little shops that lined the main street in town. As a matter of fact, it was considered to be the only street in town. Not only was he missing out on his visits but also he hadn't been able to feed Mr. Hansen's horses carrots in a few days either or visit the children's ward at the hospital. Reverend Foreland said he'd explain to the kids that Mr. Pulaski was sick, but that didn't help Mr. Pulaski feel any better. He still felt like he was letting everyone down.

The church wasn't even getting cleaned; at least, that's what Mr. Pulaski thought anyway. The women's club took on the task of cleaning the church until he recovered. But he always said that no one could clean the church as well as he could. When Mr. Pulaski dusted, he dusted the top of the coat rack and the bottom of the candleholders. Not a speck of dust got away from him; talk about your dust buster, Mr. Pulaski was the best.

Nevertheless, Mr. Pulaski enjoyed and looked forward to doing these daily tasks even if it was getting harder and harder for him to do them because of his arthritis. In fact, even the simplest tasks anymore were sometimes hard for him to do and thus made him sometimes very tired. But nonetheless, no matter what, Mr. Pulaski always enjoyed and looked forward to his daily routine each day of the week.

Anyway, now getting out of bed in the mornings was difficult enough because of his arthritis, but being tired because of the medication made it even more of a challenge. By the time he was finally able to move well enough to sit up, time slipped by faster than usual, but he still managed to make a piece of toast or two with butter and strawberry preserves and his morning coffee. After he finished eating, he refilled his cup and carried it into the living room.

In the living room, he stood in front of the window looking out toward the front lawn. Once again, big flakes of snow were being carried ever so softly by a subtle wind that could only be detected by the movement of the snowflakes as they were gently laid down upon one another as they blended into a pure white blanket stretched across the ground.

As Mr. Pulaski stood staring out, he envisioned Maria and him helping Angela and Antonio building a snowman. Maria was throwing snowballs. The first one hit him in the head, but the second missed him as he ducked and quickly made one himself. He returned fire just missing her, as he intended of course. Maria was laughing and had the biggest smile he had ever seen. Antonio was on the other side of the half-made snowman just picking up snow and throwing it with both hands at Angela as she laughed running behind Maria and then grabbing onto the back of his coat just in time for him to turn and hide her from the snow attack of Antonio.

Samuel stood at the window smiling as he watched himself chase Antonio with a big handful of snow. Then the four of them stopped and finished placing the head of the snowman on the body. Samuel lifted Angela up so she could place stones for eyes and a carrot for the nose. Antonio placed stones across the face as a smile. Then Maria took her scarf from around her neck and placed it around the snowman. As they all stood back and looked at their team efforts, they pointed and laughed, and then one by one starting with Maria, they fell into the snow and moved their arms up and down to make snow angels. As they stood up and jumped to one side looking down at their artwork, tears came to Samuel's eyes as he continued watching from the window.

Then all of a sudden, one by one starting with Samuel's image, they disappeared from his sight until the only one left was Maria. Samuel placed his hand up to the window as Maria turned and looked up at him. Samuel's smile disappeared as he was reaching for her, and she toward him. She whispered, "I love you Samuel!" Then she too vanished from the vision that he had enjoyed for what seemed to be only a few moments. As he pulled his hand back away from the window, he closed his eyes and reopened them only to see the snowman gone as well as the impressions of the snow angels that once lay on the ground a short distance from where the snowman stood. Samuel walked to his chair and sat down; he leaned to one side and once again closed his eyes to rest.

The house was quiet except for the ticking of the clock on the wall and the crackling of the fire in the fireplace. Samuel began to stretch his neck and his arms, and then as he yawned, he heard a knock at the door. He looked at the clock and wiped the tears from his eyes, wondering where the time had gone.

"Come in, Jimmie!" he yelled from his chair.

The door opened, but it was Becky who was peeking from around the door. "Mr. Pulaski, it's me, Becky!"

"Good afternoon, Becky! Is Jimmie with you?"

"No, sir. Jimmie had some things to do right after school, so I hope you don't mind. I came by myself."

"I don't mind at all, Becky. To what do I owe this honor of your visit?" he answered.

Becky hung up her coat as she said, "You said if I brought you a picture, you would put it in your room, so I brought it with me and some other things for you as well. I didn't bring very much, just a few small things if that's all right."

"Well, bring them over here and let me see what few things you have!" Mr. Pulaski said.

Becky reached in her coat pocket and pulled some small items out and carried them over to him. He straightened his blanket out over his lap, and Becky laid them down. Mr. Pulaski adjusted his glasses and began looking at the treasures that lay before him. Still a little teary-eyed, he looked down at the five-by-seven recent picture of her. Accompanying the picture was a certificate of excellence that was rolled up and tied with a red ribbon from a dance recital and a few dried rose petals. She had included a few seashells that she had found on the beach during the previous summer's family vacation.

"I know this isn't very much, Mr. Pulaski. But for now, it's all I have, and I want you to have them," she said.

Mr. Pulaski looked up at her over his glasses. "These are wonderful treasures, Becky. Why don't you put them in the room for now, and as soon as I'm able to move around a little better, I'll take care of them, okay?"

Becky smiled and did as he asked. After returning to the parlor, she smiled. "Mom was concerned about me being out after dark, so I promised her that I wouldn't stay long."

"Well, thank you for stopping by!" he said with a warm smile.

Becky put her coat on and left for home. While Becky was visiting, he had forgotten how quiet the house was, but after she left, it didn't take long for him to be reminded.

A few minutes later, Mr. Pulaski made his way into the kitchen and warmed up some soup and crackers for supper. He was happy that Becky had come to visit him. Talking to her helped to pass the time, and by the time she had left, the snow had stopped falling. The sun never had a chance to make even a short appearance that day because of the heavy clouds. Mr. Pulaski didn't mind though; he wasn't going anywhere anyway. As a matter of fact, after he finished his soup, he took his medication and climbed into bed once again and turned on the lamp that stood on an antique stand next to his bed and returned to his book that he had been reading earlier. As quickly as he opened his book, his eyes began to close; barely awake, he reached over and turned the light off as he fell fast asleep.

PART 4

AN UNEXPECTED DISCOVERY,
THE THRILL OF CHRISTMAS
BREAK, THE CHRISTMAS PRESENT,
THE MOUNTAINTOP, GOD'S
MESSENGER, AND A TOWN'S LOVE

INTRODUCTION
TO PART 4

Miracles happen; God picks when, where, and for whom they will occur. Some miracles are very subtle, like the birth of a child, a sunrise or sunset that takes your breath away, and the song of a lark first thing in the morning as the dawning of a new day.

These are miracles that are taken for granted every day of our lives. Few of us see them as miracles because we don't take the time to think about their beginning. Who created them?

Then there are miracles that are totally unbelievable and leave us mystified. A doctor gives no hope of someone surviving a terrible accident, but they do because someone took the time to pray for them. Someone loses hope and faith, and God sends an angel to help them understand and regain their faith. God creates miracles when he feels they're needed. He's in control whatever the situation is. Oftentimes, if we don't receive a miracle when we ask for it, we feel he isn't listening, or we say, "Why me?" or "Why him or her? They don't deserve this!" Well, there is a reason; we aren't given the knowledge to know why or an explanation, but we will. Someday, all will be revealed to us.

Our lives become so complicated and involved; we miss the little things that happen every day. A neighbor's smile or even a stranger's smile. A cordial greeting like "Good morning. How are you today?" When was the last time you asked that of someone and really meant it and stopped to listen? I worked for an individual that used that question as a lead into something he wanted me to do. So after a while, I just said, "I'm fine. What's up?" He didn't really want to know. As a matter of fact, there was a situation where I needed to transfer closer to home, and I explained to him that my wife had an incurable disease. When I told him the name, he said he didn't know what it was. I started to explain, and he cut me off, "Oh, you don't have to tell me what it is. I just don't know what it is." And he just went on with the procedure that I needed to follow for request of the transfer. Very caring person, wouldn't you say?

Well, there's no time like the present. And speaking of the present, I know there are two different meanings, but what a lead in—how often do we sit and try to figure out what to buy someone for Christmas? We spend hours walking through stores trying to find something that catches our eye as the perfect gift or something that we think is the perfect gift. Well, what about a gift of love and kindness? I mean if you know someone who has small children, why not offer to watch their children so they can have a day to do whatever they want to? If you don't feel you can watch small children, then pay for a babysitter for them.

Presents don't always have to be wrapped; they don't have to be things that sit on a shelf and need to be dusted every so often. Just smile and tell someone how much you appreciate him or her and love them for who they are. Bottom line: discover life all over again, go back to the basics of life, and discover the true meaning of life—the true meaning of the birth of Jesus Christ our Lord and Savior now and forever.

This is the last section of the story. I hope it helps you discover or, should I say, rediscover, faith.

CHAPTER 29

An Unexpected Discovery

We know that we live in him and he in us because he has given us of his Spirit. And we have seen and testify that the Father has sent his Son to be the Savior of the world. If anyone acknowledges that Jesus is the Son of God, God lives in him and he in God. And so we know and rely on the love God has for us.
—1 John 4:13–16, New International Version

I was just about at the bottom of the steps on my way to the kitchen when the doorbell rang. As soon as I opened the door, Becky burst in, almost knocking me over as she spoke, "Jimmie, I was thinking on my way home . . ."

"You are on your way home from where? Why were you thinking and why weren't you in school?" I asked because I was confused and had no idea what she was even talking about.

"From Mr. Pulaski's house," she said excitedly. I just stared at her. She continued to make absolutely no sense. "Did you ever notice that he doesn't have any Christmas decorations up?"

"Yeah, so? He never has had any up that I can think of!" I said, holding my hands out to my sides.

She shook her head with her eyes closed. "Okay. What time does he go to sleep?"

I looked at her, even more puzzled. "What time is it now?" I asked.

"Six o'clock!"

I looked at her with one eye closed. "With the pills that Doc Ramsey gave him, he should be asleep now if he took them on time. Why?"

Becky stood there, quiet for a few moments with her finger in her mouth. Then she suddenly said, "Okay, I want you to help me with something tonight. I'm going home, and I'll be back at seven!"

"For what?" I asked loudly as she began running down the steps.

"I'll tell you when I come back. Just be ready to go!" she replied.

I was really beginning to worry about her. I closed the door as Mom came in to see to whom I was talking. I closed the door as I answered, "It was a really strange girl, but she left. So everything's okay!"

"Is Becky all right?" Mom asked as she looked out the window.

"How did you know it was Becky?" I was amazed that mom guessed it was Becky.

She laughed. "How many girls do you know that you think are strange?"

I looked up at her. "You got a point!" I said as I continued my quest to find something to eat.

I settled for a glass of chocolate milk and returned to my room to finish some homework that I was unsuccessfully putting off. Before I knew it, the doorbell rang again.

I was closing my math book when Mom called for me, "Jimmie, there's a strange girl at our front door!"

"Very funny, Mom!" I yelled down the steps.

By the time I reached the bottom of the stairs, Becky was standing inside the entrance. I looked at Mom and smiled; then I looked at Becky. "So what's going on?"

"We have to hurry. Come on!"

At this point, I didn't ask any more questions. I just grabbed my coat as we left. I even tried not to ask any questions until we were at least a little way down the street. As we continued walking at a fast pace, Becky suddenly began walking even faster.

"Where are we going?" I asked as I tried to keep up with her.

"We're going to Mr. P's!"

I honestly had a little trouble keeping up with her because I really wasn't in the mood to be running. I was a little curious though. "Not that I don't want to. But why?"

"Because he doesn't have any Christmas decorations up, and we are going to surprise him. That is, if he doesn't wake up before we're finished!"

By the time we reached Mr. Pulaski house that evening, it was close to seven thirty. I turned to Becky and, in a loud whisper, said, "You're crazy, Becky!"

"Shhh!" she said quite loudly. "He'll hear us!" Becky went over to the big oak tree in the corner of his front yard.

"Where are you going now?" I asked.

"Just be quiet and help me with this tree!" She started dragging a pine tree out from behind the large trunk of the oak tree.

"What are we going to do with this?" I asked.

Becky just shook her head. "We, the two of us, are going to sneak into his house and put it up!"

"But we don't have any decorations!" I pointed out.

She had a very large grin on her face. "Yes, we do!" Then she started dragging a box from around the tree.

"I don't believe this!" I said in amazement.

"Mom took me to get a tree, and then she helped me pick out some decorations to put on it, just in case we can't find any in his house!"

I didn't say anything else. I just picked up the bottom of the tree as she lifted the top, and we managed to get it up the front steps without making a sound.

"Open the door!" she whispered.

I just rolled my eyes. It was a good thing it was dark so she couldn't see me.

As quietly as I could, I opened the door, and we managed to get the tree inside. Becky quietly closed the door, and we took the tree into the parlor. We stood it up, and Becky took a stand out from the box. It wasn't easy, but the two of us managed to get the tree into the stand.

"There. Now let's go see what kind of decorations he has in the cellar!"

In disbelief, I replied, "Becky! Are you nuts? Let's just put the decorations on that you brought and get out of here!"

"Jimmie, just stop complaining and follow me downstairs!" She seemed to be very impatient.

I leaned toward her. "How do you know he keeps them in the cellar?"

"Because I haven't seen them anywhere else, have you?"

"No!" But then I never looked for them.

As we were going down the steps, Becky turned on a flashlight. She never stopped surprising me that night. We got to the bottom of the steps and looked around.

"Just out of curiosity, where did the tree came from . . . You didn't cut it down out of Mrs. Kantar's yard, did you?"

"Of course not, Mom took me to get it. She thought it was a great idea!"

"Well then, why didn't you bring her with you instead of me?" I sarcastically answered back.

Becky just looked at me. Then she pulled on my coat sleeve. "There!" She pointed with the flashlight. "Over there are some boxes. Let's see what's in them!"

Then she pulled my arm so hard that I almost fell over. In the corner were some boxes piled up on top of one another. As she handed me one at a time, I set them down. Then she brushed the heavy layer of dust off them and started to open them. She whispered as she handed me the fourth box, "Here's one!"

I looked up at her. "How do you know? You didn't look inside it yet!"

"Ah, it has Christmas written on the side of it. I think that's a clue!" She kept looking through the rest of what seemed to be at least thirty more.

By the time she stopped, there were three medium boxes filled with Christmas stuff that she had found. We carried them up the steps and into the parlor. Becky went through them, picking out different things. One box was filled with lights and garland and all sorts of old decorations. A second box had other Christmas decorations in it. Then she lifted and opened the last box. As she was lifting it, she gasped. She set it down and reached inside and held up the most beautiful angel that I had ever seen. It was very old but well-kept. Becky handed it to me, and I stood on the step stool that we had brought in from the kitchen. Considering Mr. Pulaski's height, I don't know why he even had a step stool. Anyway, I placed the angel on the top of the tree and guided the cord through the branches down to the bottom of the tree where Becky plugged it into the extension cord. In admiration, we both stood back and watched for a few minutes as the glow from the angel shone all around.

Although we were counting on Mr. Pulaski's medication to keep him asleep, we unplugged it just to make sure the light didn't wake him up. We continued decorating the tree, and then we placed a few odds and ends around the room. Becky removed the wrapping from a wreath and hung it on the door as I unpackaged some other ornaments that appeared to be as old as the angel. After we finished decorating the inside of the house, to Becky's satisfaction, we cleaned up everything and took the boxes back to the cellar. That is, except for a few strands of lights and a nativity that Becky insisted we put outside. So we carried a few things with us as we were leaving and closed the door.

While Becky set up the nativity in the front yard, I put the lights up around the porch railing and stretched them across the edge of the roof. Once again, we plugged everything in and then stepped back almost to the street. I was really glad when Becky said she was happy with everything. We quickly turned them off and started for home.

As we left, Becky looked at me and smiled as she spoke, "Thanks, Jimmie, for helping me. I couldn't have done it alone, and I really wanted to surprise Mr. P!"

I smiled back. "I'm just glad that we didn't get shot or arrested for breaking in! But then again, maybe we will when Mr. P wakes up in the morning!"

After a few minutes, we returned to my house, but instead of going inside, I decided to walk Becky to hers. Since it was dark, I didn't want her to have to go walk home alone. Besides, it gave me more time to tell her how much I enjoyed breaking into Mr. Pulaski's house, going through his things, and decorating his place. Anyhow, I couldn't think of anything else to do with my time that night, so I was really happy that she thought of me to help her commit burglary. Well, we reached her house, and I said good night as she walked up the sidewalk. As she reached to open the door, I turned to leave.

Just as I was leaving, Becky's father pulled into the driveway; he must have had to work late. As he got out and closed his car door, he looked over at me and said, "Hi, Jimmie. What brings you out this late in the evening, especially in front of my house?"

I smiled and replied, "Oh, nothing much. I just helped Becky break into someone's house and go through their cellar and take things. Then I walked her home!" I smiled as I walked past him and then continued, "See ya later. I got to get home before Mom finds out I'm not in my room!" I left him standing on the sidewalk as I ran all the way home.

CHAPTER 30

Wednesday—Four Days before Christmas

Everyone who believes that Jesus is the Christ is born of God, and everyone who loves the father loves his child as well. This is how we know that we love the children of God: by loving God and carrying out his commands.
—1 John 5:1–2, New International Version

The next morning, Mr. Pulaski woke with the morning sunlight shining through his window. He rubbed his eyes and sat up on the edge of his bed. He was feeling a little better that morning. As a matter of fact, he felt like he was ready to start his town visits again. But he knew that Dr. Ramsey wouldn't think too favorably on that decision. Besides, Dr. Ramsey was due to visit Mr. Pulaski around ten o'clock in the morning right after he was finished visiting Mrs. Jenkins, who thought she was having a heart attack again. But then again, she thought she was having a heart attack at least once a month. Dr. Ramsey said that all she had to do was to stop eating spicy foods since they give her heartburn. Once she did that, she'd be all right.

Meanwhile, Mr. Pulaski showered, dressed, and made his morning coffee and oatmeal. While eating at the kitchen table, he listened as usual to the radio while he waited for Dr. Ramsey to arrive. I'd say patiently waiting, but I don't think Mr. Pulaski ever waited patiently when it came to waiting for the doctor.

In the meantime, Becky, Sam, Billy, and I got to school a little bit earlier than usual. I had no idea how that happened because we left at the same time as always. Becky leaned against the lockers while she waited for me to open mine to get our books out for our morning classes. She needed to put the books she wasn't going to use in my locker since it was closer to our classrooms than her locker was. Looking back, I didn't even remember giving her permission at the time. As I recall, she was waiting for me to get my books one morning and realized that she didn't need all of hers, so she put the ones she didn't need in my locker rather than taking them all the way back to hers. And as time went on, she ended up with all her books in my locker without me even realizing it. I didn't really mind though. After all, what are friends for if they can't share a locker, right? Besides, I really didn't think it would have been a good idea at the time to tell her she couldn't.

"I can't believe it's only four days until Christmas!"

I closed my locker. "You can't? Personally, I can't wait until Saturday when I can give Mr. P his Christmas present." I know you're not supposed to give presents until Christmas morning, but I knew that this was going to be one big surprise that he would never expect, in addition to the Christmas decorations Becky made me put up in his home; at least, that's what I hoped.

"Do you think he's noticed the tree and the decorations yet?"

I shrugged my shoulders. "I don't know, depends on if he got up yet!"

Becky leaned over in front of me so I couldn't miss her looking at me. "Aren't you even a little bit curious?" she asked in an investigative manner.

I rolled my eyes before answering, "I'm glad I'm not going to be there when he finds out, just in case he gets mad!"

"Why would he get mad?" Becky asked as her voice started to sound like she was getting a little upset.

"Oh, no reason. I'm sure he is going to be filled with joy!" I quickly replied.

Becky looked at me with a strange stare as if she didn't believe I was serious. Then she went on with her psychology. "I think he never puts any decorations up because he's alone and doesn't have anyone to share them with!"

I turned around to walk down the hall. "We'd better get to class before we're late and Mr. Keen surprises us with detention."

Meanwhile, as Mr. Pulaski stood up and put his plate in the sink. He looked at the clock on the counter. Dr. Ramsey hadn't arrived as yet, and it was fifteen minutes after ten. Mr. Pulaski scratched his forehead as he was trying to think of what he wanted to do until he arrived.

I'll write a letter to Angela, he thought.

As he left the kitchen and entered the parlor, he looked up and immediately stopped. He just stood staring at the room in disbelief. Before him stood a Christmas tree as tall as the ceiling, and on the very top was an angel dressed in a long white dress lined with gold trim and two lighted candles one in each hand. Her flowing wings stood high above her shoulders, and her head was bowed as if she was standing before God. The base was encircled with miniature lights covered by her long gown as it glowed. All the emotions that Mr. Pulaski never shared flowed through his body as his eyes followed slowly down the tree, taking in all the decorations that he had missed for so many years. The tree was covered with candy canes and miniature popcorn balls wrapped in different-colored foil. Red and silver garland encircled the tree from top to bottom. Scattered about the tree were ornaments of different shapes, which included some bells that Maria had treasured as much as the homemade ornaments that Angela and Antonio made as young children. Tears began to flow down his cheeks as he walked over and touched the golden bells that read: "Our First Christmas, Samuel and Maria, 1948."

As he looked around the room, he paused. There were candles held up by golden bases covered with evergreen on the mantel over the fireplace. Pictures of Angela and Antonio with Santa Claus were evenly spaced side by side on the coffee table, and on the stand next to his chair was a picture of Maria in a beautiful Christmas dress and Mr. Pulaski in a suit. Mr. Pulaski stood holding the photograph.

Tears fell from his eyes onto the glass frame as his memories of all the Christmases past flowed through his mind.

As he walked over and stood by the front window, he could see the decorations on the porch. Garland wrapped around the banister, and a string of colored lights lined the windows. A nativity stood on the front lawn just beneath the porch.

As Mr. Pulaski was viewing all the outdoor decorations, Dr. Ramsey pulled up in front of the house. As Dr. Ramsey opened his car door, he just stood there frozen with amazement looking up at the house. He couldn't believe his eyes. Mr. Pulaski's house hadn't ever been decorated before. As he walked up the sidewalk toward the house, Mr. Pulaski opened the door to greet him.

"Your house looks wonderful, Samuel!" he complimented as he arrived at the door.

"Thank you! But I didn't do it!"

Dr. Ramsey entered and started taking his coat off. As he hung it up, he turned toward the Christmas tree. He looked at Mr. Pulaski in amazement. "I suppose you didn't do that either!"

Mr. Pulaski smiled. "Nope!"

Dr. Ramsey smiled. "I suppose elves visited you last night!"

Mr. Pulaski looked up at the top of the tree. "Nope, angels!"

Dr. Ramsey just looked at him. "Okay, well then, let's see how you're doing."

Mr. Pulaski escorted Dr. Ramsey into the parlor where he began his examination.

Mr. Pulaski just stared at the tree and, with a calm low voice, said, "She is very caring, for one so young."

Dr. Ramsey lowered his stethoscope as he answered, "Excuse me?"

"Oh nothing," Mr. Pulaski said. Then Mr. Pulaski whispered, "God must have known you and I needed someone like her in our lives, Jimmie. Becky is a very special person!" Mr. Pulaski smiled and kept looking at the tree the entire time Dr. Ramsey conducted his examination.

As much as I wanted to visit Mr. Pulaski that week, I couldn't because I had some last-minute things to do to make sure everything was ready for the school concert on Saturday night. All the teachers were helping me with this project since I volunteered to plan this very special Christmas program. I didn't realize when I volunteered that it was going to be so much work. We even had to spend extra time after school practicing our music because Mr. Thomas said, "If we are going to put on this concert, then we were going to put on the best concert ever, and that, my friends, is going to take a lot of work!" Boy was he right because by the end of every practice, we all had very sore arms, fingers, and lips. Well, the end of school finally arrived, and we were all very, very happy.

That evening after supper, I went to visit Mr. Pulaski. I didn't want him to think that I had forgotten about him, especially since he was sick. It was six o'clock when I arrived at his home. I knocked on his door and then opened it and yelled in, "Mr. P, are you home?"

"In the kitchen, Jimmie."

"Is it okay for me to come in?" I said, trying not to be too loud.

"I can't think of any reason why you can't, can you?" he replied.

"I don't know of any!" I said as I cautiously hung up my coat and took my shoes off. I was waiting for Mr. Pulaski to yell at me or kick me out or something, but he just looked at me and smiled and then said, "Come into the parlor, Jimmie. I want you to see something." I followed Mr. Pulaski very slowly. "Look at what grew in my parlor last night!" I smiled as he stood next to the tree.

"You know, Jimmie, I haven't had a Christmas tree in my house in years, but when I saw it this morning, years of memories were awakened, and years of emotions flowed through me. If you know who the angels were that set this up for me, I'd like to thank them!"

I could feel my eyes getting really big. "Well, to tell you the truth, Mr. P, Becky and I did it. Actually, it was Becky's idea, and she made me do it!"

Mr. Pulaski smiled at me without saying another word.

Then I sat down on the couch and tried to change the subject. "Mom told me that the doctor was here today to check on you. How are you doing?"

Mr. Pulaski had gone back into the kitchen to finish his dishes. "I'm doing fine. The doc said that I may be able to start going outside again soon, just for short periods though. And how did your mom know that the doctor was seeing me today?"

"Mr. P, you know that nothing in this town gets past Mom. She works at the only diner, and everyone eats there, plus I don't think there's anyone who doesn't know Mom!"

Mr. Pulaski just smiled. "I guess you're right, Jimmie."

"Well, what did he say besides that? You're doing okay, right?"

"He said he wants me to come in for another chest X-ray tomorrow, but he suspects that my chest will be clear, and maybe by this weekend, I'll be able to get back to my normal routine."

"That's great, Mr. P, because I sure do miss you at the lake, and I'm sure everyone else does too! Mr. Peters keeps delivering wood for you to burn, so the pile is growing."

Mr. Pulaski smiled. "That's because he likes the tax deduction for donating wood he can't use, but that's okay. Without his wood, there wouldn't be a fire to keep everyone warm. Well, I miss the lake too, Jimmie, and now that I'm finished cleaning up, let's go in and sit by the fireplace!"

I followed him into the living room. He sat in his chair, and I sat on the sofa as usual; he never gets tired of sitting by the fireplace in the winter.

"Becky brought me her picture the other evening," he said, "and a few other things, so I made a place for them in the room. She's a very nice girl, Jimmie!"

I looked at Mr. Pulaski. "She's all right, I guess. She evens up the teams when we play hockey, that's for sure! Who would have thought that a girl would be playing hockey with us?"

"Is she good at it?" Mr. Pulaski asked.

"Well, she's okay. I guess she's doing pretty well. She sure does make Billy and Sam mad when they lose!"

Mr. Pulaski laughed, and then he leaned forward as he looked over the top of his glasses at me. "You know what I think, Jimmie? I think she likes being around you, not so much Billy and Sam, but I really think she likes being around you!"

I didn't know what to say; my eyes got really big with shock as I interrupted, "I don't think so, Mr. P! I know she hangs around me a lot but . . ."

Mr. Pulaski just sat there looking at me with a smile for a minute. "Jimmie, you're young yet. Have fun, play hockey, and have a great time. And when the time comes, you'll know exactly what I'm talking about!"

"Okay, Mr. P, thanks. Although I don't have a clue what you're talking about, it must be the medication you're on! Anyway, I have a lot to do between now and Saturday night. You're still planning on coming, aren't you?"

"Jimmie, I wouldn't miss it for anything!"

"Okay, Mr. Pulaski, I just wanted to see how you were doing, so I'll stop by tomorrow!" I said as I grabbed my coat and put it on and closed the door. I ran all the way home.

CHAPTER 31

Christmas Break Begins

Worship the LORD your God, and his blessing will be on your food and water. I will take away sickness from among you.

—Exodus 23:25

I tossed and turned all night waiting for morning. The anticipation of Saturday's arrival was difficult enough, but Christmas break was about to start, and that just made it twice as hard, not to mention the Christmas concert. I wanted everything to be perfect for Saturday night. It was going to be an event that the whole town was going to remember for a lifetime; at least, that was what I hoped.

On the one hand, I couldn't believe that it was only Thursday, and I still had Friday to go through. On the other hand, I only had one more day to make sure everything was ready. Thus, I spent all day Thursday worrying, which made it really difficult to concentrate during classes. And as most of my teachers said, "I wasn't focused." I even had a hard time paying attention to conversations with Becky, Sam, and Billy. By the time they were finished talking, they had to start over because I missed everything that was said the first time. Every teacher that I talked to was as excited about Saturday as I was; at least, that's what they said. Mr. Jones, the school principal, said he couldn't wait either; he was really excited to see how it was going to turn out. I'm not sure if he really meant it or if he was just saying he was, but it didn't matter. By the end of the day, I was exhausted, first from not being able to sleep and second from all the work that I did.

When the school bell rang for dismissal, I hurried out of school and went straight home. I didn't even take time to talk to Sam or Billy, and I hardly said anything to Becky. Most of the time, I did very little talking anyway; Becky usually did most of the talking, and I just agreed with everything she said. As a matter of fact, I agreed so fast that after I got home, I realized that I had agreed to wait for her before I went to Mr. Pulaski's house again.

When I finally arrived home, Mom had dinner ready, and Dad was already sitting down. Dad had to leave for work early, so Mom made dinner early. I don't know how Becky was able to do it, but her timing was always perfect. By the time I finished, she was at the door, ready to go. I asked Mom if I could be excused from the table, but I was already getting up and heading for the door.

"I'll be back by eight!" I yelled.

Mom answered with her usual "Be careful and dress warm!"

When we reached Mr. Pulaski's house, I didn't even ring the doorbell. "Mr. P, you home?" I yelled. I knew he was; my question was just a formality to let him know that I was there.

We walked in and hung up our things as Mr. Pulaski laid his book down on his lap.

"How are you two doing this evening?" he asked.

"I'm fine!" Becky answered.

"I'm fine too, Mr. P. I just wanted to stop by and let you know that Mom and Dad are going to pick you up to go to dinner and the concert on Saturday evening at four if that's okay with you."

"I'll be ready, Jimmie. I even had my suit cleaned and pressed. I can't wait. I think this is going to be the most excitement I've had in years, maybe since you graduated from elementary school!"

I didn't say a word. I just grabbed a cookie off the plate that was centered on the coffee table as usual.

"Well, I just wanted to check on you and let you know that everything is working out just fine, but I'll be glad when it's over!"

I turned to leave. "Oh, by the way, tomorrow is our school Christmas party, and we're getting out early! So I'm going to try to visit you tomorrow, but Mom said she'd help make sure everything's ready for the concert. She is going to stop by the school to ask if there's anything they need her to do. Mr. Jones, Mom, and Mrs. Garcia have really been helping me a lot since I haven't ever done this before, and I will probably never volunteer to do anything like this again!"

Mr. Pulaski laughed. "I'm sure everything will work out just great, Jimmie!"

Becky rolled her eyes. "That's what I keep telling him, Mr. Pulaski!"

"Well, we'd better go. I have to be home by eight tonight. I can't wait until tomorrow when school's out for two weeks! And hopefully, you'll be able to start going back to the lake!"

Mr. Pulaski grinned. "I sure hope so, Jimmie! The doctor took the X-rays today, and he said they looked pretty good, so I plan on calling him tomorrow to find out for sure. I think I missed enough!"

"Okay, see you tomorrow!" I yelled as we walked down the steps.

All I could think about on my way home was that the next day was going to be Friday, and I couldn't wait. Our school Christmas party was only a few hours away. Becky and I talked about it all the way home from Mr. Pulaski's house. After I walked her to her house, I ran all the way home. I was hoping for a little more snow before morning. I wouldn't mind it at all if it snowed enough so that we wouldn't have to go to school, and we'd get an extra day off. But then I thought for a second as I realized we'd have to make it up during spring break, and maybe that wouldn't be as much of a good idea, I thought. Upon arriving home, I went to bed and tried to get what sleep I could before tomorrow.

Friday morning, I showered, ate quickly, and hurried to school. I thought that the sooner I got there, the quicker the day would end, and then it would be break time. All I could think about were my big plans for Christmas vacation. My schedule was going to be filled with sleeping in late, getting up, hanging out at the youth center until the afternoon, and then ice skating at the lake until almost midnight. This was the only time of year Mom let me be out that late. I was so excited.

The morning didn't go as fast as I hoped, but we were down to the last hour and twenty minutes. Only one more hour and twenty minutes and school was officially over. I could feel the excitement building, anticipation getting stronger and stronger with every moment that passed. Then it happened; the bell rang. I don't think any of us ever moved as fast as we did when that bell rang. It was like a contest to see who could get to their locker first, put their books away, and be the first one to the gym for the school Christmas party.

Although school was officially over, most of the kids stayed for the party. If there was one event that we all enjoyed at school, it was the big Christmas celebration. Anyway, we were all rushing to get back to the gym. I was really moving fast; I had to build up speed in order to have enough momentum to slide down the part of the hallway that sloped going into the gym. You had to build up just the right amount of speed in order to slide all the way down. Everything was going well too: I had my speed just right, I hit the top of the slope, and I was sliding at record speed.

And then Mr. Jones came out into the hallway from talking to the science teacher. Wouldn't ya know it, out of all the kids running in the hallway, he yelled at me. "Jimmie!" Mr. Jones said sternly.

I stopped dead in my tracks approximately six inches from his toes, and I looked up at him and said with a smile of course, "Yes, Mr. Jones?" I gulped and squeezed my teeth together. Here it comes, I thought since this was my third time getting caught running.

Mr. Jones was six feet two inches tall and looked like Abraham Lincoln. Much to my surprise, he then said, "I need some help carrying some things to the gym for the party!"

"Sure, I'd be glad to help you, Mr. Jones!"

He smiled and told me to follow him to his office. As we walked together, he looked down at me. "By the way, isn't this the third time I caught you running in the hallway?"

Without hesitation, I answered, "I'm not sure. I don't think so!"

Mr. Jones looked at me with his hand holding his chin. "I believe the first time was September eighth, two thirty in the afternoon, right before school was getting out. And I seem to recall October thirteenth as well, eight five in the morning. Late for class, I believe?"

"Oh yeah! You sure do have a good memory, Mr. Jones. I hope my memory is that good when I'm as old as you," I answered slowly as I tried not to get caught by saying too much.

Mr. Jones just stopped and looked at me as I was smiling up at him. "I hope so too, Jimmie—I think!"

Anyhow back to the party—it was great. Billy's Mom brought ice cream and root beer. My mom made chocolate chip cookies; they're the best. No one ever makes them like she does; they're not those little flat ones; they're really big and soft. They're so big that one would be enough for anyone except for me. Time went by pretty quick; we all had a lot of fun, but I couldn't wait to get to the lake. I usually stopped at the diner where Mom worked, but since she wouldn't be there today, I asked her if I could go to the lake right after school. I wanted to get there as soon as I could. She said yes, but I needed to be on time for dinner.

After this, Becky and I stopped at Mr. Pulaski's house. While we were there, we found out that the doctor said he wasn't ready to allow Mr. Pulaski to go to the lake again just yet; he wanted Mr. Pulaski to wait a few more days. I knew it was hard for him; after all, he had been going to the lake for years, and it just wasn't the same without him, especially since we weren't able to sit and eat our polish sausages. It didn't matter though; I knew that the next day, Saturday, which also was Christmas Eve, was going to be the best ever. I made sure Mr. Pulaski didn't forget that Mom and Dad were going to pick him up at four o'clock in the afternoon for dinner and the school concert. I couldn't wait.

Becky and I only stayed for a short while, and then we left. Once again, Sam and Billy were already at the lake waiting.

"We knew you wouldn't be on time!" Billy said as he skated out on to the ice away from us. "Hurry up before spring gets here!"

We hurried putting on our skates and then grabbed our sticks and headed out onto the ice after him. We practiced until it was time to leave for dinner.

"Are you coming back later after you eat?" Sam asked me.

"I'm not sure, maybe for a little while!" I knew it wasn't going to feel the same going to the lake on a Friday night without Mr. Pulaski there. However, it had been over a week already, and I didn't want Sam and Billy to be angry with me, so I agreed to come back.

Dinner didn't take long; I really wasn't very hungry anyway. I thought going to the lake would take my mind off thinking about the school concert, Christmas Eve, and Mr. Pulaski's present. I really couldn't wait for him to get it. It was going to be the best present ever, maybe even life changing for him; at least, that's what I was hoping.

I returned to the lake as promised, but I wasn't much competition for Sam, Billy, or Becky for that matter. But it seemed the only one who understood was Becky. I left early that night; I guess my heart just wasn't in it. I was exhausted, worried, and excited about what was going to take place on Christmas Eve. I had a little trouble falling asleep that night, but as exhausted as I was, once I did fall asleep, I didn't wake up until morning.

CHAPTER 32

Saturday—Christmas Eve

*So if you faithfully obey the commands I am giving
you today===to love the LORD your God and to serve
him with all your heart and with all your soul.*
— Deuteronomy 11–13, New
International Version

The cold gentle air moved through the wind chimes that hung from
the roof over Mr. Pulaski's back porch. He could barely hear its music
as the morning sun once again crested the horizon. As he rolled over
to the edge of the bed and lay on one side, he watched the sunlight as
it danced across the wall. The window was covered with a thin frost.
Mr. Pulaski slowly opened his eyes and smiled as he looked at the
wooden cross that stood on the stand next to his bed.

"Good morning, Father. It's going to be a wonderful, glorious
day, and I thank you for your kindness." After he spoke, Mr. Pulaski
slowly pushed himself up out of bed. Once again, the stiffness from
his arthritis made it a challenge to rise as fast as he did so many years
ago when he was a younger man.

It was the morning of Christmas Eve, and Mr. Pulaski was
growing eager as he was looking forward to the evening concert. I
too had been eagerly waiting for this day. It was going to be different
this year than in past years of Christmas Eve services. First of all, it
wasn't going to be the traditional service that Mr. Pulaski, or anyone

else, was accustomed to. Knowing that I worked very hard planning everything for this event, Mr. Pulaski prayed that it would be a success, and so did I for that matter. With these thoughts in mind, Mr. Pulaski proceeded with his morning routine.

Mr. Pulaski turned the radio on as he was getting dressed. As he sat on the edge of his bed, he listened to the morning station that played the old songs that always brought back memories for him. It was going to be a few more days before the doctor was going to let him go out again except for that night's concert, so he dealt with the boredom of staying inside the best he could. As difficult as it was, he was convinced that he was coping with his situation very well. But he had also made up his mind that this was to be the last weekend he was going to miss his walks and visits with the children at the hospital. It didn't matter to Mr. Pulaski whether Dr. Ramsey agreed or not with his plans because his mind was made up. Starting Monday, he planned on escaping to the outdoors, the lake, his walks, visiting the horses, and everything else he loved to do.

By this time, Mr. Pulaski finally managed to get up off the bed and ate breakfast.

I showed up just as he finished cleaning up the table and dishes. I opened the door and stuck my head in first and then shouted, "Mr. P, is it okay to come in?"

"Sure, Jimmie, come on in! I was wondering if you were going to stop by this morning. I know you're busy getting ready for this evening, so I really wasn't expecting to see you today."

"Oh, I can't stay long. We have to practice at the school this afternoon, just for a little while though. Mr. Thomas wants us to play once more to make sure we're ready! I think he's more nervous than I am! I may not be able to ride with you to the concert tonight because I have to be there early to help set up, but Mom and Dad said they'll be by to pick you up, and I'll meet you at the restaurant before the concert, okay?"

"I'll be waiting!" he replied. And then he continued, "And don't you worry about me. Just concentrate on tonight. I'm sure everything will work out just fine!"

"Okay, Mr. P!" I agreed, but I really wasn't convinced. I drank a cup of hot cocoa and left for home. I was having a really hard time keeping Mr. Pulaski's Christmas present a secret, so I hurried and left before I accidentally slipped and told him.

Mom worked that morning so she could be home by noon: the exact time I was back from Mr. Pulaski's house. Mom wanted to make sure she was available during the afternoon in case I needed her help. At least, that's what she said, but I think she wanted a little extra time for getting herself ready.

In the meantime, Becky stopped by Mr. Pulaski's house shortly after I had left. She had been out shopping with her mother that morning and asked her mother to drop her off at Mr. Pulaski's on the way home because she thought I would still be there. Becky planned on walking home with me, but she was unaware that I had already left Mr. Pulaski's house just moments before she arrived.

Becky knocked on his door.

"Come in!" Mr. Pulaski yelled. He always yelled "come in" no matter if he knew who was at the door or not. He trusted everyone; in fact, he said he couldn't understand why he shouldn't since no one other than me, and now Becky, ever visited him, so it didn't matter. As a matter of fact, he said he'd be surprised if someone else besides one of us two ever stopped to visit him.

Anyway, Becky opened the door and went inside as she shouted, "Hi, Mr. P!"

He was sitting as usual in his chair by the fireplace reading a book. I didn't think there was a book written that he hadn't read. I really can't remember if he did anything else since the doctor wouldn't allow him to go out of the house until he was better. I can tell you from experience though, if Dr. Ramsey tells you that you can't do something, you better not do it. If there's one thing I learned, it was never to go against Dr. Ramsey's advice. For one thing, when he got angry, his face turned red, his forehead scrunched up, and then you were given a very loud, long, and scary lecture about how he doesn't say things to hear himself talk and how he wasn't going to waste his time on someone who wasn't going to follow his instructions anyway. And oh yeah, he also said that he didn't become a doctor for the money. He said he was there to help, and if you felt you didn't need his help, then just go on and do what you want and not waste his time. When have you ever heard a doctor tell you that he wasn't in it for the money? His lecture ended with how he could have worked at the hospital instead of visiting people in their homes and that he was probably the last of the doctors on earth that still made house calls because it was more convenient for his patients. Anyway, enough about Dr. Ramsey. Let's get back to Becky and Mr. Pulaski.

Becky came into the living room where he was and sat down on the couch. "I think you'll really enjoy the concert tonight, Mr. Pulaski!" she said.

"I'm sure I will, Becky, and I understand you're the only one in the school orchestra that plays the piccolo."

Becky was excited. "I sure am! I play the flute too, but Mr. Thomas said that it would be really nice if I played the piccolo since there are five flutes, especially for tonight since it's a Christmas special."

"I'm sure you'll be great, Becky. And to be the only piccolo in the whole band, why, that's an honor!"

Becky was quiet for a minute. Mr. Pulaski just rocked in his chair as he read his book.

Suddenly, Becky broke the silence, "Mr. Pulaski!"

"Yes, Becky?" he answered.

"Can I ask you a question?"

Mr. Pulaski stopped rocking. "You just did!"

"Dad is worried that all my friends are boys, and I don't hang around with any girls. I told him that I'm just not the slumber party, shopping, cheerleading kind of person. I like action, being involved in sports and other things that are challenging. For instance, I want to climb mountains and do competition-type things."

Mr. Pulaski smiled. "I know just the mountain for you to climb, but when the time comes and when you do, don't do it alone!" Then he paused for a moment thinking. "Becky, everyone's different. You have to follow your own path wherever it leads you. As I told you and Jimmie, if you don't know what to do and you need guidance, you need to listen to your parents and God. Your parents and I can help you look at the positive and negative reasons for your decisions and help you see the consequences. But in the end, you must make your own choices. Whether they're right or wrong, they're yours to make. God gave you parents to guide you as you grow up. Of course, there are some choices your parents have to make for you . . . Your parents have God's authority to make those decisions until you become an adult. The values you learn from your parents help you choose right from wrong. The Bible tells us to honor our mother and father. Becky, if you pray and ask God for help no matter how old you are, he will help, and so will your parents!"

Becky smiled. "Can I ask you another question? I mean kind of a serious question?"

Mr. Pulaski tilted his head and looked at her as if he knew what she was going to ask. "Do you think or I mean do you know, Mr. P, if Jimmie has ever said anything about me?"

Mr. Pulaski acted like he was thinking for a minute, and then he shook his head. "Depends on what you mean, Becky. Sure, he's told me that you eat lunch with him, Sam, and Billy, and that you're pretty good at playing hockey, and—"

"No, that's not what I mean," she interrupted. Then she said, "What I mean is did he ever say anything about me, like does he mind being around me, or does he think I'm . . . never mind. Just forget I said anything." She then sat back on the couch.

Mr. Pulaski looked at her for a second or two before he said anything. "Becky, let me tell you something about Jimmie or about young boys in general. If you're asking me if he likes you, yes. However, it depends on what you mean by does he like you! If you mean does he like you more than just as a friend? I couldn't tell you. I know he plans on going to college, and he's hoping for an athletic scholarship, for track or hockey or both, so I don't think a girlfriend is on his mind right now. But I do know that he's very lucky to have you as a friend! Becky, Jimmie may not realize how much he likes you yet, but give him some time. And one day, he'll wake up, and you just might be the first thing on his mind instead of sports. You're both young, and you both have a lot of time to figure out what you want to do with your lives, so just have fun and enjoy the way things are right now. Who knows, maybe God's plan for the future will be for you two to become more than just friends."

Becky smiled a little. "I guess I'd better be going. I have things to do to get ready for tonight too! Thanks, Mr. P!"

Mr. Pulaski nodded his head. "You're welcome. Just give it time. You're young, and you have your whole life ahead of you. If it's meant to be, it will be!"

Becky stood up and walked toward the door.

Mr. Pulaski stood up. As she looked at him, he made one more comforting remark to her. "When Jimmie realizes how special you are, he'll be a very lucky young man!"

Becky smiled as she opened the door. "Thank you again, Mr. P!"

After Becky left, he turned and looked at the antique clock on the fireplace mantle. "Look at the time! I'd better get ready myself. I don't want to be late." He stood up and stretched and then went into the bathroom to wash up and groom himself. After he was finished, he went to his closet, but when he started to take the suit out that he wore to church every Sunday, he stopped and looked at a garment bag that was hanging on the end of the rack behind all the rest of his clothes. Then he hung his suit back up and slowly took the garment bag out of the closet. He held it up as he looked at himself in the mirror, then hung it up on the hook on the back of the door, and began to open it very slowly.

Once it was open, he gently took it out from the bag that had protected it for so many years. This was the suit that he wore to Maria's funeral so many years ago. Flooded with memories, he took a step back, and he put his hand to his mouth as he looked at it and held it up in front of him. Once again, it all came back to him: the ride to the church, the service, the drive to the cemetery, and the many hours he stood in the rain next to her grave after everyone had gone. Then he proceeded to take it off the hanger one piece at a time as he laid it on the bed. He knew it was out of style by now, but he didn't care. He just gently put on the pants, the shirt, the tie, and then the coat.

After he dressed, he walked over to the mirror and adjusted his tie. He wanted it to be just right. In fact, he even untied it several times because he couldn't get it just right. By this time, his hands were slightly shaking; he must have tried a half a dozen times to retie it. In frustration, he took it apart one last time. He was determined to get it right. Finally, he adjusted it for a minute and then proceeded to comb his hair while he remained standing in front of the mirror.

How did I get so old? he thought to himself. *Where did the years go? It seemed like only yesterday I was struggling just to survive after arriving in New York City from Poland.*

Remembering back to those times, Mr. Pulaski remembered how hard times seemed to plague his father and mother, but they managed to save enough money to send their son to America in search of a better life. As a young boy, he promised them that he would take care of himself and do well. After getting completely ready, Mr. Pulaski walked down the hall and sat in his chair and waited.

There was still a little time before Mom and Dad were to arrive. As he sat in his chair thinking, he decided to change. It was a mistake to put this suit on, he thought. It just wasn't going to work. However, just as he stood up and had started toward the bedroom, he heard a car out front of the house and then looked at the clock. It must be Jimmie's parents, he thought, so there wasn't any time now to change. So he brushed off the front of his jacket with his hands and started to open the door. As he looked up, he gasped, closed the door again, and reopened it more slowly than the first time.

Upon opening the door a second time, Mr. Pulaski yelled to the man standing next to the car holding the car door open next to the curb. "Can I help you?"

"I'm here to pick up Samuel Pulaski. Are you him?" the driver asked.

Mr. Pulaski swallowed. "Yes, I am him. I mean, yes, I'm Samuel Pulaski. But there must be some mistake!"

Mr. Pulaski stood at the top of the porch steps as the driver replied, "No, sir, there isn't any mistake. I am here to drive you to the concert!"

Just then, Mom opened the other door and walked toward him. She stood at the bottom of the steps and looked up at him. "Merry Christmas, Samuel. Jimmie wanted this night to be very special for you. Come on, your chariot waits!" she said as she stretched out her hand.

As they were walking toward the car, Dad stepped out of the car. "This was entirely Jimmie's idea, Samuel. You're a very special friend to our son, and we couldn't be any luckier."

Samuel smiled, leaned over, and looked in the car. Then he slowly got in, followed by Mom and then Dad.

Once everyone was back in the car, the driver asked, "Is there anyone else in your party, sir?"

"No, I'm alone!"

The driver smiled. "Well then, shall we go?" he remarked as he closed the door.

On the way to dinner and then the concert, Dad was telling Mr. Pulaski of the plans for the night.

"Since the concert is at the Mountain Inn, we thought we would have dinner there. Jimmie is going to meet us since he had to be early for practice and to help set up," Mom said.

Mr. Pulaski didn't answer; he just silently stared at a picture of both Antonio's and Angela's families. He missed them very much, and he had made his decision to move back with them and their families after winter, but he wasn't ready to say anything to Jimmie. He just didn't want to be alone anymore, and he missed Angela and Antonio terribly. But he didn't plan on saying anything until after dinner.

Mom asked with concern, "Samuel, are you all right? Did you hear what I said?"

Mr. Pulaski just looked at her. "I'm sorry. What did you say?"

Mom simply repeated, "I said Jimmie is going to meet us there at the restaurant since he had to help set up and practice. Are you all right?"

"Oh yes, I'm fine. Thank you. Just fine." He slipped his picture back in his coat pocket. Mr. Pulaski was quiet the rest of the drive.

It was exactly four o'clock in the afternoon when they arrived at the Mountain Inn. The car pulled up to the front door. The driver got out and opened the back door for Mom, Dad, and Mr. Pulaski.

As they entered the restaurant, they were met and greeted by the Mountain Inn host. "Good evening, welcome to the Mountain Inn. I believe we have your table ready, so please follow me."

Mr. Pulaski didn't move. He just stood there looking around. This was the first time he had been in a restaurant in twenty years, other than the diner where Mom worked.

The hostess looked back as she started to walk away. However, when she noticed that Mr. Pulaski wasn't moving, she stopped. "Sir, would you like to follow me? I'll take you to your table."

Mr. Pulaski smiled. "Oh yes. I'm sorry!" He kept looking around as he followed behind. At one point, he even walked backward, unable to take his eyes off the very large crystal chandelier that hung in the main entrance.

The hostess led them through the main dining room and stopped in front of two very large solid decorative doors with two very large brass handles. There were two more hostesses standing on each side of the doors. As Mom and Dad moved behind Mr. Pulaski, the two hostesses opened the doors at the same time.

When the doors opened, the room was filled with over two hundred people. The school band started playing, and people were standing all around clapping as hard and as loud as they could. Mr. Pulaski didn't move. He just looked around the room, and then he looked at Mom and Dad. They too were clapping and smiling at.

Then Dad grinned as big as if it was all for him. "This is for you, Samuel. Everyone in the whole town is here in your honor, and this is your Christmas present that Jimmie has been working on ever since Thanksgiving."

In amazement, Mr. Pulaski walked slowly with weekend knees toward the crowd as they were clapping. The men were shaking his hand. The women hugged him, and even little Katy ran up to him and smiled. Then she took his hand as they walked through the crowd. Everyone was still clapping as they moved to one side to allow him to walk to his table at the front of the room close to the stage.

As he grew closer to the end of the crowd toward his table, he stopped and put his hand up to his face as tears began to fall from his eyes. There in front of him stood Angela and her husband, Antonio and his wife, and Mr. Pulaski's four grandchildren. Angela and Antonio moved toward him with tears in their eyes. They all took turns hugging him as they wrapped their arms around him, and the three of them cried together. Mr. Pulaski held on to them as tight as he could, for he was unable to let go. The band stopped playing, and I stood up from my place in the orchestra. He opened his eyes and looked up at me.

The room grew quiet as he stood in front facing me. I walked down the steps from the stage and stood in front of him. "Mr. P, you have been a very special friend to me, and I wanted to make this year's Christmas the best one ever for you. Do you like it?"

Mr. Pulaski just wiped the tears from his eyes and smiled. "Jimmie, my very special friend, you have made me the happiest I have been in a very long, long time! You are a very special young man!"

Then Mr. Jones walked to the microphone. "Okay, everyone, we have a full evening planned, so take your seats, and Pastor Foreland will say the blessing, and then we'll begin serving. Of course, Mr. Pulaski's table will be served first and then the rest, so we must be patient, and the Mountain Inn staff will serve us as quickly as possible."

After everyone found their seats, Pastor Foreland raised his hands and began the Christmas Eve prayer. "Father, we thank you for the birth of your Holy Son Jesus Christ so long ago in a manger. Tonight, we come together to celebrate the love that you've shown us by the birth and sacrifice of your son. Tonight, Father, we come together to honor you and Jesus with praise. Tonight, we will lift our voices in praise so that we may demonstrate our love for you. We are very grateful for the opportunity to come together to show our friendship to Samuel. Father, we ask that you bless the food that is to be set before us and forgive our sins as we share in celebration this night. We ask this in the name of Jesus Christ our Lord and Savior. Amen."

Mr. Pulaski was so excited that night that he could barely eat his dinner. He just kept looking at his family and smiling. Every once in a while, during dinner, he'd glance over at me since I was seated at the table directly to his right. I would have sat with him, but there wasn't enough room for Mom and Dad and me. With so many of Mr. Pulaski's family, I thought it would be best for him to be seated alone with them. He never looked so happy; as a matter of fact, I couldn't ever remember Mr. Pulaski smiling as much as he did that night.

After dessert was served, Pastor Foreland walked up to the microphone, made some announcements, and then began the evening program. He began by stating, "I want to thank Jimmie for his hard work and his idea for this evening's program. Tonight, we will enjoy the school orchestra playing a number of Christmas songs. We will also be entertained by both the church and high school choirs, including two solos by April. And somewhere in the program, we will make the evening complete with a few words from our honored guest, Mr. Samuel Pulaski. And just so you know, Samuel, since this is your night, you can take as much time as you need. If anyone falls asleep, we'll wake them up!" Everyone laughed as Pastor Foreland returned to his table.

After a few minutes, Mr. Thomas walked up on stage and went to the microphone. "If there are no objections, I would like to make a change to this evening's program. That is, if it's all right with you, Jimmie." I shook my head yes in agreement with Mr. Thomas's suggestion. He was probably going to do it anyway.

Then Mr. Thomas looked at Mr. Pulaski. "Samuel, if you wouldn't mind, I would like to ask you to come up to the microphone before we begin our music program. But first let me explain why. When Jimmie first came up with this idea, he said he wanted to do this because you told him what it was like when you first came to this town. He said you told him how friendly everyone was and how we all pulled together during the terrible snowstorm that year. Well, I guess we all forgot about that year. It was so long ago, and time moved on very fast, and so did we. I don't know at what point this town changed, and I don't think any of us will be able to figure it out, but it doesn't matter. What does matter is after Jimmie told me what you said, I began thinking how right you were! We were a friendly town; everyone used to stop on the street and inquire as to how one another was doing. And back then, we really wanted to know. We don't take time to do that anymore. Oh, sure, we still say hello to one another, and there are conversations when people are eating lunch at the diner or in line at the grocery store, but we're all in too much of a hurry to notice how we have all changed over the years. Samuel, I am so sorry I never took the time when we were at the lake ice skating to come over and really talk to you!

"I guess we all just got used to you being there every weekend lighting the fire and making cocoa and hot dogs for everyone. I guess we all just got so used to how things were that no one noticed until you became sick and the fire didn't burn anymore and your friendly smile wasn't there serving the hot dogs! Now there's just a big pile of wood sitting there waiting for your return, and so are we, Samuel. You have done so much for the children at the hospital, and every one of us has been touched by your smile and warmth during your short visits with everyone. I guess what I'm trying to say is we've all missed you the past week, and our lives have been too busy to stop by to see you. I guess as long as Jimmie was telling us how you were doing, we felt that that was good enough. Well, I'm sorry, Samuel! I know I'm speaking for everyone here when I say, from now on, we'll be there for you just as you've always been there for us. I only hope that we all can return the love and attention to you that you have shown us all these years. Now I would like you, Samuel, to come up here and say a few words or as many as you want to say. As we celebrate the birth of Christ this evening, we also celebrate a new birth of our town. Come on up, Samuel! This is your night to remember!"

Everyone clapped as Mr. Pulaski stood up from the table. As he stood, he grabbed Angela's hand, patted Antonio on his shoulder, and kissed his grandchildren. Then he walked up on stage, stood in front of the microphone, and paused as he looked out at everyone and waited for the room to quiet down.

The heavens praise your wonders, O LORD, your
faithfulness too, in the assembly of the holy ones.
—Psalm 89:5, New International Version

CHAPTER 33

Samuel's Speech— The Mountain

*Out of the brightness of his presence bolts of light-
ning blazed forth.*
—2 Samuel 22:13, New International Version

Mr. Pulaski stood behind the podium as he looked out over the room filled with family and friends. Slowly, he reached into his coat pocket and took out a picture of Maria. He looked down at Angela and Antonio as they sat almost directly in front of him smiling and looked up at him waiting for him to speak. They were so proud of him and so very happy to be able to share in this special occasion. He laid the picture on the podium in front of him. With trembling hands, he grasped the sides of the podium and cleared his throat.

"I'm not very good at giving speeches, but I think I'm fairly good at telling stories. At least that's, what I've been told. So here goes. This is a true story that I think is most appropriate for the eve of our Savior's birth, and I hope I don't put any of you to sleep."

Mr. Pulaski cleared his throat again. Then he looked at Angela and Antonio again. "I want to start out first with an explanation that is long overdue. Angela and Antonio, I'm so very sorry for leaving the way I did when you were both in college. I love both of you with all my heart! But I struggled inside with the loss of your mother for a long time. Then after the two of you left, I was alone again, and I found myself counting the days until you returned. I loved every minute with you when you came home, even if it was only for a short time. But every time you left, it became harder and harder for me to be alone. Please don't misunderstand what I'm saying. I did everything I thought was best for the two of you. You see, your mother made me promise that I would make sure that the two of you would receive the best education possible and your hopes and dreams would be fulfilled. So I sold the house to both pay for your education and because I couldn't stand being there with so many memories of you two growing up and the life I had with your mother. I missed her so much that I just couldn't bear living there without her anymore."

Mr. Pulaski wiped his eyes. "After I sold the house, I bought a bus ticket to anywhere. It didn't matter at the time. I just wanted to get away for a while. I had every intention of returning at some point, honest I did! But it didn't happen that way. My adventure brought me to this little town. When I arrived, I had no idea that God had a plan for me. I was totally unaware of what was to take place during the two years that followed. First of all, he got my mind off everything when he arranged for the snowstorm the first night I arrived. He also planned for me to run into Betty when she handed me a stack of blankets to carry to the shelter." Mr. Pulaski looked at Mrs. Brandt. "Remember Betty?" Mrs. Brandt smiled and shook her head yes.

"Well, one thing after another happened, and before I knew it, time was flying by, and people liked to listen to my stories. Well, after I started teaching Sunday school, Jimmie showed up in my third-grade class, and for some reason, he adopted me as his grandfather.

"Now I must remind some of you or, should I say, most of you, about the year you all thought I was crazy. Oh, you were all too polite at the time to tell me to my face, but I knew what you were thinking, but I didn't mind." Mr. Pulaski laughed a little as he continued, "I think it's safe to tell you that I thought some of you were crazy too, so I felt we were even." Laughter filled the room as Mr. Pulaski spoke.

"I didn't know it at the time, but our Father in heaven thought it was time that he and I spent a little time together. So God had a mission for me, and he was going to make sure that I completed it. Just in case, let me refresh your memories. It was the third winter after my arrival to this town. I kept telling you that I could hear a sound coming down through the mountains. It was a sound that I only heard during the winter months. So I asked some of you if you knew what might be causing it. Many of you said you weren't sure. Others said they never really paid much attention to it, and a few of you said that you thought it might have been the wind blowing through the crevasses in the snow. Well, I accepted that answer for a year or two, but later, I gave it some thought. I wasn't totally convinced, so I began thinking that it had to be something more. Something on that mountain was compelling me to find out for myself exactly what it was that was causing it. It was as if I was being drawn to that mountain by some force. So I set out on my own to find out.

"That was when I knew you all thought I was crazy! I began planning for a very long and tiring journey up that mountain in the middle of winter. As a matter of fact, I actually began to think I was crazy too, but it didn't matter to me nor did it stop me. I had no idea how long and tiring it was going to be, but I was bound and determined to make that trip. I put a lot of time into preparing for that trip, and when the day came, I packed everything that I was told I was going to need and started hiking up the mountain about a week before Christmas Day. Some of you may remember seeing me practicing my hiking during the summer with a full backpack during the hottest time of year. I really began trying to persuade myself not to go, especially when I passed people sitting on their front porches drinking lemonade, but I knew when winter came, so would the sound from the mountains, and so I continued to prepare!"

Mr. Pulaski paused and took a drink of water. As I looked around the room, I could see everyone's attention was truly focused on Mr. Pulaski's every word.

"Well, winter arrived on time, right after fall, and as I expected, the sound came down from the mountains. It was the most beautiful sound I had ever heard except when Maria used to play her flute. The first few days, I hesitated, and I must admit I was a little scared. I'm certainly not going to deny that. You all know that there was a bad storm, but what you don't know is that I wasn't the only one on that mountain. During the storm, I met a man who said he lived on the other side of the mountain and that he had become lost during the storm. Well, his name was Jacob. He never told me his last name, and I never asked. I guess when you're in the middle of a snowstorm and a man shows up out of nowhere seeking shelter, you don't really think to ask what his last name is. And under those circumstances, it really doesn't matter.

"Anyway, by morning, the storm had stopped, and Jacob asked if he could hike with me for a while. Of course, by that time, I couldn't see any reason why not, so Jacob and I hiked together and talked. I couldn't put my finger on it at the time, but there was something special about him. There was something about him that made me feel calm inside, and I hadn't felt that way in a long time. After Maria died, I had trouble sleeping, and I didn't feel whole anymore. You see, a very important part of my life was missing, but Angela and Antonio were still young, and they needed me. Then when the time came for Antonio and Angela to return to college, I lost all will to live. I wanted to hide somewhere from life, anywhere; I didn't care. So you might say that I was running away from home. Jacob made me realize that I was actually trying to escape from God. Nothing mattered to me anymore, nothing at all! But while I was on that mountain, Jacob helped me find the peace I was missing. He helped me to find my inner peace with God, and he helped me to regain my life and faith all at the same time!

"Well, after the third day, Jacob told me he needed to return home, so he left, and I continued my journey alone, or so I thought. You see, as I got closer to the top of the mountain, I saw lights. They were the brightest lights I had ever seen dancing across the sky. As I watched them, I remembered seeing them before. I remembered seeing them when Maria was in the hospital the night she died. I remember sitting by her side and holding her hand when she opened her eyes for the last time. When I looked down at her, I could see that she was staring out of the window." Mr. Pulaski paused once more and wiped his eyes with his handkerchief. He cleared his throat again.

"She told me to go to the window and look out. I always did what Maria asked me to do, so I stood up and turned toward the window and looked out into the sky and into the darkness. With tears in my eyes, I asked God to forgive my sins, and I prayed that he would hold Maria's hand and let her know that I would always love her. The sky lit up that night, and I knew it was a sign that she was happy. I knew as I turned around at that moment that Maria had gone to be with God and my life was over!

"Those lights on that mountain helped me to remember the promise I made to Maria just before she died. She made me promise that I would never stop loving God and that I would find the strength to go on and finish whatever work God had planned for me. As I continued to hike, I saw the most beautiful sight God could ever have made; even the terrible storms somehow seemed to be a wonderful sight because they demonstrated God's power over the land. I also realized I wasn't paying any attention to the days, nor did I realize that the last night I was up there was Christmas Eve. Even though I grew very tired that night, I didn't want to stop. Then the wind began to pick up. As it blew harder and harder, I could hear tree branches breaking off in the distance. I looked up at the sky as it was beginning to be overtaken by fast-moving clouds. The closer I got to the top, the stronger the wind blew. With every step I took, I had to struggle to keep my balance. I grew more tired with every step, and I began to feel the cold through my snowsuit. I began to question if God really wanted me to climb that mountain. I thought if he did, why he made it so difficult for me.

"The wind became so strong that I was having difficulty moving. The snow began falling faster and faster, and then the force of the wind caused the snow to blow into my face. I was so tired I couldn't walk anymore, so I dropped my backpack on the ground, and within a matter of minutes, it was covered with snow. I lost one of my snowshoes because the strap broke as I collapsed with exhaustion. I was desperately trying to reach the top, but it was just too difficult, and finally my legs stopped moving, and I gave up.

"As I fell down and leaned against a tree, I pulled my hood over my face and closed my eyes. As I began to give into the cold and fall asleep, I began recounting my life. I thought about Maria, Antonio, and Angela. I wanted them to know how much I loved them and how proud I was of them! I had no doubt at that point that I was going to die on that mountain without one last opportunity to tell them how much they meant to me! I'm not sure if I was actually yelling out to God or if the words were very loud in my mind, 'I can't go on, and I'm so tired! Father! Please let me come home!'"

As Mr. Pulaski intently recalled his thoughts of that last night on the mountain to an audience that was totally mesmerized by every word, Angela's thoughts drifted back to that same day when she and Antonio arrived in town to surprise him with an unscheduled Christmas visit. It was a tradition for the two of them to visit Mr. Pulaski every Christmas in the past, but like most people, life had taken hold, and it became harder and harder to keep their ongoing visits. So that year, they decided to visit him unexpectedly as a surprise. Just to make it extra special, they were going to extend that year's visit through New Year's as well. It was to be a very special year.

Antonio and Angela arrived in town early that afternoon on Christmas Eve. Apparently, the storm that Mr. Pulaski was experiencing on the mountain was only hours away from reaching town. As they pulled up in front of Mr. Pulaski's house, Angela was so excited that she jumped out of the car before Antonio came to a complete stop. She was in so much of a hurry to get out she almost slipped, and Antonio had to press on the brake to completely stop and hope that the car wouldn't slide on the ice. She ran as fast as she could up to the door and started knocking and yelling, "Papa! Papa!" But there wasn't any response from the darkness of the house. Antonio had just reached the porch as she turned around and looked at him. Antonio tilted his head forward with unrevealing concern. "He must have gone to the store. Let's go see!"

The small store was on the corner at the end of his street, so it didn't take them long to get there. As they entered, the store owner was stocking shelves.

"Hi, Mr. Pratt!" they said.

Mr. Pratt turned around and almost fell off his stool as he was putting some sales signs over a display case. "Well, I'll be . . . When did you two get here? Samuel didn't tell me you were coming!" Mr. Pratt hugged them both. "That's not a secret he would have been able to keep. What's going on?"

Angela looked at Antonio. "We just arrived! We wanted to surprise him. He didn't know we were coming. Actually, we didn't know we were coming until the last minute. Have you seen him? We stopped at his house, but he's not at home. We thought he might have come here. Have you seen him?"

Mr. Pratt put his hands in his pockets and looked down at the floor. "Well . . . yes, as a matter of fact, I do know where he is!"

Angela looked at Mr. Pratt, her smile changed to an expression of concern. "Is he all right? Mr. Pratt, where is he?"

Mr. Pratt pointed out the window. "He's on that mountain!"

Angela put her hand over her mouth as she remarked, "Oh, God, no!"

Mr. Pratt interrupted with excitement in his voice, and he began shaking his head. "Oh no, he didn't die . . . He's not buried up there . . . He's climbing that mountain! We all tried to stop him, but he wouldn't listen! He said he had to climb to the top for some reason! You see, there's a noise that comes down from the mountain every year around this time. We never paid much attention to it, but Samuel, well, he—"

Angela interrupted, "By himself?"

"Yeah, he wouldn't let anyone go with him! He said he had to do this himself. He wouldn't even let the local guide go with him! He's been planning this trip all summer, and I don't think anyone could have stopped him!"

Just then, a state policeman walked in the door. "Hi, Jim. It's getting really cold out there, and that storm is moving this way pretty fast! You might want to think about closing early and going home before you get stuck here overnight. It looks like it's going to be a bad one!"

Angela just looked again at Antonio, and with tears in her eyes, she interrupted Mr. Pratt's conversation. "My father is up there!" Now as she looked at the trooper, she pleaded, "You have to find him . . . Please you have to find him!"

Mr. Pratt looked at Angela and said, "Jim, this is Samuel Pulaski's son Antonio and his daughter Angela. They just arrived to surprise Samuel, but he's somewhere on that mountain. You remember when he kept saying all summer that he had to climb that mountain? Well, he did!"

Trooper John looked at Mr. Pratt as he exclaimed, "Alone? By himself?"

Mr. Pratt sort of smiled and looked up at Antonio.

Trooper Jim looked at them. "I told him he was crazy and to forget about it! Well, I should have known he never listened to anything else I ever told him either!"

Mr. Pratt began explaining to Antonio and Angela, "A couple of days ago, he just packed up and left and said he'd see us in a couple of days. I tried to talk him out of it too, but you know how he is! 'No way!' he said. 'I got to go, and that's just what I'm going to do.' You remember?"

Trooper John thought for a minute and answered, "Oh yeah, so he really went up there?"

Mr. Pratt nodded his head yes.

Angela held on to Antonio as she pleaded, "Please you have to find him!"

Trooper John looked at Angela as he replied, "I'd love to, but . . ."

Angela, almost in tears, just looked at Trooper John as she asked, "But what?"

"But we can't! Look at that storm! It's too dangerous to send a search party up there! I couldn't even get a helicopter up there in that wind! Everything is grounded! Besides, a dog sled couldn't even make it up there! Although I never really tried operating a dog sled, I don't have one! Matt Hollander does, but he lives fifty miles from here."

Angela sat down with her arms on the table and her hands over her face, crying.

Antonio put his arm around her, kissed the top of her head, and looked up at Trooper John as he began. "Our father and mother adopted us both when we were very young. They adopted Angela one year after they adopted me. Before then, we never really know what it was like to belong to a real family. Angela never really knew her birth father, so Samuel is the only father she ever knew. Her mother brought her to Samuel when he was a counselor at a youth center because she was dying. We lost our mother, Maria, about twenty-five years ago. It was hard on all of us! But it took Dad two years before he started smiling again! We can't lose our father! Not now! Please help us find him! Please!"

Trooper John knelt and looked at Angela. "Look, I promise. As soon as the storm passes and I get clearance from the FAA, I'll go look for him myself. But until then, we have to sit and wait. Now why don't the two of you go back to Samuel's house and wait there. He never locks it. He always says he doesn't have anything worth taking, and if someone needs what he has, then they're welcome to it. So go home and get something to eat and rest, and the minute the storm breaks, I'll let you know, okay?"

Angela looked up, smiled, and nodded her head yes as she wiped her tears away.

As they were leaving, Trooper John asked, "By the way, how did you get through the pass? It's been closed because of the snow for the past two days!"

Antonio was getting into the car. "We stopped at a gas station on the way up, and the clerk told us it was closed, but a man who was drinking a cup of coffee said he was headed up this way, and if we wanted to follow him, he'd plow through for us. I'd never seen a plow as big as what he had before!"

Wrinkles furrowed Trooper Jim's forehead. "Wow! The last I heard, all the plows were being used to maintain the main roads for emergency vehicles. Oh well, you two stay warm, and as soon as I hear something, I'll let you know."

Angela faintly began to here Mr. Pulaski's voice again, just as he was describing the cold windy storm and how tired he was on the mountain.

"As I sat on the cold snow and leaned against the tree," Mr. Pulaski continued, "I closed my eyes. I was so tired, and I just wanted to sleep. The wind, snow, and darkness just didn't matter anymore, and no matter how hard I tried to get up and continue on, I couldn't.

In fact, the more I tried to get up, the harder the winds blew. I can still hear tree branches breaking from the weight of the snow and ice. I must have sat by that tree for hours with my eyes closed. My mind wanted to continue, but my body wasn't moving. I knew my time had come. I knew it was time to see Maria again, but my heart was breaking because I didn't get to say good-bye to Antonio and Angela! I wanted so desperately to let them know how proud I was of them!"

As Mr. Pulaski looked down at Angela and Antonio again, Antonio began to remember that night too. He remembered taking Angela back to the house with hope that Trooper John would call soon with news that they could begin looking for him. Hours passed, and then finally, the storm began to break toward early morning; it was Christmas morning. He and Angela had fallen asleep when Antonio heard the sound of a jeep out front of the house. As he jumped up and looked out the window, he saw Trooper Jim getting out and running up to the front door.

As Antonio was opening the door, he yelled, "Angela, wake up! Trooper Jim is here!"

Angela opened her eyes, threw the blanket off, and ran to the door looking out over Antonio's shoulder.

"The storm is breaking, and we have a small window to get a helicopter up to look for him, but we have to hurry!" Trooper Jim explained.

Antonio and Angela grabbed their coats and scarves, slipped their boots on, and followed Trooper Jim to his jeep.

Trooper Jim drove as fast as he could through the deep snow to the helicopter pad at the end of town. It was an emergency pad next to the forest ranger's cabin, which was mainly used during hunting season. It was only a few minutes before the helicopter arrived.

At that moment, someone at the table next to him began coughing, and Antonio once again returned his attention toward Mr. Pulaski. Mr. Pulaski looked down once again at Angela and Antonio as they were looking up at him with tears in their eyes.

"All my energy was gone!" "At that moment as I sat leaning against the tree, I thought I was closing my eyes for the last time: my life with Maria, my search for Antonio, and the moment that Angela held me tight because she was scared all came back to me. And then, all of a sudden, I saw a bright light shining all around me. This light was so bright that I had to cover my eyes with both hands.

"Suddenly for some reason, I began to feel the warmth that I had never felt before. Then I heard a voice speaking to me. 'Rise, Samuel!' the voice said, but I couldn't.

"'I can't! Who are you?'

"Then I heard the voice say, 'I am Jacob! Your Father in heaven sent me! You must finish your journey!'

"Again, I cried out, 'I can't! I'm so tired and cold and scared! Please! I just want to sleep!'

"Then Jacob reached down with his hand stretched out toward me. 'Take my hand! Take my hand and feel the strength of our Father, and we will finish the journey together! Samuel, your Father has been with you every step of your life. When Antonio was in the hospital, your Father talked with you. When Maria was dying, he comforted you. And when you served the many people of this town, Samuel, you gave him a blanket to keep warm! Samuel, there were so many times your Father sent his angels to you! You have been receiving strength from your Father in heaven every step of your life! And now! Samuel, take my hand and once more feel the strength of your Father's hand and walk with me!'

"I reached up and took Jacob's hand, and the warmth I felt gave me a strength that was remarkable, a strength that I had never felt before, and once again, I heard the music that I was so determined to find. Then I realized the minute our hands came together that it wasn't the music I was seeking; it was courage to live that I was searching for, and so I stood up. I picked up my backpack, and we continued to walk. I forgot about the snowshoes. I didn't need them anyway. I couldn't believe what was happening to me! I was walking on top of the snow! I could see the wind blowing, the falling snow all around us. But with every step that we took, I couldn't feel the cold wind or the snow or anything else. Jacob and I walked together to the top of the mountain. As Jacob promised, we finished the journey together.

"When we reached the top, Jacob walked away from me, and the minute he let go of my hand, I fell to my knees. As I raised my head up and I looked out across the horizon, I saw angels holding their hands up to the sky as the sun began to rise. There were so many I couldn't count them all! Then all the storm clouds disappeared, and the wind stopped. The sound that I had been searching for was louder than ever and more beautiful than ever before! Jacob looked down at me, and he raised his hands. As he did this, it was like he was floating in midair. And once more, he smiled with the radiance of heaven! 'God is pleased with you, Samuel. Pick up your flute and play. Play with all your heart, for God's blessed Son has been born on this day, and he blesses those who witness his love and glory and those who call upon his name for forgiveness! Samuel, you are his messenger, and he wants you to go forth and tell all who are willing to listen of his greatness and his love!'"

Mr. Pulaski wiped the tears from his face. "Well, I did as he asked. I played for hours. And as I played, my hands trembled as tears rolled down my face, as they do now. Then the angels stopped singing. I opened my eyes, and they were gone, and so was Jacob. I sat down on the ground and held my flute across my lap and just stared at the sun as it rose over the mountaintops. It shone more beautifully than ever that morning. Then I heard a loud noise. It became louder and louder as it grew closer and closer. As I turned around, I saw a helicopter coming toward me. I stood up and began waving. It landed a few yards away from me. The doors opened, and to my surprise, Angela and Antonio climbed out, and they ran toward me. I was never as happy as I was that Christmas morning.

"As the helicopter landed, Angela, with tears in her eyes, ran to me. She was so excited that she almost knocked me down as she hugged me. Then she smiled and whispered, 'Let's go home, Papa!'

"We walked back to the helicopter, and within a short time, a lot shorter time than it took me to climb up that mountain, we returned home."

Then Mr. Pulaski looked up from his podium with tears in his eyes. "I believe that this night is the night that God wanted me to be his witness. You all may still think I'm crazy, and perhaps some of you thought I was delirious from cold on that mountain that night. But I lived it, and I believe that God wants me to deliver his message to you tonight! And that message is that he loves you. He loves every one of you, and he wants you to know that he sent his Son Jesus Christ as your Savior because of his love for us. Jesus was born, and he died so that we would have eternal life!"

That night, after Mr. Pulaski finished with his story, there wasn't a dry eye in the place. He delivered God's message to many people that night. It was a simple message, but it was a very important one. And it was one that was told by a very special man, a man that loved everyone and who was a friend to all.

After he was finished, Pastor Foreland walked up on stage. He put his arm around Mr. Pulaski. "Samuel, I had prepared a sermon for Christmas Eve, but there is no way I can do any better than what you just did. So how about we skip my sermon?"

Everyone instantly clapped. Knowing what everyone meant by this action, Pastor Foreland simply remarked, "Okay, I get the message. Just remember when you all least expect it, my sermon will be twice as long! Anyway, Mr. Thomas, let's get the music started!"

Pastor Foreland turned and walked away from the stage but suddenly stopped. "I have one more thing I want to say to all of you before I go." He looked at Mr. Pulaski. "Samuel, I'm sorry. And I know I promised to keep your secret, but I think it's time they knew." Pastor Foreland looked out over the room. "I think now is the time for you all to know that Samuel is an ordained minister and has been for many years, but he gave up preaching when Maria passed away. However, I think it's time he started again as an associate pastor of our church! Anybody object?" Everyone clapped again as loud as they could.

"Okay then, Samuel, you have the sermon next Sunday!"

After that, Mr. Thomas called us all up on stage to take our seats. Mrs. Gray began playing the piano as Mr. Thomas turned down the lights and turned up the stage lights. Mom sang the first song that night, "O Holy Night," and you know, Mom sounded great. I mean she always sounded wonderful, but that night, I think she sang better than she had ever sung before.

That night turned out to be the best night ever, and I was so happy. I don't know if you ever had to plan something like that, but I sure can tell you it's exhausting, and I didn't have any trouble falling asleep that night. As a matter of fact, I didn't even remember the trip home.

Hear my prayer, listen to my cry for mercy; in your faithfulness and righteousness come to my relief
—Psalm 143:1, New International Version

And you will sing as on the night you celebrate a holy festival; your hearts will rejoice as when people go up with flutes to the mountain of the LORD, to the Rock of Israel.
—Isaiah 30:29, New International Version

Let the heavens rejoice, let the earth be glad; let them say among the nations, "The LORD reigns!"
—1 Chronicles 16:31,
New International Version

CHAPTER 34

Samuel's Reward

*Giving thanks to the Father, who has qualified you
to share in the inheritance of the saints in the kingdom of light.*
—Colossians 1:12, New International Version

The concert and banquet couldn't have been any better. The look on
Mr. Pulaski's face made all the planning and frustration I experienced
worthwhile. Morning came, and I awoke fully rested. But since I
wasn't in any hurry to get up, I lay in my bed as my mind ran through
everything from start to finish once more. I was trying to think of
anything that I may have forgotten, but there wasn't anything. It was
a night to remember, and everything was truly perfect, but it wasn't
because of me. It was Mr. Pulaski that made it a success. All I did was
the planning; it was Mr. Pulaski's story that he finally finished that
made it complete.

After a few minutes, it occurred to me that it was Christmas
morning. I suddenly ran out of the room, down the hallway, and halfway down the steps before stopping. I stood gazing at the Christmas
tree. There were presents everywhere; under it, beside it, they were
even stacked one on top of another. I couldn't help but think how
happy I was that Mom didn't go with Mr. Pulaski's idea of only one
or two presents.

Mom and Dad must have heard me running down the hallway because they were right behind me. Dad was mumbling about not getting quite enough sleep while Mom was checking to see if she remembered to put film in the camera the night before. I was so excited that I didn't waste any time. I went straight to work opening presents. I managed to get halfway through the first present before Mom stopped me. "We need to pray before you go any further, Jimmie."

I stopped on her command, but since I had some of the paper off, I quickly tried to see what it was before she prayed. Needless to say, I didn't have any luck. So I hoped it was going to be a short prayer. As soon as Mom ended with amen, I continued where I had left off.

I got a new hockey stick, skates, and a watch. The watch was Mom's idea. She said I wouldn't have any more excuses for being late for classes at school or getting home on time for dinner. There was a new fishing pole and some gear and a locking tackle box. I was really happy though when I removed the wrapping from some more houses and track for my train set. Mom got some new earrings and a necklace with a cross from Dad and me. Dad gave her some different kinds of perfume. Dad got a new fishing pole too. Mom gave him some new flannel shirts and work pants and a new winter coat and gloves.

After we finished opening all the presents, I ran all the way to Mr. Pulaski's house. I couldn't wait to show him everything I got, but I couldn't carry everything, so I only took my fishing pole, hockey stick, and watch. I figured I could tell him about everything else or bring it the next time I visited him. Mom said I could invite him and his family for Christmas dinner too. With all the excitement, I didn't think they had time to plan anything.

Finally, I reached his house, but I stopped just a short distance from the steps. I couldn't believe my eyes—there were more people at his house than I've ever seen. But then again, more than two are more than I had ever seen. There were so many that I thought something had happened to him. So I ran up the steps and pushed open the door. There must have been a hundred people in his house.

WALT DEECKI SR.

Well, maybe twenty or so, but it seemed like it was a hundred. The kitchen was covered with trays of ham, turkey, potatoes, stuffing, and desserts, which included things like pumpkin pie, apple pie, cookies, and a whole lot of other stuff. However, none of them looked as good as Mom's. Continuing my search for Mr. Pulaski, I walked back out of the kitchen and into the living room. I moved through the crowd until I finally saw Mr. Pulaski talking to Pastor Foreland. I didn't want to interrupt, so I started to leave, but just as I reached the door, I heard Mr. Pulaski call me.

"Jimmie!" he yelled. "You did a terrific job last night! I don't know how you kept it all a secret all that time, but I want to thank you. It was the best Christmas present I've gotten since Maria passed away. And what you did really means a lot to me! Thank you very much, my friend!"

I just looked up at Mr. Pulaski, and as I did, I forgot all about showing him my new stuff; besides, I had left it on the front porch.

"You're welcome, Mr. P!" Then as I began to go out the door, I looked back at him and saw someone else to talking to him. Happy for Mr. Pulaski and the satisfaction of knowing that he was pleased, I just simply smiled and left for home.

Mr. Pulaski's home seemed like a train station that entire week. People were in and out of his house every day. Antonio and Angela had a great time and promised to visit every year from then on. Mr. Pulaski even changed his mind about leaving town and moving back with Angela. He seemed to be much happier in the years that followed.

My friends and I graduated and were accepted to the colleges we all chose. Mr. Pulaski was very happy for us all, but he wasn't happy that I wasn't going to be able to visit him as much. I was very happy that everyone in town kept him busy until I returned for the summer. It was only four years that I was gone or, I should say, four winters, and I visited during all my breaks too.

After I finished college, I returned home, and thanks to Mr. Pulaski and our church, I opened a center for kids in our small town. It was almost like the one he worked at. As a matter of fact, Mr. Pulaski helped me with organizing it. He helped me with legal stuff such as getting the license and encouraged everyone at church to donate most of the money. Pastor Foreland took up a special collection every Sunday until we had enough. We even received money from other churches; it was wonderful. Mr. Pratt even talked the bank's board of directors into donating the building. Heck, anyway, it was a building that needed a lot of work, and they couldn't sell it. Fortunately, everyone in town volunteered to help fix it up, and we had it open within seven months. The boys and girls came from all over. I really didn't have any experience with this sort of thing, but again, everyone in town helped, and Mr. Pulaski spent a lot of time there. I never saw him so happy at the end of a day. Thanks to him, everything fell into place.

The biggest help, however, was my bookkeeper, which just happened to be my wife. I never thought that Becky and I would grow up and become husband and wife, but I think this was her plan since the day we met. She finished her degree in accounting at the same time I finished my degrees in both child development and social services. We were kept so busy with the center that it was a challenge for us to finish graduate school, but we did. Becky talked me into working toward my doctorate. I never thought it would be possible, but I did.

Time passed though. The seasons changed, and the years slipped by unnoticed by everyone except Mr. Pulaski. After I grew up, he wanted me to call him Samuel, but it just didn't feel right. I had more respect for him than anyone else, except for Mom and Dad. I guess it was really because calling him "Mr. P" kept me connected with both my childhood years of growing up and the memories of visiting him.

With the passing of each year, Mr. Pulaski's walks into town became fewer and fewer. Antonio and Angela continued their annual visits just as they had promised. Time seemed to pass by quickly, and Mr. Pulaski began to have difficulty remembering his stories. Then his health began to deteriorate and made it harder for him to make the trips to the lake. It took some convincing, but he finally agreed to let me drive him to the lake. On the way, he still insisted on stopping by the horses so he could feed them carrots. They didn't run to him like they used to. And then one day, they weren't in the pasture anymore. I could tell his heart was broken that day. In a way, I think he thought that as long as the horses were there, he didn't feel as old as he was. It wasn't too long after that that I built the fires and did the cooking of hot dogs and cocoa. While Mr. Pulaski sat in a chair next to the fire to keep warm, visitors took time to sit with him and talk while Becky and I skated with the boys and girls.

Again, the summers came, and winter slipped by. Mr. Pulaski and I didn't go fishing anymore, but Becky and I took the kids from the center. We spent more time untangling lines than we did fishing, but we had fun just the same. Becky even fixed a picnic basket or, I should say, baskets, with enough food to feed the whole town.

I loved every minute growing up with Mr. Pulaski, and if I had to do it all over again, I wouldn't change a day. More years passed, and Mr. Pulaski's visits to the lake stopped. In the evenings though, I helped him put his coat on, and we'd sit on the front porch, just so he could listen to the sounds of the people passing by. Many of them stopped by his house on their way down to the lake and on weekends just to talk. I think it was more for their benefit than his.

Mr. Pulaski began to grow tired faster, and he had a hard time walking. Eventually, all he could do was listen to the sounds of the townspeople echoing through the quiet nights. Not just in the winter from the lake though but in the spring and summer as well. Many of them walked together in the quiet spring and summer evenings past Mr. Pulaski's house just to say hi. He began to have difficulty remembering their names at times, but nonetheless, he smiled and waved as they passed by, just so he wouldn't feel bad. I'd wave as well and call out their names as I yelled, "Good evening, Mr. and Mrs. Jones. How are you this evening!" or whoever it might have been. Antonio and Angela increased their visits to twice a year and at different times. Pastor Foreland posted a schedule in the church of whose turn it was to look in on Mr. Pulaski each day.

Then the time came when it was almost impossible for him to leave his home. Mr. Pulaski missed his trips to town terribly, so every few weeks, Dr. Ramsey came with us as I drove him through town. I think Dr. Ramsey came along more for his own benefit than Mr. Pulaski's. Most of all though, I liked bringing Mr. Pulaski to the center every now and then, even if it was only for a short period of time. I know he enjoyed it too. Mr. Pulaski gave so much of himself to this little mountain town, and now it was time for the town to give a little of itself back to him.

Christmas after Christmas, Becky and I spent the day making dinner at the church in the same tradition as Mr. Pulaski did for so many years. Everyone still helped to prepare a wonderful meal for Thanksgiving and Christmas Day to celebrate together like one big happy family.

Little Katy wasn't little anymore. As a matter of fact when she married, she made sure that Mr. Pulaski sat right up front. Also, he was still the first one she hugged and kissed before leaving the church every Sunday until he couldn't leave his home anymore. Then when Katy's little girl, Christy, was born, she continued to fill Mr. Pulaski's heart with love and warmth whenever she smiled. Christy too wrapped her arms around his neck just as her mother did as a little girl whenever they visited.

Mr. Pulaski's visitors grew in numbers over the years, so many that they couldn't all fit in his house at the same time. So they wandered in and out during the holidays except for Antonio, Angela, Becky, and me. Antonio's and Angela's families were constant company, and we often engaged in conversation about Mr. Pulaski's stories, although we could only remember fragments. His legendary kindness toward everyone was a constant topic of conversation, and we often laughed together. Together, the four of us took care of and looked after Mr. Pulaski.

The first year that Mr. Pulaski wasn't able to leave his home, we decided to plan a small gathering of friends and family for Christmas dinner at his home, but it didn't turn out that way. To our surprise, word got out that he would not be attending any more Thanksgiving or Christmas dinners at the church. Anyways, Becky and Angela cooked the turkey and ham, and I helped Mr. Pulaski to the table. We all sat down. Mr. Pulaski said the blessing, and as I started to carve the turkey, the doorbell rang.

"I wonder who that could be," Antonio said as he pushed his chair back to stand up. He walked over to the door and pushed the curtain back a little so he could see out. "I don't believe it!" he exclaimed. Then he looked back at us with a big smile.

We all stood up except for Mr. Pulaski, but he almost fell out of his chair trying to see what the commotion was about.

"Who is it?" Mr. Pulaski asked, squinting and trying to see out the window around us.

Angela looked out as Antonio opened the door. She gasped and put her hand up to her mouth, and then she looked back at Mr. Pulaski.

"Well . . . who is it!" he demanded.

Becky looked at him. "It's the town!"

"What?" he replied in amazement.

Antonio just opened the door, and people started entering the house with Pastor Foreland leading them. Each one entered, carrying a dish of food.

Pastor Foreland walked over to Mr. Pulaski as he sat in his wheel-chair and looked down at him with a smile. "Samuel, there was no way we were going to have a dinner without you there. It just didn't seem right! As I stood in front of everyone ready to say the blessing, I couldn't help but feel as if a part of me was missing! Samuel, your chair was empty, and I just couldn't continue. So here we are! And we have another surprise for you! Bring them in!" Pastor Foreland yelled.

One at a time, nurses came through the door, either carrying or pushing one of the children from the children's ward at the hospital. Tears came to Mr. Pulaski's eyes. He couldn't believe this day turned out to be one of the most special Christmases of his entire life, even though he had had a few others from time to time.

Mr. Pulaski looked up at Pastor Foreland and asked a question, but he already knew the answer. "Where is Little Toni?"

Toni was one of the smallest children and one of the last that Mr. Pulaski was able to visit at the hospital. He had been fighting leukemia for five years and was very special to Mr. Pulaski.

Pastor Foreland grinned. "Little Toni is holding hands with Maria. He passed away last week."

Mr. Pulaski closed his eyes and prayed for Little Toni, and then he smiled. "Maria loves children. He's in good hands!"

Pastor Foreland smiled again with great joy. "Well, let's eat. Shall we?"

The table wasn't big enough for everyone, so they filled their plates and ate wherever they could find room. Whether they sat, stooped, it didn't matter.

Mr. Pulaski was so happy to have all his friends around that day. People were in and out of his house visiting from late morning until early evening.

As the last visitors left, Mr. Pulaski closed his eyes and whispered to Angela, "God planned this. Wasn't it a wonderful surprise?"

"Yes, Papa, it was!" she replied.

Christmas dinner at Mr. Pulaski's house became a tradition after that year. But once again, time passed on.

Then one year, just as everyone had just about left, Mr. Pulaski whispered to Angela, "I'm feeling a bit tired. I think I'll lay down for short time."

"Okay, Papa, let me help you to your room," she whispered back. Angela escorted him to his bedroom, helped him take off his shoes, and covered him with a blanket.

"I'll be back in a few minutes to check on you, Papa!" she told him as she kissed him on the forehead and then returned to the living room.

The only ones that hadn't left yet were Pastor Foreland and his wife. "Is Samuel all right?" he asked.

"I'm not sure. He looked a little pale. I'll check on him in a few minutes," Angela said.

Then they all sat and talked about how wonderful and special this day was to Mr. Pulaski, especially the children.

"It was their parents' idea the first year!" Pastor Foreland replied. Then he added, "When we decided to bring all the food here, the children's parents called the hospital and gave their consent for the children to be released for the afternoon. There were a few that couldn't leave, but the hospital staff planned something special for them!"

After an hour had passed, Angela stood up. "I'm going to go check on Papa."

She entered his room and whispered, as not to startle him. It was dark, and she couldn't see him very well. "Papa, Papa. Are you all right? Do you need anything?"

Mr. Pulaski didn't respond, so she quietly moved on tiptoe a little closer and asked again, "Papa, Pastor Foreland is getting ready to leave. Would you like to say good-bye?" Still, she was unable to get a response. So she stood next to his bed and leaned over him. In a little louder quivering voice commanding him to get up, she said, "Papa! Would you like to say good-bye to Pastor Foreland?" Still, there wasn't any response from him.

Now she felt a little weak and scared, and she called out, "Antonio! Come quick! Papa isn't waking up, and I think something is wrong!"

Antonio ran into the room. Pastor Foreland and I followed.

Antonio picked up Mr. Pulaski's hand and patted it. "Papa, can you hear me?"

I ran back into the living room and called for an ambulance. Antonio and Angela continued trying to wake him up, but he didn't respond. Pastor Foreland called home to let them know he was going to the hospital with us and instructed Mrs. Foreland to meet us there.

The ambulance soon arrived, and the emergency medical technicians went straight to work trying to revive Mr. Pulaski. First, they attached a heart monitor and oxygen to him, and then they radioed the hospital that they were en route and to stand by for their arrival. Angela rode in the ambulance with him, and Pastor Foreland drove Antonio, Becky, and me. The ambulance drove with lights flashing and sirens screaming, but because of the ice and snow, they had to drive cautiously.

When we arrived at the hospital, Antonio and I got out while Pastor Foreland parked the car. As instructed, the doctors were waiting at the door when we arrived. Mr. Pulaski was taken out of the ambulance and right into the treatment room. Antonio, Angela, Pastor Foreland, Becky, and I waited outside the double doors that led into the treatment area.

Pastor Foreland put his hand on Antonio's shoulder. "They'll call us as soon as they finish examining him, and that could take a while, so let's get a cup of coffee since all we can do now is wait. He's in good hands."

Angela, unable to speak, just nodded her head in agreement.

Once we had our coffee, we returned to the waiting area as Angela held on to Antonio as she was unable to let go.

Moments later, Mrs. Foreland arrived. "As soon as we find out something, your families want you to call and let them know if they should bring your children."

Antonio smiled and put his face in his hands. I was scared. What was I going to do without my best friend?

After a while, the doctor came out and removed his glasses. "They'll be taking Mr. Pulaski up to his room in a few minutes. If you want to go up and wait for him, he'll be in room two hundred five. I want to prepare you though. Mr. Pulaski had a stroke. He's still not responding, but he is stabilized for the moment. We need to run some more tests over the next couple of days. We'll do everything we can, okay?"

Thanking the doctor, we walked to the elevator and went up to his room; no one spoke a word. After a short time, he was brought in, and Pastor Foreland placed his hand on Mr. Pulaski's shoulder. "Please pray with me." We all bowed our heads. "Father, we ask that you place your hand on Samuel and help him to recover. We ask that you give him the strength to overcome this illness if it is to be your will. Samuel has given us great joy for many years. We know as a father, he has fulfilled your expectations of what a father should be. And as a friend, he has shown us what a great joy life is when we have been blessed by your grace. If it is your will that Samuel enter your kingdom, then we ask that you give us the strength to continue living as Samuel has taught us. We thank you for the blessing of Samuel's friendship and love. In the name of your Holy Son, Jesus, amen."

After a while, as suggested by the doctor, we all left for the night except for Angela. She stayed and slept in the large chair in the corner of his room. Antonio promised to bring her a change of clothes in the morning and her toothbrush and other items to freshen up.

By morning, the entire town had been notified of Mr. Pulaski's condition. We returned to the hospital by eight o'clock in the morning, and as we walked toward the elevator, there was a crowd of visitors waiting for the elevator as well. When they saw us coming toward them, they all burst out with questions as to his condition. We answered as many as we could before the elevator arrived. There were so many of us that we filled all three elevators.

Mr. Pulaski was still unconscious when we arrived, and Angela was sitting by his side holding his hand and talking to him with tears rolling down her face. Antonio gave Angela her small suitcase, and she left the room to freshen up. We all took turns visiting Mr. Pulaski all day; there just wasn't enough room for all of us. Besides, Nurse Crouch wouldn't allow all of us in his room anyway. Yes, she was still there. She mellowed out a little over the years, but she still looked mean.

It was a long day. We couldn't get Angela to leave his side even to eat. Antonio brought her some food. Angela wanted to be there in case he woke up. Most of the people visiting Mr. Pulaski stayed even when he was taken for tests.

The day passed, and night came once again with no change in his condition. Pastor Foreland prayed again before he left for home. Mom and Dad tried to talk Becky and me into going home, but we didn't leave until Nurse Crouch kicked us out for the night. The doctor didn't say anything more except that he was going to run more tests, but we could tell by his expressions and his voice that he was concerned and perhaps even worried. This would be the second day that Mr. Pulaski hadn't responded to treatment. Antonio and his family, Angela's family, Becky, and I returned to Mr. Pulaski's home for the night. I just couldn't go home in case the hospital called.

As I sat in Mr. Pulaski's chair for the first time in my life, I thought about all the times I went to him for advice and the joyous expression on his face when I came running over the hill toward the lake because we both were eager to sit and eat polish sausages and drink hot cocoa as I listened to him tell me his stories. I missed hearing them so much. That night seemed like it was never going to end, but eventually, it did. And once again in the morning, we returned to the hospital.

By the time we arrived, they had moved Mr. Pulaski into a larger room. He had this room all to himself so that there would be more room for visitors. It wasn't every day the hospital had a patient as popular as Samuel Pulaski; even the nurses and doctors visited him. I don't think there was one person whose life hadn't been touched by him.

Still another day ended, and we returned to Mr. Pulaski's house for the night. Then again, morning came, and again we returned to the hospital. Every day we returned to the hospital, the larger the crowd became. His room had gotten filled up with flowers, cards, and all sorts of things. Angela read everything that everyone had brought to Mr. Pulaski, but still she didn't get any type of response from him. After a while, when someone approached the nurses' station for directions to his room, they just simply said, "Just look for the room that is going to break all the world's record for the most people in a hospital room at one time!"

Then suddenly during the afternoon on the third day as Angela was reading his favorite verse from the Bible out loud, Mr. Pulaski opened his eyes. Angela called out for the nurses. "Papa's awake. Get the doctor. Papa's awake!"

The nurse ran in and asked everyone to leave quickly, and she began to check his blood pressure, temperature, and all his vital signs.

The doctor also came in and examined him, and then he came to the waiting room where we all were waiting. When he approached us, he said, "I know you want me to tell you that everything is okay, but I can't. God knows how much I wish I could give you all good news, but Samuel is very weak. Although he's awake, I'm still worried. Pastor Foreland, you and his family members can go back in now but only for a little while. Please understand his condition is still serious."

We entered Mr. Pulaski's room, and we all stood around his bed.

Angela kissed his forehead, and with tears rolling down her face, she whispered, "I love you, Papa! We all love you with all our hearts!"

Mr. Pulaski didn't respond. Antonio walked around to the other side of the bed and held his other hand. As we all stood quietly next to his bed, we tried our best to smile and to let him know how much we cared for him.

After what seemed to be a longer time than it really was, he looked up and smiled with a surprised look on his face. "Jacob! What are you doing here?"

"Who is he talking to? Who's Jacob?" the nurse asked.

I looked at Mr. Pulaski. I could see the excitement in his eyes, and I knew he wasn't going to be with us much longer. "Jacob is a very special friend of his. Actually, he's Mr. Pulaski's angel," I explained.

He raised his head a little. "Am I going to see Maria? Are you here to take me home?"

I knew that my friend was going to be leaving us that very night. No matter how hard the doctors tried to revive him, I knew he was leaving, and oh, how I was going to miss him.

Then Mr. Pulaski smiled again and turned toward Angela. "I'm going to see your mother. Antonio, I'm going to see Maria. Jacob is here to take me home!"

Just then, Angela started crying, and Antonio raised Mr. Pulaski's hand to his face and gently kissed his hand.

Then Mr. Pulaski smiled at me and slowly turned away. As he turned away, he talked to Jacob again. "Jacob, who is going to take care of Antonio and Angela?"

It appeared by the way Mr. Pulaski was staring that Jacob must have been standing at the foot of the bed.

Smiling, Jacob replied, "They're going to be just fine, Samuel. They have each other."

"What about Jimmie and Becky?" Mr. Pulaski asked him.

Again, Jacob smiled. "Samuel, you don't have to worry. Their futures are wonderful, and the angels will guide them as they have always guided you! You did a fine job helping to raise them, and God is very pleased with you! Samuel, you delivered God's message, and you've touched so many people's lives! You singlehandedly changed the direction of many people's lives as you did Jimmie's. Now it's time. Rise and walk with me! Samuel, as we enter the light of heaven, your Father is waiting for you."

"Jacob, can I have just one more minute? Please. And then I'll be ready."

"Sure, Samuel, but only one minute!"

Mr. Pulaski turned back toward Antonio, Angela, and me. "I have to go now. I love you all with all my heart, and so does Maria and God."

We each kissed him.

Then he spoke his final words, "You're all going to be just fine without me. But I want you to promise that you will take care of one another and never ever stop believing in God. You are all very special to me. And remember that Jesus said, 'I will always be with you!'"

Then Mr. Pulaski turned his head toward the end of his bed and looked up. There was a bright light dancing all around Jacob, and with a smile, Mr. Pulaski passed from this earth and walked with Jacob into eternal life.

As they walked, Jacob looked at Mr. Pulaski. "By the way, I have one more thing to tell you. You know that very special angel I mentioned that will guide Angela, Antonio, and Jimmie?"

"Yes," Mr. Pulaski replied.

"It's you!"

Mr. Pulaski just looked at Jacob as they walked.

"And did I mention that Maria is going to be with you?"

> *Then a voice came from heaven, "I have glorified it, and will glorify it again." The crowd that was there and heard it said it had thundered; others said an angel had spoken to him.*
> —John 12:29, New International Version

> *The sun will no more be your light by day, nor will the brightness of the moon shine on you, for the LORD will be your everlasting light, and your God will be your glory.*
> —Isaiah 60:19, New International Version

CONCLUSION

So what do you think? Here's an elderly man whose life was filled with happiness and love, and then all of a sudden, a terrible tragedy happened that resulted in the loss of his wife. Then eventually, his children grew up as all children do, and he lost his faith in God. Perhaps we should say he fell into "depression." Not knowing how to deal with his loss, he left home in search of answers. Then he sold his home and traveled to a town that he knew nothing about and had never even heard of in search of his faith.

What do you think he was looking for? An escape from life perhaps? Imagine that, running away from his problems. Do you think that climbing a mountain during the winter and during the coldest storm of the year was a little drastic? Did I mention he did this in the middle of winter and slept in a tent. And for what? Was it to find out about a sound that he heard coming from the top of a mountain, or was there some other purpose?

Why was Samuel Pulaski so driven to leave his home and to climb that mountain? Because he had to. It's as simple as that. He had to. He could have said no and ignored the sound. He could have turned away from it, but he didn't. Don't you hate that word "but"? But this was his life's path, "his destiny."

Well, guess what? Don't you hate it when someone says that? I mean when someone says, "Guess what?" Do you really want to guess? I don't. Anyway, what Mr. Pulaski did, he did because it was the path that God knew he had to take to find a renewed faith. And somehow, Mr. Pulaski had to make the tough journey to get back "home." Notice I said he lost his faith in God. God didn't lose his faith in him. God was willing or, should I say, patient enough to wait as he guided Mr. Pulaski to regain his faith. Mr. Pulaski's faith was with him all the time. It's just that it was a flicker, not a burning flame in his heart. All through Mr. Pulaski's life, God sent an angel (Jacob) to help guide him.

Jacob didn't just appear and say, "Hi, I'm an angel, and God sent me to help you find your faith." Jacob appeared as a man, a human just like you and me. He talked to Mr. Pulaski. He had a conversation with him. He let Mr. Pulaski tell his story, and he listened to him. Then he left him with the suggestion to talk to God.

Jacob planted a seed, and it grew. That seed provided the strength that Mr. Pulaski needed to pray and to continue his battle. Guess who won. I'm sorry, but go ahead: guess who won. Mr. Pulaski's battle was within himself. And when he didn't have the strength to go on alone with his depression and anger all tied up inside, he gave it up to God. He fell on his knees, and he prayed. And I believe God rejoiced in Mr. Pulaski's return to life after so many years of trying to deal with it alone because he was angry.

Why me? Right, why did this happen to me? Well, guess what? Nothing in life is a guarantee, except God's love and his faithfulness to us. He never abandons us. We abandon him, maybe not intentionally but something gets in the way like pride or pain or the lack of ability to understand or some other reason or excuse, and then Satan takes advantage of that, of us. But the bottom line is you need to find your way back. If you haven't lost your faith and you're confident that you're secure in your faith, great. But if you're not, trust in our Lord. Jesus was sent to earth as a man, a human being, and as flesh and blood. So do something for yourself, right now.

Even if you are secure in your faith, I want you to kneel if you can. Sometimes our health doesn't allow us to do things like that, so in that case, do the best you can. Anyway, kneel, close your eyes, picture in your mind that there's a man standing in front of you, and he's wearing a white robe. Got that picture?

Okay, here's the next step. Hold out your hands in front of you and picture this man reaching out to you, and he holds your hand in his. Now open your eyes and see his gentle smile as it warms your heart and melts your pain. No matter what it is that's troubling you, it's gone because the words that he is whispering to you are "I love you as my Father in heaven loves you, who has sent me. Rise and walk with me in faith. Go and deliver this message in the name of my Father."

Now he has left, and you are standing with a renewed love for God and a renewed faith in his Son, Jesus. So take a deep breath and be thankful that you didn't have to climb a mountain in the middle of winter and in the worst snowstorm you could ever imagine.

You will still have mountains to climb, and there will still be storms to battle, and then there's your pride, feelings of loneliness, and pain. But now, you know you can win because God is with you. Faith in his Son, Jesus Christ, who died for our sins, will win your battles. You still may not understand why they happen, but someday God's promise is that you will. So now go and deliver God's message.

Now in most cases, "that's the end of the story." But in this case, it's not. Your story will never end, for God truly loves you, and I believe that there will always be an angel close by. All you have to do is ask and believe. One way to ask is through prayer. Here is a prayer that you can say:

> Father, forgive me in my time of pain and weakness. I believe that your Son Jesus died for me, and his blood washed away all my sins. Father, I ask that you come into my heart and comfort me in my time of need. Please take away the pain and the hurt from my mind and soul and make me whole again. Help me to renew my faith, and from this moment forward, Father, I place all my fears and troubles in your loving hands. I ask this in the name of your Holy Son, Jesus Christ, my Lord and Savior. Amen.

ABOUT THE AUTHOR

Walter G. Deecki Sr. is retired from the US Air Force and Boy Scouts of America as a district director. His education is in organizational management, elementary education, and curriculum and instruction. He enjoys working with youth organizations and teaching them how to accomplish goals.

His greatest joy is serving God through helping others who are struggling with their faith. His experiences working with children and adults alike as well as his father's stories have given him the wonderful experiences that form the basis for his adventures. Personal observations of real-life events and the hand of God have provided the ability for his stories to come alive. Walter believes that it was the hand of God that guided his hand and chose the words that have been penned. He believes that God gives us the choice to follow him even though we can't control events in our lives. We can make the decision whether or not to follow him and to trust in him for comfort and guidance.

His goal is to spark a renewed faith in God. Every Christian is chosen to lead others to Christ in their own calling. Throughout his life, he faced many struggles, many to the point of questioning his own faith, but he believes that by the grace of God, he found his faith and understood that God had a purpose for him. And that purpose was to tell others about the never-ending love that God has for each and every one of us through his Son Jesus Christ.

At times, it seemed frightening as to where God was leading him, but through faith and courage, he followed, and the result was his writing.

CPSIA information can be obtained
at www.ICGtesting.com
Printed in the USA
BVOW03s0525011217

501415BV00001B/7/P

9 781641 403009